IT'S ALL CONNECTED

THE UNOFFICIAL AND UNAUTHORISED GUIDE TO THE MARVEL CINEMATIC UNIVERSE

VOLUME THREE
PHASE FOUR (2020 - 2022)

IT'S ALL CONNECTED
THE UNOFFICIAL AND UNAUTHORISED GUIDE TO THE MARVEL CINEMATIC UNIVERSE

VOLUME THREE
PHASE FOUR (2020 - 2022)

RYAN ALCOCK

This book is dedicated to my haters. In the words of Everglow:
Got no time for haters, fuck it all and throw it away..

Published by Tribeca Studios in Austraila.
Copyright © Ryan Alcock 2023

Ryan Alcock has asserted his right to be identified as the author of this work.

Cover art by Ryan Alcock.

First published in 2023.

NATIONAL LIBRARY OF AUSTRALIA

A catalogue record for this book is available from the National Library of Australia

CONTENTS

/ INTRODUCTION

Welcome to the third volume of *It's All Connected*, a series of books about the Marvel Cinematic Universe written by someone who has an obsession with "episode guides". COVID created a number of delays for everyone in the world everywhere, but cinema was noticeably hit as the distribution companies struggled to work out what to do with the movies they had to release, and production companies tried to determine how they could make movies (and money). Marvel joined in the series of delays that every other company was going through, and its well-planned schedule ended up being pushed back by a year (except for **SPIDER-MAN: NO WAY HOME** because there was no way Sony wasn't getting its movie released).

As such, 2020 remained something of a "non-year" for Marvel, with only three television shows released, and none of these had any input from Marvel Studios. Ironically, however, big things were on the horizons, as Marvel Studios not only took back their characters from Fox, but they also took on the television production as well. Now, not only were we getting three MCU films a year, but we were also getting at least that many television shows as well actively under the control of Marvel Studios. The MCU was becoming much bigger than the silver screen could contain.

A lot has been said about Phase Four as people have tried to attack Marvel for failing to deliver on their past successes. Most of what has been said, however, seems vitriolic at best. Once COVID stopped being a problem for cinemas, the Marvel movies proved their pulling power, with **SPIDER-MAN: NO WAY HOME** in particular making an enormous profit.

Phase 4, though, has embraced the diversity that the comics have already delivered. Marvel's new superheroes are a variety of ethnic backgrounds and genders; Ms Marvel, She-Hulk, Moon Knight, Shang-Chi and the new Captain America stand alongside Thor, Spider-Man and Ant-Man, bringing a more varied and interesting universe that only strengthens the stories they have to tell. And just to prove that the fans are still important to them, Marvel have brought back the characters like Daredevil and the Kingpin, keeping the casting from the television shows they originated in, and respecting those original works. And that's not even mentioning the Reed Richards cameo.

The fear that the MCU had nowhere to go after **AVENGERS: ENDGAME** has been swiftly put to rest. There are still plenty of stories to tell, and still plenty of heroes to join on adventures. In truth, the MCU has never been bigger.

And this book series will be here to chart it.

How to Use the Book…

Each entry has the following format:

Title *(Date of initial release – **Original television station where applicable**)*
Short summary of the story.

Cast: For television shows this is the regular credited cast. For movies it's generally the cast that feature in the credits sequence. Cast and characters that are italicised are characters lifted from the comics.

Crew: The principal production crew involved. **Writers, Directors, Producers, Composers, Executive Producers**, **Directors of Photography, Production Designers, Editors, Costume Designers, Production Companies** (all where applicable); running time (mins), budget, box office (information gathered from Box Office Mojo).

Notes: Background notes on the movie, and general points of interest. This book tends to avoid unsubstantiated rumour, but where there are recorded details of back stage controversy, it's mentioned.

Stan Spotting: Where to look out for the cameo appearances of Stan "The Man" Lee.

Should I Stay To The End?: A note on whether the post-credit sequence is worth waiting for.

It's All Connected: This section details recurring characters in the MCU, as well as important plot points that echo across the films.

Comic Notes: A somewhat in-depth section on the comic appearance of the characters that appear in the movie. For comic fans, this will provide background details; for those less that way inclined, hopefully it will be an interesting look at the different path the movies take.

Ratings: The ratings from IMDb, Rotten Tomatoes and Metacritic, where available.

Review: The author's own personal opinion on the media.

// PREVIOUSLY IN THE MCU

During World War II, Dr Erskine, Colonel Phillips, SSR Agent Carter and Howard Stark work on recreating the Super Soldier serum, and with scrawny volunteer Steve Rogers, they create the powerful Captain America. After assembling a team of Howling Commandos, Rogers goes into battle to locate and stop Johann Schmidt – the Red Skull, and former recipient of the serum – from using a powerful energy source called the Tesseract. In the process, Rogers loses his best friend, James "Bucky" Barnes, and is himself frozen in ice. Peggy Carter continues working with the SSR, uncovering a plot by Leviathan to kill Howard Stark and Whitney Frost's insane plan to harness dark matter. With the help of Stark's butler Jarvis, Carter stops them both, though is unrecognised until Stark invites her to join him in creating SHIELD.

In the 1990s, Carol Danvers and Maria Rambeau work for Wendy Lawson, but Danvers is captured by Yon-Rogg, a Kree commander, who turns her into one of his weapons. The brainwashed Veers returns to Earth as she hunts down Skrulls, the enemies of the Kree, only to join forces with Nick Fury and Skrull leader Talos when she discovers the truth about her past and the part Yon-Rogg played in her abduction. She leaves Earth, but gives Fury an intergalactic pager to summon her if he ever needs her help.

Ironically due to an explosion from a weapon designed by himself, Tony Stark becomes a prisoner of the Ten Rings terrorist organisation, led by their mysterious leader, the Mandarin, and builds a suit of armour to escape. Deeply changed by this experience he abandons weapon research and concentrates his interests on developing a suit of armour to help him fight injustice. With this he becomes Iron Man! At much the same time, Bruce Banner works hard to develop a way to stop becoming the Hulk when he is angered, and though pursued by General Thaddeus Ross, it seems, after a battle with the Abomination in Harlem, Banner is successful. Having bested Obadiah Stane in his Iron Monger armour, Stark finds the arc reactor in his chest is killing him. Though Nick Fury tells him there is no place for him in The Avengers Initiative, Stark is directed towards his father's research which helps him build a better arc reactor, and deal with Anton Vanko – the son of Ivan Vanko, Howard Stark's old partner – who has developed his own Whiplash armour. After attempting to teach the Frost Giants a lesson, Thor is exiled to Earth to learn humility, though this leaves Asgard open to the machinations of Loki, who seizes power when Odin goes into a deep sleep. Thor learns his lesson as he tries to defend an Earth town from the Destroyer, and returns to Asgard to restore his father's power – in the process destroying the Bifrost bridge and cutting him off from Jane Foster, for whom he has developed romantic feelings. Subsequently, Loki leads the Chitauri, the alien army of

Thanos, in invading Earth and seizes the Tesseract. With no other option, Nick Fury assembles Tony Stark, the newly recovered Steve Rogers, Bruce Banner, SHIELD agents Natasha Romanoff and Clint Barton, and Thor himself to create the Avengers to stop Loki – which they do, though sadly SHIELD Agent Phil Coulson dies in the process.

Dealing with PTSD from the Chitauri invasion, Tony Stark goes after the Mandarin and Ten Rings when his friend and bodyguard Happy Hogan is hurt, but discovers that they are a front for mad scientist Aldrich Killian, who has harnessed the power of Extremis, though with the help of Colonel James Rhodes who has his own War Machine armour, Tony is able to defeat him. Fury orders the resurrection of Coulson using the TAHITI project, which injects him with Kree blood. Coulson forms a team to investigate superhumans, during the course of which he is forced to inject Agent Skye with the same blood. Dark Elf Malekith the Accursed hunts down the Aether to convert the universe to darkness. When Jane Foster accidentally stumbles on it, Thor and Loki are able to team up to stop the Elf. Though considered dead, Loki actually exiles Odin and takes his place on the throne. Steve Rogers discovers that after all these years, SHIELD has actually been infiltrated and controlled by HYDRA and with Fury's blessing, he tears SHIELD apart in the eyes of the world. Fury goes dark, assumed dead, but instructs Coulson to rebuild SHIELD as its new director. In the process, Rogers learns that Bucky Barnes is still alive, refashioned as the assassin, the Winter Soldier. With SHIELD apparently gone, Rogers and his friend Sam Wilson, set out to find Barnes. During the eighties, Peter Quill is abducted by aliens not long after his mother dies. Twenty-six years later, he steals an orb ahead of his mentor Yondu, and is forced to team up with four other criminals to keep the orb out of the hands of Ronan the Accuser. Ronan, though, is one of many agents seeking out the Infinity Stones for Thanos; both the Tesseract and the Aether are stones. Coulson's new SHIELD faces a number of threats to its stability, including former agent Grant Ward, a number of HYDRA cells, and a separate SHIELD faction. Attorney Matt Murdock – in actuality a gifted human being – becomes embroiled in Wilson Fisk's empire building among the criminal community, and becomes Daredevil to bring Fisk and his organisation to justice. Loki's staff contained a fourth Infinity Stone which is retrieved by the Avengers, though the stone has already given power to Wanda and Pietro Maximoff, and it creates the robot Ultron, who determines the Avengers must die in order for Earth to be peaceful. The Avengers team up with the Maximoff twins, and a new lifeform called Vision, to stop Ultron, but in the process a devastating blow is dealt to the city of Sokovia. The majority of Sokovians are saved thanks to Coulson and Fury.

Meanwhile Coulson's SHIELD encounters a group of powered

humans called Inhumans, led by Agent Skye's mother. Inhumans get their abilities from a process called terrigenesis, which gives Skye – actually Daisy Johnson – vibration powers. Daisy's mother's operation is shut down when the woman decides to unleash terrigenesis on the Earth. A Kree artefact takes Agent Jemma Simmons to another world, which is needed by HYDRA, though when Grant Ward crosses over, he is killed and absorbed by a creature called the Hive. Private eye Jessica Jones discovers her rapist, the superhuman Kilgrave, is alive and loses control, going after him. A number of missteps bring the pair together and Jones kills Kilgrave. Matt Murdock encounters an old flame named Elektra, and a vigilante named Frank Castle as he tracks down an organisation known as the Hand that seem to be kidnapping children. The trio stop the Hand, though Castle appears to die, and Elektra certainly does. Murdock reveals his secret to Karen Page, and gives up his role as Daredevil. Having encountered Jessica Jones and learned that she killed his wife, Luke Cage returns to Harlem, but keeps a low profile to prevent his rearrest and return to jail for escaping. However, he comes into conflict with Cornell "Cottonmouth" Stokes and his cousin Mariah Dillard, and their associate Willis "Diamondback" Stryker. Teaming up with cop Misty Knight, Cage stops Stryker – in actuality his own brother – and Dillard kills Stokes. Danny Rand, heir to the Rand legacy, arrives in New York after being presumed dead for a number of years. He resumes his place at Rand Industries, developing an uncomfortable relationship with Joy and Ward Meachum, little knowing that their father Harold is still alive and working with the Hand. Alongside Colleen Wing, he stops Harold and his Hand controller, Bakuto. SHIELD, under the new directorship of Jeffrey Mace, encounters the Ghost Rider – Robbie Reyes, who is possessed by the Spirit of Vengeance – as they find Eli Morrow has stolen the Darkhold and is using its magic to gain power. With Ghost Rider's help they stop Morrow, but the Darkhold falls into the hands of AIDA, a Life Model Decoy built by Holden Radcliffe, who uses it to build a computer system in which she attempts to subdue SHIELD while she builds a real body for herself. She is successful, but her human emotions create instabilities and the Ghost Rider returns to deal with her and the Darkhold. When the Hand attempt to dig up the skeleton of a dragon underneath New York, Matt Murdock, Jessica Jones, Luke Cage and Danny Rand team up to stop them, and while they are successful, Misty Knight loses her arm. Frank Castle discovers that there is more to the murder of his family than he originally thought when he encountered Daredevil, and takes up arms to fight against those still responsible, including his old friend Billy Russo. Jessica Jones is approached by a man calling himself the Whizzer, but when he is killed, she suspects someone is trying to kill those experimented on by Karl Malus. Malus is now working with Jessica's mother Alisa, but Trish Walker, in order to protect

Jessica, not only tries to get superpowers, but then kills Alisa. Luke Cage comes up against Bushmaster, a man with a vendetta against Mariah Dillard, but in order to stop them, Cage realises he may have to make a deal with the darker side of Harlem. Joy Meachum and Davos employ Typhoid Mary to kill Danny Rand, but Rand opts for a different approach and gives up the power of the Iron Fist to Colleen Wing. Matt Murdock recovers from his battle with the hand, only to discover someone is masquerading as Daredevil to destroy the hero's reputation. Suspecting that Wilson Fisk is involved, Murdock sets out to deal with his nemesis once and for all. Jessica Jones investigates a serial killer, while at the same time encountering a man who has the ability to sense evil. Both assisted and hindered by the newly powered Trish Walker, Jessica finds and stops her killer, but realises that Trish has gone too far and also has to be dealt with by law enforcement. Meanwhile Frank Castle becomes involved in the murder of a woman which leads him back into conflict with the horrifically scarred Billy Russo.

After being released from prison, Scott Lang is talked into robbing the house of Hank Pym, little knowing this is Pym's attempt to find someone to replace him as Ant-Man and stop industrialist Darren Cross. Lang complies and stops Cross, earning the respect of his family in the process. After the Avengers confront Crossbones and a number of innocents are killed when Crossbones takes his own life, new Secretary of State, General Thaddeus Ross, insists on the Avengers signing the Sokovian Accords to make them answerable to the UN. A guilty Tony Stark immediately agrees, but Steve Rogers is convinced this will make them pawns of warring governments, bringing the two into conflict. Meanwhile Helmut Zemo blows up the UN conference, killing King T'Chaka of Wakanda and framing the Winter Soldier. Rogers, Clint Barton, Wanda Maximoff, Sam Wilson, Bucky Barnes and new recruit Scott Lang find themselves in a fight against Stark, Natasha Romanoff, Vision, James Rhodes and new recruits Peter Parker (the amazing Spider-Man) and Wakandan prince T'Challa (the Black Panther). Though Stark learns that Zemo framed Barnes, on discovering that Barnes killed his parents, a rift is created between him and Rogers that cannot be repaired. Stark ends up with the Avengers – now just Vision and Rhodes – while Rogers disappears with his secret Avengers aided by T'Challa. Stephen Strange is badly wounded in a car accident, and the brilliant surgeon becomes desperate to regain the use of his hands. He ultimately travels to Kamar-Taj where he meets the Ancient One who teaches him that there is more to life than what Strange thinks. As Strange learns what is effectively magic, he finds himself forced to confront Kaecilius, one of the Ancient One's former students, who has made a deal with Dormammu, a creature that exists in a completely different physical plane. Meanwhile, out in space, the Guardians of the Galaxy encounter a Celestial called Ego who is actually Quill's father. Though Quill is delighted to meet him, the other Guardians are a little more concerned. With a vengeful Nebula and Yondu and his Ravagers chasing them, the Guardians find themselves in unusual alliances to stop Ego's ultimate plan of seeding the entire galaxy. Peter Parker attempts to gain membership to the Avengers, but realises that his place is actually on the streets helping his family and friends. Thor finds himself confronting his long-lost sister in a battle which results in the destruction of Asgard. As the remainder of the Asgardians depart, their ship encounters another, far more powerful vessel.

On the moon, the original Inhumans find themselves at the centre of a civil war when leader Black Bolt's brother Maximus seizes control of the city of Attilan. Though Black Bolt and his family stop Maximus, Attilan is destroyed in the process and the Inhumans are forced to come to Earth to make a new home. Coulson's team are kidnapped and taken deep into space to a space station controlled by the Kree. Though they are able to return home (and indeed their own time, as they were taken by Chronicons), they find General Hale waiting for them, starting her own version of Hydra. A group of children with a variety of special abilities learn that their parents are a cabal of criminals and together the kids – Niko, Karolina, Alex, Chase, Molly and Gert (and her pet dinosaur, Old Lace) – battle the Pride and the mysterious Jonah who controls them. They are able to destroy Jonah's body, but he has the ability to take control of others, which he proceeds to do, but ultimately the Runaways join forces with the Pride to stop Jonah. In Wakanda, T'Challa takes leadership of his country, but his cousin, Kilmonger, returns to wrest the mantle of the Black Panther from T'Challa. Two Louisiana teens – Tandy and Tyrone – discover they have unusual abilities, even as a strange black sludge starts to turn the locals into zombies. Forced together, the pair set out to stop the strange force. Tandy and Tyrone then find themselves up against the dark entity known as Deschaine, who feeds on the despair of those in New Orleans. The pair then opt to leave the city to explore new paths.

Thanos takes the Tesseract from Loki, the aether from the Collector and the power stone from Xandar, before killing Gamora on Vormir to get the soul stone. He attempts to get the time stone on Earth, but ends up fighting Iron Man, Dr Strange, Spider-Man and the Guardians of the Galaxy on Titan to get it. Returning to Earth, in Wakanda Thanos' forces take on the other Avengers and the Wakandan army, but takes the mind stone from Vision and then destroys half of all life in the universe. With the help of General Talbot, Coulson's team are able to stop Hale, but Talbot absorbs enormous amounts of gravitonium, becoming the powerful Graviton. In the process of stopping the now insane Talbot as he goes to confront Thanos, Fitz appears to die (though another version of him still exists) and Coulson's life also comes to an end.

Scott Lang is recruited by Hank and Hope to help them get Janet Van Dyne back from the Quantum Realm. The mysterious Ghost also needs the technology, though after battling, they are able to work together. When Scott returns to the Quantum Realm, Thanos' snap removes Hank, Janet and Hope. When Fury and Hill are also snapped away, Fury uses his last moments to summon Captain Marvel. She rescues Tony Stark and Nebula – the only survivors of Titan and returns them to Earth. The Avengers then track down and kill Thanos, but he has already destroyed the Infinity stones and there is now nothing that can be done. Post snap, Steve Rogers leaves the Avengers, and Natasha Romanoff takes over as the new leader, working with Okoye and Captain Marvel to resolve problems. With Alphonso "Mack" Mackenzie now in charge of SHIELD, they encounter a group led by what appears to be Coulson. This "Coulson" wants to destroy a being called Izel. They are successful, but also come under attack by Chronicoms. With the help of Chronicom Enoch, the team opt to jump back in time.

Five years after the snap, Scott Lang escapes the Quantum Realm and approaches Rogers, Romanoff and Stark with a plan to go back in time and collect the stones before Thanos, allowing them to undo the snap. Assembling the remaining Avengers, including Rocket and Nebula, they travel through time. Nebula and War Machine get the power stone from Star-Lord, but Nebula is captured by an earlier version of Thanos. In 2012, Banner is able to get the time stone from the Ancient One, but Loki uses the Tesseract to escape his capture. Thor and Rocket get the aether, and the remainder of the team get the mind stone. Rogers and Stark travel back to the forties to get hold of the Tesseract from Howard Stark, where Tony is able to say goodbye to his father, and on Vormir, Natasha gives up her life for Clint Barton to take the soul stone. Back in 2023, Banner is able to return everyone, but the past version of Thanos travels through time to attack them. As every single one of Earth's heroes unite as the ultimate Avengers, Tony gets hold of the Infinity Stones and uses them to stop Thanos and his army, dying in the process. Peter Parker finds himself viewed as Tony Stark's protégé and struggles with the responsibility of it, as Nick Fury seeks him out to help him with a new threat – Mysterio, someone who claims to be from another universe. However, Peter finds that Mysterio is simply an embittered former Stark employee, though when Mysterio is accidentally killed, a video is leaked revealing Peter's true identity to the world. Fury also has a secret – he is actually the Skrull Talos; the real Nick Fury actually being on a giant space station above Earth…

/// PHASE FOUR

RUNAWAYS
[Season 3]*(13 December, 2019 - Hulu)*

Cast: *Rhenzy Feliz (Alex Wilder), Lyrica Okano (Nico Minoru), Virginia Gardner (Karolina Dean), Ariela Barer (Gert Yorkes), Gregg Sulkin (Chase Stein), Allegra Acosta (Molly Hernandez), Angel Parker (Catherine Wilder)* [31-3.3,3.8]*, *Ryan Sands (Geoffrey Wilder)*[3.1-3.3,3.6-3.7,3.9-3.10]*, *Annie Wersching (Leslie Dean)*[3.1-3.4,3.6-3.7,3.9-3.10]*, Clarissa Thibeaux (Xavin)*[3.1-3.4]*, *Ever Carradine (Janet Stein)*[3.1-3.2,3.6-3.10]*, James Marsters (Victor Stein), Brigid Brannagh (Stacey Yorkes), Kevin Weisman (Dale Yorkes)*[3.1-3.3,3.6-3.10]*, *Brittany Ishibashi (Tina Minoru)*[3.1-3.7,3.9-3.10]*, James Yaegashi (Robert Minoru)* [3.3-3.7]* special guest star *Elizabeth Hurley (Morgan Le Fay)*[3.1-3.4,3.6-3.7,3.9-3.10] *guest starring Olivia Holt (Tandy Bowen)*[3.7-3.8]*, Aubrey Joseph (Tyrone Johnson)*[3.7-3.8]

*Credited on all episodes

Prod: P Todd Coe, Kirk A Moore; **Music:** Siddhartha Khosla; **Exec.Prod:** Quentin Peeples, Alan Fine, Joe Quesada, Karim Zreik, Jeph Loeb, Josh Schwartz, Stephanie Savage; **Created by** Josh Schwartz & Stephanie Savage; **DOP:** M G Wojciechoski; **Prod.Des.:** Colin de Rouin; **Costumes:** Leoisick Castro [3.1-3.3], Samantha Rattner [3.4-3.10]; **Marvel Television/ABC Signature Studios/Hulu**; 45

Episodes:

3.1 SMOKE AND MIRRORS
Trapped in the algorithm, Karolina, Chase and Janet Stein all experience perfect realities, though each of them starts to realise all is not what it seems. Xavin confirms that Jonah is now in Victor's body, Stacey hosting Jonah's wife and Tina hosting his daughter. The remaining Runaways have only one thing on their minds, however – the rescue and recovery of Karolina, Gert and Chase.

Cast: Myles Bullock (Anthony "AWOL" Wall), Jeremiah Birkett (Londell Kendricks), Susan Papa (Ultra Sound Technician)
Dir: Larry Teng; **Writer:** Tracy McMillan; **Ed:** Jesse Ellis

3.2 THE GREAT ESCAPE
Chase begins to learn how to gain a degree of control over the

algorithm and is able to pass this onto Janet. Together they unite with Karolina as they wait for Alex to free them. Alex starts work on this, but Nico's fear of using the staff continues. Meanwhile Molly and Xavin bond as they try to track down the Yorkes, but are confronted by Jonah and his family. Dale decides it's for the best to release Gert and Old Lace to escape on their own.

Cast: Anjali Bhimani (Mita Nansari), Aaron Anastasi (Security Guard), Chase Ellison (GrubMates Guy), Dan Sanders-Joyce (Engineer)
Dir: Philip John; **Writer:** Warren Hsu Leonard; **Ed:** Joseph Mitacek

3.3 LORD OF LIES

Alex comes up with a plan to discover which of them is Jonah's son, and as they go to the Minoru's house to get what they need, Alex is summoned by Catherine who wants to heal old wounds. Tamar, however, has other plans for Catherine and she soon meets with an accident in her cell. The Runaways use the test but are somewhat shocked to discover that Alex is the host for Jonah's son.

Cast: Kathleen Quinlan (Susan Ellerh), Cody Mayo (Vaughn), Ozioma Akagha (Tamar), Anjali Bhimani (Mita Nansari), Tim Halling (Guard), Dizzie Harris (Leader)
Dir: Allison Liddi-Brown; **Writer:** Kirk A Moore; **Ed:** Karen Casteñeda

3.4 RITES OF THUNDER

While "Alex" takes Leslie to meet with Jonah, the Runaways are able to get to them with help from Tamar, where Leslie has her baby. Xavin realises that her prophecy actually involves the new baby rather than Karolina. However, "Alex" has the baby stolen away, and with weapons provided for them by Chase and Gert, the Runaways, with Xavin, go to confront Jonah's family.

Cast: Ozioma Akagha (Tamar), Michelle N Carter (Nurse), Akaash Yadav (Clerk)
Dir: Jeremy Webb; **Writer:** Russ Cochrane; **Ed:** Jesse Ellis

3.5 ENTER THE DREAMLAND

The Runaways new home seems to have reverted to the days when the Great Quinton owned it, and when they meet the magician, he suggests that they are in a different realm, one where Alex, Victor, Tina and Stacy are as well. The group set out to track down their friends, each in their own personal hells, though Gert finds Stacy, Chase finds Victor and Niko finds firstly Amy, and then Tina, who tells her they are in the Dark Dimension. They have to leave as the longer they stay, the more their memories will fade away.

Cast: John Ales (Quinton the Great), Myles Bullock (Anthony "AWOL" Wall), Amanda Suk (Amy Minoru), *Carmen Serano (Alice Hernandez), Vladimir Caamano (Gene Hernandez), Nicole Wolf (Destiny Gonzalez),* Marilyn Tokuda (Akair Minoru), Minae Noji (Tokiko Minoru), Brianna Ishibashi (Judith Minoru), Granville Ames (Curtis)
Dir: Rob Hardy; **Writer:** Quinton Peeples; **Ed:** Joseph Mitacek

3.6 MERRY MEET AGAIN
With six months of time missing, the Runaways try to reconnect with the outside world. Niko attempts to get Tina to help her retrieve Alex from the Dark Dimension, but she refuses, and both women are shocked to find Morgan Le Fay is in a relationship with Robert Minoru, now the CEO of Wizard. Gert is attracted to Max who gives her a mobile phone that seems to have a magical feather in it. Meanwhile, Karolina and Molly find Leslie has revamped the Gibboram Church, which includes Dale.

Cast: Cody Mayo (Vaughn), Ozioma Akagha (Tamar), Scarlett Byrne (Bronwyn), Elliot Fletcher (Max), Martin Martinez (Bodhi), Lauri Hendler (Mediator), Charlie Charbonneau (Survivor 1), Tom Proctor (Survivor 2), Ali Kinkade (Survivor 3), Grant Jordan (Gil), Ashley Wigfield (Jules)
Dir: Vanessa Parise; **Writer:** Ashley Wigfield; **Ed:** Karen Castañeda

3.7 LEFT-HAND PATH
Nico recovers from her ceremony but is curious that she can't remember anything. Molly attacks Karolina, Chase and Gert after being hypnotised by her phone. When she recovers, the four realise they have to get the message out, but Morgan stops them. Nico rescues Tina from the psychiatric care Morgan put her in, and she breaks Robert free from Morgan's spell, even as Morgan hypnotises Geoffrey. As everyone is taken by Morgan's followers, Robert gives Nico a chance to get Alex back.

Cast: Cody Mayo (Vaughn), Scarlett Byrne (Bronwyn), Martin Martinez (Bodhi), Emily Alabi (Cassandra), Beth Hawkes (Nurse)

Dir: Katie Eastridge; **Writers:** Tracy McMillan & Kendall Rogers; **Ed:** Jesse Ellis

3.8 DEVIL'S TORTURE CHAMBER

Nico convinces Tandy and Ty to help her and they rescue Karolina, Chase, Gert, Dale, Stacy and Victor before Ty takes the Runaways into the Dark Dimension where they run into Quinton the Amazing again. Alex is currently held by Darius who agrees to let him go only on the condition he kill Catherine. Forced to confront the darkness, Nico is inadvertently exposed to her hopes thanks to Tandy, while Ty reveals Gert's greatest fears.

Cast: John Ales (Quinton the Great), Myles Bullock (Anthony "AWOL" Wall), Scarlett Byrne (Bronwyn), Emily Alabi (Cassandra), DeVaughn Nixon (Darius Davis), Evelyn Angelos (Young Molly)
Dir: Jeff Woolnough; **Writers:** Warren Hsu Leonard & Stu Selonick; **Ed:** Joseph Mitacek

3.9 THE BROKEN CIRCLE

Geoffrey reassembles the Pride and together they are able to rescue Molly from being used as a sacrifice by Morgan in her spell. The Runaways and the Pride decide to work together to stop Morgan, Tina assuring everyone that Morgan will arrive to get the Staff of One. As the group work together, one of the solutions forces Gert to realise she may lose her connection to Old Lace forever.

Cast: Ozioma Akagha (Tamar), Scarlett Byrne (Bronwyn), Emily Alabi (Cassandra), Jamal Dennis (Security Guard)
Dir: Geeta V Patel; **Writers:** Russ Cochrane & Kirk A Moore; **Ed:** Karen Castañeda

3.10 CHEAT THE GALLOWS

In 2022, things have changed since Gert's death and the return of Nico reunites the group, but with a surprise visitor – Chase from the future, along with an Alex who is bitter and angry at his former friends. Future Chase reveals that while he wants to stop future Alex, his principal aim is to go back further and stop Gert from getting killed.

Cast: Scarlett Byrne (Bronwyn), Timothy Granaderos (Lucas), Claudia Sulewski (Julie), Keisuke Hoashi (Mr Kwan), Derek Luh (Brayden),

Cooper Mothersbaugh (The Gert), Rob Parks (Buzzcom Reporter), Rachel Gage (Brianna), Allison Beteta (Molly Cast Double), Biz Betzing (Karolina Cast Double), Courtney Kato (Nico Cast Double), Tyler Lofton (Alex Cast Double), Nathan Varnson (Chase Cast Double)
Dir: Ramsey Nickell; **Writer:** Quentin Peeples; **Ed:** Jesse Ellis

Notes: Again, for this season, Hulu decided to release all episodes at once rather than one a week. A decision was taken early on (with a lot of fan support) to have Cloak & Dagger make an appearance in the series. Additionally, to increase focus on the children, the adult cast members were given a reduced episode count (though all were credited in the titles for the series).

It's All Connected: Obviously it wouldn't be the Runaways without Alex, Gert, Chase, Karolina, Nico, Molly and Old Lace (though obviously separated as they were last season, with Chase and Karolina part of the Wizard systems), and their parents all put in return appearances. For the Steins, Victor is still possessed by Jonah while Janet becomes one with the Wizard computer systems. With the Yorkes, Stacey remains possessed by Jonah's wife (though when this is undone, she and Victor find themselves in an unusual relationship), and Dale initially trains Gert on how to make the most of her connection to Old Lace before joining Leslie Dean's church. Leslie herself has her new child, Elle, with some surprise help from Tamar. Tamar's return also directly involves the Wilders, as Catherine decides to confess to the murder of Darius and is imprisoned as a consequence. Tamar has her revenge by having Catherine murdered in prison, and though Geoffrey is shattered by this, his guilt over Darius' death brings him a surprise relationship with Tamar. Tina Minoru is still possessed by Jonah's daughter, and Robert finds himself getting into a relationship with Morgan Le Fay, that costs Tina her company after she is trapped in the Dark Dimension. The Dark Dimension is fairly significant, in that it is what frees Victor, Stacey, Tina and Alex from Jonah and his family, though when the Runaways attempt to rescue them, they can't save Alex. Robert ultimately realises he is being manipulated by Morgan and turns on her (thanks to Nico and Tina), though this costs him his life. As Morgan's grand plan to enslave the world comes to fruition, the Runaways (rejoined by Alex – more on this soon) team up with what remains of the Pride to stop her. This also costs Gert her life. The final episode is set some years after the ninth, and sees future versions of Alex and Chase attempting to change the course of history. With the help of the younger Runaways, they are successful and manage to save Gert's life (ironically at the cost of the older Chase…which would surely cause a paradox? Best not to think about it…). Xavin gives up on

17

her plans to marry Karolina when Leslie has Elle, as she realises that the love that was foretold is actually a maternal love for a child rather than a romantic love. She uses Jonah's teleport system to take Elle away from Earth before the Runaways destroy the system.

There are considerable references to the wider MCU in this series, not just with the mentions of Roxxon, but also the fact that Morgan has the Darkhold, and, of course, appearances by Cloak and Dagger who assist the Runaways in getting Alex free from the Dark Dimension (obviously Cloak has this force within him, as we know from the last season of *CLOAK & DAGGER*). Alex ultimately frees them by seemingly taking on the responsibility of his mother's death. Interestingly, Dagger's powers allow her to see Alex's hopes, which are to have all the powers of the Runaways. The Darkhold is what Morgan uses to try to enslave the world, but Nico's magic proves to be impressively strong. Tina also mentions that she trained in magic, something Robert knows little about. As such, it's now quite possible that the Tina Minoru we saw in **DOCTOR STRANGE** is indeed the Tina Minoru from this series.

Comic Notes: *Morgan*: or Morgan Le Fay is a character who originated in Arthurian legends, but was later adopted by Marvel to be part of its enormous history. She was first featured in *Black Knight #1 (May, '55)* and this version was created by Stan Lee and Joe Maneely. She is indeed the half-sister of King Arthur, but also part of the Darkhold cult, and often fought Sir Percy, the Black Knight. Interestingly, during these medieval times, she also encountered Doctor Doom and Iron Man. When she appeared in modern times, acquisition of the Darkhold was generally her primary motivation, and she often clashed with the likes of Spider-Woman, Doctor Strange and Dane Whitman, the modern-day Black Knight. She has been killed repeatedly, but always resurrects. Her television appearance isn't too far removed from the comic version, and her powers are almost identical.

And: Gert did indeed die in the comics (*Runaways Vol 2 #19 (Sep, '06)*), killed by Geoffrey Wilder as the Runaways were falling apart due to Nico and Chase sharing a kiss. Poignantly she passed on mental control of Old Lace to Chase. Interestingly, though, Chase did go back in time to rescue her and she was saved by Nico's magic (*Runaways Vol 5 #1 (Nov, '17)*).

Ratings: *IMDB:* 7.0; *Rotten Tomatoes:* 91%; *Metacritic:* 68

Review: This season is a departure from the first two as the Pride take a definite backseat to the Runaways themselves, and Jonah's story is dealt with quickly in order to give us a more magical story, with Morgan taking on the new villain role. This is great, not least because it gives the kids a real opportunity to shine. The Pride get quite a nice role, despite the reduced episodes, and most of the out and out comedy comes from them. What's great, though, is the opportunity for the Runaways to meet Cloak & Dagger, which is a crossover that works really well. It's sad that the end of Marvel Television has meant the end of both of these programs, given how enjoyable the crossover was. Moreso, given that *Runaways* had really hit its stride, its cancellation is a genuine loss.

AGENTS OF SHIELD
[Season 7] *(May 2020 – ABC)*

Regular Cast: *Clark Gregg (Phil Coulson), Ming-Na Wen (Agent Melinda May), Chloe Bennet (Daisy Johnson/Quake)[7.7]*, Elizabeth Henstridge (Agent Jemma Simmons), Henry Simmons (Agent "Mack" Mackenzie), Natalia Cordova-Buckley (Elena "Yo-Yo" Ramirez),* Jeff Ward (Deke Shaw) special guest star *Iain de Caestecker (Leo Fitz)[7.11-7.13]*

*Credited, but does not appear.

Prod: Chris Cheramie; **Music:** Bear McCreary, Jason Akers; **Exec.Prod:** Craig Titley, Drew Z Greenberg, Garry A Brown, Brent Fletcher, Alan Fine, Stan Lee, Joe Quesada, Jeph Loeb, Jeffrey Bell, Maurissa Tancharoen, Jed Whedon, Joss Whedon; **Created by** Joss Whedon, Jed Whedon, Maurissa Tancharoen **DOP:** Allan Westbrook, Kyle Jewell; **Prod.Des.:** Gregory S Melton; **Ed:** Eric Litman, Dexter Adriano, Kelly Stuyvesant, Joshua Charson; **Costumes:** Whitney Galitz Berger, Jessica Torok; **Marvel Television/ABC Studios/ Mutant Enemy**; c 45

Episodes:

7.1 THE NEW DEAL *(27/5/2020)*
Finding themselves back in the 1930s without Fitz, SHIELD encounter dead men without faces who force Mack to make finding the Chronicoms their first order of business. The new Coulson leads Mack to an early version of the SSR where they meet one of Keonig's ancestors. Meanwhile Simmons and Yo-Yo watch over May's recovery, while Daisy and Deke run into a Chronicom and are forced to capture it.

Cast: Joel Stoffer (Enoch), Tobias Jelinek (Luke), Joe Reegan (Chronicom), Darren Barnet (Freddy Malick), Nora Zehetner (Freddy's

Contact), Greg Finley (Tillman), Luke Baines (Chronicom) and Patton
Oswalt (Ernest Hazard Koenig)
Dir: Kevin Tancharoen; **Writer:** George Kitson

7.2 KNOW YOUR ONIONS *(3/6/2020)*
Having learnt the true identity of Freddy Malick, Daisy is keen to have
him killed to avoid the future, and tells Deke to do so, though he is
stopped by Mack. Simmons realises that Freddy is smuggling the key
ingredient of the super soldier serum to the future Red Skull, but
Coulson is insistent they keep history correct. Meanwhile both May and
Yo-Yo show signs of having been affected by their previous adventures.

Cast: Joel Stoffer (Enoch), Tobias Jelinek (Luke), Darren Barnet
(Freddy Malick), Nora Zehetner (Freddy's Contact) and Patton Oswalt
(Ernest Hazard Koenig)
Dir: Eric Laneuville; **Writer:** Craig Titley

7.3 ALIEN COMMIES FROM THE FUTURE! *(10/6/2020)*
Unable to control their jumps, when the team arrive in the 1950's they
realise that the Chronicoms are nearby at a government base, and
Coulson and Simmons go undercover as Peggy Carter and her aide,
though this is destroyed the moment they run into Daniel Sousa. With
little choice, Daisy, May and Yo-You go in to rescue Coulson and
Simmons before the Chronicoms begin their mission.

Cast: Enver Gjokaj (Daniel Sousa), Tobias Jelinek (Luke), Julian
Acosta (Pascal Vega), Michael Gaston (Gerald Sharpe) and Tamara
Taylor (Sibyl)
Dir: Nina Lopez-Corrado; **Writers:** Nora Zuckerman & Lilla Zuckerman

7.4 OUT OF THE PAST *(17/6/2020)*
Coulson recalls the events leading up to Daniel Sousa's death, as they
negotiate Sousa's handover of a very special item to Howard Stark's
associates. However, knowing that Wilfred Malick is interested in
acquiring the same item, Coulson and the team work to ensure the
changeover goes smoothly, while debating whether they should save
Sousa's life.

Cast: Joel Stoffer (Enoch), Tobias Jelinek (Luke), Neal Bledsoe
(Wilfred Malick), Larry Clarke (Bar fly) with Enver Gjokaj (Daniel Sousa)

Dir: Garry A Brown; **Writer:** Mark Leitner

7.5 A TROUT IN THE MILK *(24/6/2020)*
In 1973, the team try to track down Enoch, but in the bar are a little surprised to find that Freddy Malick is alive, contrary to established history, and that General Rick Stoner is preparing to launch Project Insight, about forty years ahead of schedule. In an attempt to stop both these things, the team try to make a plan, but the Chronicoms skip forward three years to foil them.

Cast: Joel Stoffer (Enoch), Tobias Jelinek (Luke), Thomas E Sullivan (Nathaniel Malick), Neal Bledsoe (Wilfred Malick), Dawan Owens (Ford), Cameron Palatas (Gideon Malick), Sedale Threatt Jr (John Mackenzie), Paulina Bugembe (Lila Mackenzie) with *Patrick Warburton (General Rick Stoner)* and Enver Gjokaj (Daniel Sousa)
Dir: Stan Brooks; **Writer:** Iden Baghdadchi

7.6 ADAPT OR DIE *(1/7/2020)*
At the lighthouse, May and Coulson are arrested and brought before Stoner, and they try to warn him about the threat of the Chronicoms. Nathaniel Malick captures Daisy and Sousa, with a plan to take Daisy's blood and give himself her powers. Mack organises a plan to rescue his agents, but is shocked to find that his parents are being held in a SHIELD base under imminent threat.

Cast: Joel Stoffer (Enoch), Tamara Taylor (Sibyl), Tobias Jelinek (Luke), Thomas E Sullivan (Nathaniel Malick), Paulina Bugembe (Lilla Mackenzie), Dawan Owens (Ford), Sedale Threatt Jr (John Mackenzie), Shakira Barrera (King) with *Patrick Warburton (General Rick Stoner)* and Enver Gjokaj (Daniel Sousa)
Dir: April Winney; **Writer:** DJ Doyle

7.7 THE TOTALLY EXCELLENT ADVENTURES OF MACK AND THE D *(8/7/2020)*
Stuck in 1982, Mack retreats away, still devastated by the deaths of his parents, while Deke attempts to work with him to get him through it. Elsewhere, Sybil reveals she survived the destruction caused by Coulson, and works with a computer technician to rebuild her army. However, she's not the only one building an army, and strangely not the only one to have survived the explosion.

Cast: Jolene Anderson (Olga Pachinko), Austin Basis (Russell), Ryan Donowho (Cricket), Tipper Newton (Roxy Glass) and Tamara Taylor (Sibyl)
Dir: Jesse Bocho; **Writer:** Brent Fletcher

7.8 AFTER, BEFORE *(15/7/2020)*

With the Zephyr's time jumps occurring more rapidly, only Yo-Yo has the speed to shut the machine down, but without her power is unable to. May and Yo-Yo go to Afterlife to meet Jiaying in the hope she might know a way to restore Yo-Yo's power. Jiaying agrees to help Yo-Yo, but the agents are concerned about a young Inhuman with enormous power that seems to be a prisoner.

Cast: Joel Stoffer (Enoch), Thomas E Sullivan (Nathaniel Malick), Dichen Lachman (Jiaying), Dianne Doan (Kora) with Byron Mann (Li) and Enver Gjokaj (Daniel Sousa)
Dir: Eli Gonda; **Writers:** James C Oliver & Sharla Oliver

7.9 AS I HAVE ALWAYS BEEN *(22/7/2019)*

Daisy awakens to find herself watched over by Sousa before a sequence of events results in the destruction of the time drive, whereupon she awakens again and goes through the same events. She soon becomes aware she is trapped in a time loop and gets help from Coulson who also seems to be aware of the situation. Together the pair try to work out how to save the ship – except they discover that they are getting closer and closer to the center of the time vortex.

Cast: Joel Stoffer (Enoch) and Enver Gjokaj (Daniel Sousa)
Dir: Elizabeth Henstridge; **Writer:** Drew Z Greenberg

7.10 STOLEN *(29/7/2019)*

Stranded back at the Lighthouse in the 1980s, Coulson suggests they have to stop Nathaniel Malick, who has already recruited Garrett to his cause. They are visited by Jiaying and Gordon, and the latter then teleports Coulson back to Afterlife where Malick is injecting his people with Inhuman blood to give them powers. But as Malick and Garrett penetrate the Lighthouse, it seems they are looking for someone very specific.

Cast: Enver Gjokaj (Daniel Sousa), Dichen Lachman (Jiaying), Thomas

E Sullivan (Nathaniel Malick), *James Paxton (John Garrett)*, Dianne Doan (Kora), Tipper Newton (Roxy Glass) and Byron Mann (Li)
Dir: Garry A Brown; **Writers:** George Kitson & Mark Leitner (Teleplay), Mark Linehan Bruner (Story)

7.11 BRAND NEW DAY *(5/8/2020)*
Kora claims to want to work with SHIELD but in a planned fit of anger allows Sybil to enter the Lighthouse computer systems, though Coulson is surprised to find he has gained the ability to understand those systems. Meanwhile, Malick continues his search for Fitz, and even threatens Zeke to get Simmons to talk, but finds himself unsuccessful.

Cast: Joel Stoffer (Enoch), Thomas E Sullivan (Nathaniel Malick), Dianne Doan (Kora), *James Paxton (Garrett)* and Enver Gjokaj (Daniel Sousa)
Dir: Keith Potter; **Writer:** Chris Freyer

7.12 THE END IS AT HAND *(12/8/2020)*
Daisy, Mack and Sousa head toward the zephyr with Chronicom ships around them destroying the SHIELD bases. Simmons is injected with a substance that aims to destroy the memory chip in her head. Coulson, May and Yo-Yo manage to capture Garrett and reveal the truth about Malick to him, while Daisy does the same to Kora. But with a coded message beamed to them, the team decide to abandon the Lighthouse.

Cast: Tamara Taylor (Sybil), Thomas E Sullivan (Nathaniel Malick), Dianne Doan (Kora), *James Paxton (Garrett),* Stephen Bishop (Brandon Gamble) with Bill Cobbs and Enver Gjokaj (Daniel Sousa)
Dir: Chris Cheramie; **Writer:** Jeffrey Bell

7.13 WHAT WE'RE FIGHTING FOR *(12/8/2020)*
With Simmons' mind in tatters, Fitz tries to get the team ready to return to their timeline, but they are against the idea of leaving the new timeline to deal with the Chronicoms. Fitz reaches Simmons, and the team come up with a plan to return to the prime timeline taking the Chronicom ships with them. However, to do this, someone needs to remain in the new timeline to activate the Quantum Bridge.

Cast: Joel Stoffer (Enoch), Thomas E Sullivan (Nathaniel Malick),

Dianne Doan (Kora), Briana Venskus (Piper), Stephen Bishop (Brandon Gamble), Maximilian Osinski (Davis), Coy Stewart (Flint), with Tamara Taylor (Sybil) and Enver Gjokaj (Daniel Sousa)
Dir: Kevin Tancharoen; **Writers:** Brent Fletcher & Jed Whedon

Notes: There are a number of different logos used through the series: the first two episodes have a 1930's style logo, while the second two 1950's episodes have two different logos that reflect the pulp sci-fi nature of the first, and the noir version of the second. Episode 5 has a 70's inspired title sequence (which is astonishing), while 6 uses the "future" version of the logo. Episode 7 has a simple 80's style type-face, but 8 has a glam 80's version of the original logo. From this point, the episodes swap between the "future" logo and the glam 80's version. The series was filmed after season six, and so remained ready to go despite the real-life global pandemic.

It's All Connected: The final season of *AGENTS OF SHIELD*, perhaps unsurprisingly, has a lot of connections to mention. Mack is back, still as the Director of SHIELD, along with Daisy, Simmons, Yo-Yo and May, while Coulson returns as a LMD struggling to identify if he's the real deal or not. He gets destroyed once, ends up in a computer, and then gets a new body…again. May has gained an empathic ability since her resurrection from the last season, and for the first part of the series has difficulty determining if her feelings are hers or others. Fitz makes an appearance in the last three episodes, apparently lost in time for the first part of the season. Simmons has an implant to deliberately keep her from remembering Fitz's location, as they are being hunted by the Chronicoms. Sybil returns, leading the Chronicoms to find Fitz, as there is no future where they succeed that has Fitz in it. Enoch also returns to assist, though he is stranded in the 1950's and has to wait a considerable time for the team to show up again. His death is one of the most genuinely poignant moments the series has ever delivered. The crew encounter Koenig's ancestor in the 1930's, who sets up a bar that will become a secret SHIELD hangout over the next century. Freddy Malick also resurrects Hydra and later fathers Gideon and Nathaniel, though it is Nathaniel that becomes SHIELD's antagonist when he learns of Daisy's abilities. There is a mention of Whitehall's theories that the blood of Inhumans can give other's abilities, and both Jiaying and Gordon appear in the 1980's episodes, though Nathaniel kills Jiaying. Jiaying also has a daughter named Kora – the sister Daisy never had, which brings us neatly to….

    The majority of the season takes place in an alternate timeline that seems to be generated from the 1950's after they save the life of Daniel Sousa (he of *AGENT CARTER* fame). Sousa joins the crew, forming a relationship with Daisy, but it is made clear that everything that happens in the 70's and 80's all takes place in an alternate timeline (such as the deaths of Mack's parents). In the final two episodes, Fitz shows them how to use the Quantum Realm (*ANT-MAN*) to get back to the normal universe as the Chronicoms destroy SHIELD, including the Triskelion (*CAPTAIN AMERICA: THE WINTER SOLDIER*). Nathaniel also recruits a young John Garrett (played neatly by Bill Paxton's son) and turns him into an Inhuman – though he is later shot by a SHIELD agent after leaving Nathaniel's gang (rather callously, no one seems to care). In the seventies SHIELD is under the control of General Rick Stoner, who appeared as a hologram previously, and in the eighties, it is clear that Victoria Hand is a member of SHIELD. Deke Shaw is still a regular character, but it's worth giving him some time, as his murder of Freddy might also be the catalyst for the alternate history. Stranded with Mack in the eighties, Deke forms a rock group by stealing old songs and then uses this as a front to form a second SHIELD, using the Lighthouse as a base. Someone needs to stay in the alternate universe to allow the others to return and Deke opts to do this, remaining as the new Director of SHIELD.

The coda for the series is set a year after the return of the team (it's unclear when they return – potentially it is 2019, but it could just as well be 2023 after the blip) and we learn of the fates of the SHIELD team. Mack is still a high-ranking member of SHIELD and at the very least commands a helicarrier. May teaches at the Phil Coulson Academy, training, amongst others, Flint. Fitz and Simmons have retired from SHIELD and are raising their daughter Alya – the real reason Simmons hid Fitz's location. They still act as advisors. Yo-Yo has her own SHIELD team, including Piper and an LMD of Davis. Daisy continues to explore space, with Sousa and Kora (who went to the prime universe) helping her. Coulson remains uncertain of his future, but has Lola back – upgraded by Mack, so the car can now not only fly, but change colour.

Comic Notes: Again, nothing new for this season, though given it's tying up the television show, that's perhaps not surprising.

Ratings: *IMDB:* 7.5; *Rotten Tomatoes:* 100%; *Metacritic:* 74

Review: After proving that space travel didn't make for particularly good *Agents of SHIELD*, it's fortunate that the creative team didn't make the same mistake with time travel. Setting episodes in the thirties, fifties, seventies and eighties gives the show the chance to really have some fun, and from the outset the series seems to be a step up from last season. As the series goes on and it gains a new semi-regular in the form of *AGENT CARTER* regular

Daniel Sousa, everything clicks. Everything works perfectly, every character in fine form (despite Fitz's disappearance for most of the season), and there are some truly emotional moments (Enoch's finale being particularly powerful). Perhaps the thing that works least well is villain Nathaniel Malick, who is nowhere near the threat that, say, Talbot was two seasons ago. However, season seven is **AGENTS OF SHIELD** going out in style and this is easily one of the best seasons the show ever did.

HELSTROM
[Season 1]*(16/10/ 2020 – Hulu)*

Regular Cast: *Tom Austen (Daimon Helstrom), Sydney Lemmon (Ana Helstrom), Elizabeth Marvel (Victoria Helstrom), Robert Wisdom (Henry the Caretaker)*[1.1-1.5,1.7,1.9-1.10], *Ariana Guerra (Gabriella Rossetti), June Carryl (Louise Hastings), Alain Uy (Chris Yen)*[1.1-1.2,1.4-1.7,1.9-1.10]
Prod: Vail Romeyn, Blair Butler; **Music:** Danny Bensi and Saunder Jurriaans; **Exec.Prod:** Daina Reid, Joe Quesada, Karim Zreik, Jeph Loeb, Paul Zbyszewski; **Created by** Paul Zbyszewski; **DOP:** Bernard Couture [1.1-1.4,1.6,1.8,1.10], Christopher Charles Kempinski [1.5,1.7,1.9]; **Prod.Des.:** Todd Fjelsted; **Costumes:** Aieisha Li [1.1-1.2], Farnaz Khaki-Sadigh [1.3-1.10]; **Marvel Television/ABC Signature**; 45

Episodes:

1.1 MOTHER'S LITTLE HELPERS
When a nurse kills a security guard and frees two patients at St Teresa's psychiatric ward, Hastings informs Daimon who talks with his incarcerated, and seemingly possessed, mother, but gets no real answers. At much the same time, Henry summons Ana to show her something he has uncovered – something that comes with the corpses of those associated with St Teresa. With little choice, Daimon and Ana find themselves meeting again.

Cast: Jesse James Baldwin (Archer Cavallo), Daniel Cudmore (Keith Spivey), Sandy Robson (Alex Tilden), Eric Gustafsson (Edward Tate), Nolan Hupp (Young Daimon), Erica Tremblay (Young Ana), Todd Thomson (Mr Cavallo), Jessie Fraser (Mrs Cavallo), Shayn Walkor (Ellis), Shane Leydon (Hock), Mig Macarlo (Liddle), Kat Pasion (Rose), Nicole Anthony (Auctioneer)

Dir: Daina Reid; **Writer:** Paul Zbyszewski; **Ed:** Hunter M Via

1.2 VIATICUM

Ana asks Daimon if she can see Victoria, and Daimon agrees, against Hastings better judgement. Initially she gets nowhere, but when alone, Ana asks Victoria what creatures had been released, though Victoria claims release wasn't her plan. Meanwhile Daimon and Gabriella go to a highway accident where they find a survivor possessed by a demon, and Yen's interest in the skull Ana found, marks him for possession by it.

Cast: Deborah Van Valkenburgh (Esther Smith), Daniel Cudmore (Keith Spivey), Erica Tremblay (Young Ana), Hiro Kanagawa (Father Sean Okamoto), Sandy Robson (Alex Tilden/Magoth), Kyle Warren (Cameron Tate), Andres Collantes (Kevin)
Dir: Anders Engström; **Writer:** Blair Butler; **Ed:** Kelly Stuyvesant

1.3 THE ONE WHO GOT AWAY

With Victoria briefly lucid, Ana agrees to help Daimon, and they join Gabriella who has found one of the Helstrom's father's victims still alive, though Ana is convinced this is impossible as she remembers as a child when her father killed the victim. They meet the woman but Ana's conviction has the three thrown out. Meanwhile Henry visits Hastings and discovers the truth of his friend's health, and that Victoria has given over to Mother.

Cast: Zachary S Williams (Bryce/Magoth), Daniel Cudmore (Keith Spivey), Erica Tremblay (Young Ana), David Quinlan (Tooms), Camille Sullivan (Zoe Richards/Aubrey Richards), Jordan Burtchett (Chad), Sean Kuling (Jake)
Dir: Michael Offer; **Writer:** Marcus Dalzine; **Ed:** Brian G Addie

1.4 CONTAINMENT

Henry reveals that the mysterious skull is a Keeper demon that can be used to trap the Helstroms' father, and Ana and Daimon go back to San Francisco where they discover Yen has disappeared with the skull, after killing someone. A demon attempts to attack Gabriella but Henry stops it and takes the possessed priest to a hotel where the possessed are watched over by The Blood. Meanwhile Hastings has a surprising conversation with Victoria.

Cast: David Meunier (Finn Miller), Zachary S Williams (Bryce/Magoth), Trevor Roberts (Father Joshua Crow), Kyle Warren (Cameron Tate), Shayn Walker (Ellis), Hamza Fouad (Officer Derrick Jackson), Shauna Hansen (Nurse), Joe Buffalo (Orderly)
Dir: Amanda Row; **Writer:** Sheila Wilson; **Ed:** Hunter M Via, JD Sievertson

1.5 COMMITTED

While Gabriella meets with Bryce to see how the student is dealing with the removal of Magoth, Victoria finds herself trapped in a repeating cycle of the day she was committed. However, this changes as she is confronted by Kthara who needs her help. Meanwhile, Daimon and Ana try to find the skull and Yen, realising he must be somewhere nearby.

Cast: Fiona Dourif (Mother/Kthara), Zachary S Williams (Bryce), Nolan Hupp (Young Daimon), Erica Tremblay (Young Ana), Brody Romhanyi (The Keeper), Veenu Sandhu (Psychologist), William Valenzuela (Social Worker), Marcel Zadeh (Orderly)
Dir: Jovanka Vuckovic; **Writer:** Ian Sobel and Matt Morgan; **Ed:** Kelly Stuyvesant

1.6 LEVIATHAN

As Daimon and Gabriella clean up at the hotel, they realise that the demons have been let loose. Ana tries to get through to Yen, but Hastings suggests she talk with Victoria, and Ana is surprised to find her guard drops. Spivey arrives and takes control of the hospital, and Daimon and Gabriella are forced to go to a mechanics. In both cases the demons are lying in wait.

Cast: Samantha Sloyan (Joelene Spivey), Daniel Cudmore (Keith Spivey), Trevor Roberts (Father Joshua Crow/Raum), Jan Bos (Dr Lawrence), Magda Ochoa (Emaciated Woman/Yessenia Flores), Shayn Walker (Ellis), Andrew Wheeler (Naren), Xavier deSalaberry (Brian), Leif Bridgman (Jeff), Alan Yu (Manny), Leah Hennessey (Tanya), Arkie Kandola (Mechanic)
Dir: Sanford Bookstaver; **Writer:** Amanda Segel; **Ed:** Brian G Addie

1.7 SCARS

The fallout from the attack on the hospital sees Ana and Yen returning home, where Ana is desperate to kill someone to ease her rage, though

Yen is very reluctant and has to rebuild bridges with Derrick anyway. Daimon learns about Hastings' decision to separate Ana from him as a child and is contacted by the Blood who want to form an alliance to destroy his father.

Cast: Samantha Sloyan (Joelene Spivey), Daniel Cudmore (Keith Spivey/Basar), Trevor Roberts (Father Joshua Crow/Raum), Deborah Van Valkenburgh (Esther), Tom Everett (Archbishop Terrazi), Hamza Fouad (Derrick Jackson), Erica Tremblay (Young Ana), Nolan Hupp (Young Daimon), Tarun Keram (Lee), Eugene Lipinski (Loman), Melice Bell (Client)
Dir: Bill Roe; **Writer:** Mark Leitner; **Ed:** Hunter M Via

1.8 UNDERNEATH

With the knife half retrieved, Daimon and Gabriella set off to get the other half, but when they go to the Helstrom's old home, they are acutely aware of the Blood agents also there. Daimon comes up with a plan but knows that Gabriella probably won't approve. Meanwhile Ana and Hastings are summoned to a trap, but the possibility of saving Victoria motivates them into doing so, regardless of the consequences.

Cast: David Meunier (Finn/Magoth), Daniel Cudmore (Keith Spivey/Basar), Trevor Roberts (Father Joshua Crow/Raum), Deborah Van Valkenburgh (Esther), Nolan Hupp (Young Daimon), Shekhar Paleja (Ahmad), Christine Horn (Real Estate Agent), Olivia Poon (Doctor)
Dir: Cherie Nowlan; **Writer:** Maggie Bandur; **Ed:** Kelly Stuyvesant

1.9 VESSELS

Gabriella awakens to find that she is now carrying Daimon's child; however, she is a prisoner of Magoth and Raum, who anxiously await Kthara's rebirth through the child. Shockingly Gabriella realises that despite Kthara's visitations, she has no real power. Meanwhile Basar – in the form of Daimon, tries to kill Victoria, leaving Ana to determine a way that she might exorcise her brother.

Cast: David Meunier (Finn/Magoth), Trevor Roberts (Father Joshua Crow/Raum), Hamza Faoud (Derrick Jackson), Jasmine Lukuku (Nurse), Jean-Paul Najm (Blood Thug #1), Franckie Francois (Blood Thug #2)
Dir: Kevin Tancharoen; **Writers:** Ian Sobel and Matt Morgan; **Ed:** Brian G Addie

1.10 HELL STORM

Hastings and Victoria try to protect Gabriella, who flees to the church to get help from the Blood. Hastings is badly wounded and goes to hospital, while Yen discovers he is a Keeper, and tells Ana how to repair the dagger, which she can then use to free Daimon. Gabriella is forced to go with Basar and the other demons to give birth to Kthara's new form, and Ana and Yen confront Daimon in an attempt to free him.

Cast: Mitch Pileggi (Papa), David Meunier (Finn/Magoth), Trevor Roberts (Father Joshua Crow/Raum), Deborah Van Valkenburgh (Esther), Tom Everett (Archbishop Terrazi), Jen Landon (Dr Katherine Reynolds), Nolan Hupp (Young Daimon), Tarun Keram (Lee), Grace Sunar (Lily), Michael Sangha (Surgeon)
Dir: Jim O'Hanlon; **Writer:** Paul Zbyszewski; **Ed:** Hunter M Via, JD Sievertson

Notes: The series was cancelled in December, 2020, though this was unsurprising as Marvel Television had been shut down a year earlier. Like all Marvel television programs, the series was intended to be, technically, **MARVEL'S HELSTROM**, but Disney requested the **Marvel** be dropped, along with the logo at the beginning of each episode. It had the working title *Omens*.

It's All Connected: We are introduced to Daimon and Ana Helstrom, the children of Victoria Helstrom and her husband, both of whom have powers such as telekinesis, as well as the ability to immolate – though Ana can also sense people's thoughts, and Daimon can exorcise demons. Their father was a demon himself, and he took Ana when they were young, leaving Daimon with Victoria who was possessed by a demon named Kthara. Daimon had his mother locked away to protect her, and she remained in care for decades. Ana was ultimately rescued by Henry – also known as Caretaker – while Daimon remained in church care under the eye of Louise Hastings. When the show picks up, Daimon is a lecturer who does the odd spot of exorcism, while Ana is an antiques dealer who, with her partner Chris Yen, tracks down criminals and kills them. We also meet Gabriella Rosetti, a novice in the church, who reports to the Archbishop on Daimon, and is broadly intended to replace Hastings, who is dying from cancer. By the end of the season, Gabriella and Daimon have a child who is the reincarnation of Kthara, after Victoria is freed from the demon. Ana and Daimon have patched up their family history, along with Victoria, but Gabriella, who fell in love with Daimon, now believes that demons are truly terrible and joins the Blood. In the final scene of the series, the young Kthara meets Papa – Daimon and Ana's father – and joins him, revealing her real name to be Lily.

In the opening episode we do see a fuel station that belongs to Roxxon, but outside of that there is no connection at all to the wider MCU.

Comic Notes: Daimon and Ana Helstrom are known in the comics as *Daimon and Satana Hellstrom*, but television viewers are more sensitive than comic book readers so the spelling was changed. If Satanism offends, you might want to skip this section and go straight to the review.

Daimon Hellstrom: first appeared in *Ghost Rider #1 (Sep, '73)* and was created by Roy Thomas and Gary Friedrich. Now, as times changes and the sensitivities change as well, so backstories are often retconned. Initially, Daimon was the son of Victoria Wingage and Satan (the actual Satan). Daimon tried very hard to cling to his humanity, and was indeed raised in an orphanage, and later did become a professor of anthropology. He has the ability to heal, project fire and use dark magic. Daimon has been a member of a number of supergroups, including the Hellfire Club, but spends a lot of his time with the Defenders. He even married Patsy Walker/Hellcat, but this ended when Patsy summoned his father to save him, and she got a glimpse of Daimon's "true face of evil" driving her insane. At one point he told Patsy that he was actually the son of Satannish, and intended on taking control of all the hell dimensions, but this was later revealed to be a lie.

Satana Hellstrom: first appeared in *Vampire Tales #2 (Oct, '73)*, created by Thomas and John Romita Sr, and like her brother can project fire, use dark magic, but can also absorb souls. Like the series she was abducted by her father, but in the comics, she was taken to a hell-like dimension and become a servant to her father, bonding with a spirit called the Basilisk and gaining a familiar named Exiter. When she grew up, she became a succubus and was banished to Earth where she crossed her father to save the soul of a man named Michael Heron. She died at one point trying to save Dr Strange, but was resurrected, and died and resurrected... At one point she joined the Thunderbolts to work with Man-Thing, and even married Deadpool. Currently she is dead, killed by the human-Asgardian crossbreed Tier. The television version is quite a good visual interpretation of the comic version.

Victoria Wingate Hellstrom: was a woman who was rejected by a convent and she was sold to the Chapel of Dresden where she was marked to be the mother of demon children. When she was at Fire Lake, she apparently met Satan – though this later turned out to be a demon named Marduk Kurios who was just posing as Satan, and who impregnated her. She gave birth to her son

Daimon, and a year and a half after that, Satana. When she found Satana performing a ritual sacrifice, it drove her mad and she was institutionalised. She carried an ankh as protection from her husband. She first appeared in *Marvel Spotlight #13 (Jan, '74)* and was created by Gary Friedrich and Herb Trimpe.

Kthara: also played a part in the Hellstrom's lives. She was a demon who served Satan, but later was released from Hell by Satanist Gloria Hefford. On Earth she wanted to perform a rite which would give her control over the world, and involved killing eleven people, with Daimon to be her twelfth. She manipulated Daimon into battling Satana, and Daimon apparently killed her, but the Basilisk revived Satana, and she saved Daimon before Kthara could sacrifice him. She was sent back to Hell, but was later released and beaten by Daimon with help from the Fantastic Four's Thing. Kthara also made her first appearance in *Marvel Spotlight*, but in #24 (Oct, '75) and was created by Chris Claremont and Sal Buscema.

Louise Hastings: first appeared in *Darkhold: Pages from the Book of Sins #1 (Oct, '92)* created by Christopher Cooper and Richard Case. She is a member of the Darkhold Redeemers and has worked alongside Ghost Rider in order to destroy the Lilin. Sadly, she was killed by Morbius who was possessed by one of the Lilin at the time.

Gabriella Rosetti is a gender swap of *Gabriel Rosetti:* a teacher who joined a seminary after his wife appeared to have taken her own life. He was possessed by a demon named Catherine who made him rip his own eye out, and as such he seared a cross onto his chest, driving the demon out. He became a professional exorcist with the help of a woman named Desadia who he later married. He helped Agatha Harkness stop her son Nicholas Scratch possessing Franklin Richards, but he encountered Daimon Hellstrom on a number of occasions which ultimately drove him insane. With Desadia killed by evil forces, Daimon left Rosetti with Gargoyle to be looked after. He first appeared in *Haunt of Horror #2 (Jul, '74)* and was created by Doug Moench and Billy Graham.

Caretaker: is never given a name in the comics, but he is a member of the Blood and has worked with Dr Strange and two different Ghost Riders. He also has an apprentice named Seer. Oddly enough, while he worked with the Midnight Sons and fought the Lilin, he, like Louise Hastings, never actually encountered the Hellstroms. He also appears to be free from aging and has a degree of superhuman strength. He first appeared in *Ghost Rider Vol 3 #28*

(Aug, '92) created by Howard Mackie and Andy Kubert. His comic book appearance is very different to his television version, being white-haired and blue eyed.

Ratings: *IMDB:* 6.8; *Rotten Tomatoes:* 27%; *Metacritic:* 40

Review: If ever there was something that felt like an afterthought, *HELSTROM* is it. There's a huge lack of energy in the show, as if the production team were going through the motions to meet their contractual obligations. The lead cast struggle to engage, either with each other or the audience, and only Elizabeth Marvel really stands out. Everyone else has the same inertia, doing what has to be done. The story is serviceable but makes the huge mistake of leaving the big stuff for season two. Mitch Pileggi's appearance at the end is hugely exciting, but really only works if you know there's going to be a pay off, and in this case, we know there's absolutely not. You can't help but wonder why the production team didn't just leave the scene out. At its best, the series is average. At its worst, it's boring. Marvel can do much better.

ADVENTURE INTO FEAR

In May, 2019, after Netflix had cancelled all their Marvel television series, an announcement was made that two new series for Hulu were going into development – *Ghost Rider* and *Helstrom*. Gabriel Luna was on board to return as Robbie Reyes, the Ghost Rider, while Tom Austen and Sydney Lemmon would be Daimon and Ana Helstrom. Though no further details were released about what was being called *Spirit of Vengeance*, Jeph Loeb indicated that there would be other series, and that *Adventure into Fear* (as the new title of *Spirit of Vengeance* became) would rise to fill the void that the Netflix series left.

This was seen as slightly odd. By this point Disney had acquired much of Fox and its properties, and in 2018 Disney+ was also moving ahead. As such there was a fair bit of speculation that the Netflix MCU programs would be cancelled so that Disney could start work on them for their own platform. When Netflix cancelled them, to many it was seen as a pre-emptive strike, before Marvel Television simply didn't renegotiate. The cancellation of *AGENTS OF SHIELD* as well as *RUNAWAYS* and *CLOAK & DAGGER* all seemed to suggest that Disney was bringing everything back under one roof.

But still, Ingrid Escajeda was announced as the showrunner for *GHOST RIDER* while Paul Zbyszewski was appointed to *HELSTROM*. In July 2019, Loeb assured people that Robbie Reyes would still be the character from **SHIELD**, and that would be referenced, but in August, Zbyszewski made the confusing announcement that **HELSTROM** would not tie into the MCU. Then in September 2019, Hulu announced they were not moving forward with **GHOST RIDER**, much to the surprise of Luna. At this point, many believed that *Helstrom* would probably follow, and in December 2019, Marvel Television was folded into Marvel Studios, and would now be under the direct control of Kevin Feige.

So it was a little surprising when it turned out that **HELSTROM** entered production in October, 2019, and would be delivered to Hulu for an October, 2020 release. But, of course, it was no surprise when it was cancelled in December.

It's unclear precisely how the *Adventure into Fear* plans came undone, but it's not hard to guess that the launch of Disney+, and the need to get content for that platform was the primary reason. What's more confusing is why **HELSTROM** actually went ahead. It has been speculated that it did simply because of the contracts with Hulu, and Marvel Television/ABC Signature Studios were obligated to complete the project. It's hard to tell if the viewers were the ultimate winners of this situation, but whatever the case, *Adventure into Fear* became a very disappointing missed opportunity.

WANDAVISION
[Season 1] *(Disney+)*

Regular Cast: Elizabeth Olsen (Wanda Maximoff *[1.1-1.9]*/The Scarlet Witch *[1.9]*), Paul Bettany (Vision *[1.1-1.9]* & The Vision *[1.9]*), Teyonah Parris (Monica Rambeau *[1.4-1.7,1.9]*/Geraldine *[1.2-1.3]*), Evan Peters (Pietro Maximoff *[1.5-1.7,1.9]*/Ralph Bohner *[1.9]*), Randall Park (Jimmy Woo)*[1.4-1.7,1.9]*, Debra Jo Rupp (Sharon Davis aka *[1.8-1.9]* Mrs Hart *[1.1-1.2,1.7-1.9]*), Fred Melamed (Mr Hart)*[1.1]* with Kat Dennings (Darcy Lewis *[1.4-1.7,1.9]*/The Escape Artist *[1.7]*) and Kathryn Hahn (Agnes *[1.1-1.7]*/Agatha Harkness *[1.8-1.9]*/Agnes the Nosy Neighbour *[1.9]*)
Prod: Chuck Hayward; **Music:** Christophe Beck, Kristen Anderson-Lopez (Themes), Robert Lopez (Themes); **Exec.Prod:** Kevin Feige, Louis D'Esposito, Victoria Alonso, Matt Shakman, Jac Schaeffer; **Created by** Jac Schaeffer; **DOP:** Jess Hall; **Prod.Des.:** Mark Worthington; **Costumes:** Mayes C Rubeo; **Marvel Studios**; 25 - 45

Episodes:

1.1 FILMED BEFORE A LIVE STUDIO AUDIENCE *(15/1/2021)*

Wanda and Vision discover a heart on their calendar, but neither can remember what it's for. Wanda meets her new next-door neighbour and they plan an evening to celebrate an anniversary, while Vision remembers they are actually hosting his boss, Mr Hart, for dinner. During dinner, however, Mr Hart gets ill and Vision has to save his life.
Cast: Asif Ali (Norm), David Lengel (Phil Jones), Ithamar Enriquez (Commercial Man), Victoria Blade (Commercial Woman), Amos Glick (Dennis the Mailman)
Dir: Matt Shakman; **Writer:** Jac Schaeffer; **Ed:** Tim Roche

1.2 DON'T TOUCH THAT DIAL *(15/1/2021)*
Vision practices his magic act for the talent show before he meets with the neighbourhood watch. Meanwhile Wanda and Agnes head off to meet Dottie and the rest of the planning committee – except before they go, Wanda finds a toy helicopter that, unlike the rest of her black and white world is colour. At the meeting, Dottie expresses her concern about Wanda as the radio plays a strange message directed at her.

Cast: Asif Ali (Norm), Emma Caulfield Ford (Dottie), Joelene Purdy (Beverly), Amos Glick (Dennis the Mailman), David Payton (Herb), David Lengel (Phil Jones), Zac Henry (Beekeeper), Victoria Blade (Commercial Woman), Ithamar Enriquez (Commercial Man), Yuuki Luna, Eric Delgado (Tap Dancers)
Dir: Matt Shakman; **Writer:** Gretchen Enders; **Ed:** Zene Baker

1.3 NOW IN COLOR *(22/1/2021)*
Wanda's pregnancy is extremely quick, so much so that Vision roughly calculates that the baby will be born Friday afternoon, and the parents aren't sure what to call him. However, reality is starting to break down, and Vision senses that there is something wrong. But it is when Geraldine tells Wanda that Pietro was killed by Ultron that things take a surprising turn.

Cast: Emma Caulfield Ford (Dottie), David Payton (Herb), David Lengel (Phil Jones), Randy Oglesby (Doctor Nielson), Rose Blanco (Mrs Nielson), Ithamar Enriquez (Commercial Man), Wesley Kimmel (Commercial Boy), Sydney Thomas (Commercial Girl), Victoria Blade (Commercial Woman)
Dir: Matt Shakman; **Writer:** Megan McDonnell; **Ed:** Nona Khodai

1.4 WE INTERRUPT THIS PROGRAM *(29/1/2021)*

Three weeks after returning from the dead, Monica Rambeau returns to SWORD and is sent to work with FBI Agent Woo who has lost a witness…and a town. Though the town is directly in front of them, and when Monica moves forward, she is sucked into the strange reality of Westview. SWORD moves in, bringing in experts including Dr Darcy Lewis, who discovers a very strange television show being broadcast from Westview – starring someone who is definitely dead.

Cast: Josh Stamberg (Director Hayward), Alan Heckner (Agent Monti), Selena Anduze (Agent Rodriguez), Lana Young (Dr Highland), Sam Younis (Doctor), Viviana Chavez (Nurse), Bobby Hernandez (Security Guard), Shaun Maclean (Orderly), Brian Brightman (Sheriff), Zac Henry (SWORD Agent/Beekeeper), Vince Canlas, Archith Seshadri (Men in Van), Michaela Cronan (Woman in Van), Janet Song, Christopher James (Blip Back People), Lloyd Pitts (Man)
Dir: Matt Shakman; **Writers:** Boback Esfarjani and Megan McDonnell; **Ed:** Tim Roche

1.5 ON A VERY SPECIAL EPISODE… *(5/2/2021)*

The twins are stressing out Wanda, not least when they age themselves up, but things get more complicated when they get even older after finding a dog. Vision, however, is starting to notice some strange goings on in Westview, and is very puzzled when he releases Norm's mind only for him to beg for help. On the outside world, Wanda confronts Hayward, but it does not go well.

Cast: *Julian Hilliard (Billy), Jett Klyne (Tommy), Baylen Bielitz (Billy (5 years old)), Gavin Borders (Tommy (5 years old)),* Josh Stamberg (Director Hayward), Amos Glick (Postman), Asif Ali (Norm), Alan Heckner (Agent Monti), Selena Anduze (Agent Rodriguez), Jenna Kanell (Med Tech), Victoria Blade (Commerical Woman), Ithamar Enriquez (Commercial Man), Sydney Thomas (Commercial Girl), Wesley Kimmel (Commercial Boy), Eli Everett (SWORD Drone Pilot), Christine Renaud (Darcy Double), Jackson Robert Scott (Billy Reference)
Dir: Matt Shakman; **Writer:** Peter Cameron and Mackenzie Dohr; **Ed:** Nona Khodai

1.6 ALL-NEW HALLOWEEN SPOOKTACULAR! *(12/2/2021)*

With tension between Wanda and Vision, Halloween arrives and

Tommy and Billy are excited to go out with their uncle Pietro, even though Wanda is still puzzled at why he looks so different. Rambeau pushes her luck too far, and she, Woo and Darcy are expelled from the SWORD base, though Rambeau has a plan to reenter the hex. When Vision escapes the hex and starts to die, Wanda reveals the full strength of her power.

Cast: *Julian Hilliard (Billy), Jett Klyne (Tommy),* Josh Stamberg (Director Hayward), David Payton (Herb), Alan Heckner (Agent Monti), Selena Anduze (Agent Rodriguez), Sophia Gaidarova (Young Wanda), Joshua Begelman (Young Pietro), Stephanie Astalos-Jones (Toothless Old Woman), Amor Owens (Parent), Tamara Hetzel (Suburban Woman), Jon Zimmerman (Suburban Man), Christine Renaud (Darcy Double), Jackson Robert Scott (Billy Reference), Adam Gold (Commercial Shark (VO)), Tristen Chen (Commercial Kid (VO))
Dir: Matt Shakman; **Writers:** Chuck Hayward and Peter Cameron; **Ed:** Zene Baker

1.7 BREAKING THE FOURTH WALL *(19/2/2021)*
Vision makes contact with Darcy and manages to bring her out of Wanda's hex, but their attempt to return to his home is constantly hindered, to the point where Vision suspects they are being deliberately kept away. Meanwhile Wanda becomes aware that she is losing her control over Westview, but when Agnes takes the children, she comes into contact with a far more powerful Monica Rambeau, who has broken through the barrier.

Cast: *Julian Hilliard (Billy), Jett Klyne (Tommy),* Josh Stamberg (Director Hayward), Emma Caulfield Ford (Dottie), Jolene Purdy (Beverly), David Payton (Herb), David Lengel (Phil Jones), Asif Ali (Norm), Alan Heckner (The Strong Man), Rachael Thompson (Major Goodner), Selena Anduze (Agent Rodriguez), Amos Glick (Dennis the Delivery Man), Jackson Robert Scott (Billy Reference), Victoria Blade (Commercial Woman), Ithamar Enriquez (Commercial Man), Wesley Kimmel (Commercial Boy), Sydney Thomas (Commercial Girl)
Dir: Matt Shakman; **Writer:** Cameron Squires; **Ed:** Tim Roche

1.8 PREVIOUSLY ON *(26/2/2021)*
Agatha is keen to know more details about Wanda's powers and takes her back through her own past, examining the night she and Pietro were trapped in a room with a Stark bomb, when she volunteered for

Hydra and when she became part of the Avengers. Agatha notes Wanda's powers were always present, and that the she has essentially lost everything. Realising she is the Scarlet Witch, Agatha threatens Billy and Tommy.

Cast: *Julian Hilliard (Billy), Jett Klyne (Tommy),* Josh Stamberg (Director Hayward), David Payton (John Collins aka Herb), David Lengel (Harold Proctor aka Phil Jones), Amos Glick (Pizza Delivery Man), Selena Anduze (Agent Rodriguez), Kate Forbes (Evanora Harkness), Ilana Kohanchi (Iryna Maximoff), Daniyar (Olek Maximoff), Michaela Russell (Young Wanda), Gabriel Gurevich (Young Pietro), Hans Obma (Hydra Scientist), Stephen Goldbach (Hydra Tech), Aaron Gillespie (Security Guard)
Dir: Matt Shakman; **Writer:** Laura Donney; **Ed:** Nona Khodai

1.9 THE SERIES FINALE *(5/3/2021)*
As Wanda confronts Agatha to rescue her children, their fight is interrupted by the arrival of the white Vision who attempts to kill Wanda. Wanda's Vision appears and the two Visions fight, though discussion ceases the fight and brings perspective. Wanda reduces the hex when she realises what she has done to the town, but in doing so allows Hayward and Woo's teams to enter, giving her family a whole host of threats to stop.

Cast: *Julian Hilliard (Billy), Jett Klyne (Tommy),* Josh Stamberg (Director Hayward), Asif Ali (Abilash Tandon (aka Norm)), Emma Caulfield Ford (Sarah Proctor (aka Dottie)), David Payton (John Collins (aka Herb)), David Lengel (Harold Proctor (aka Phil Jones)), Amos Glick (The Delivery Man (aka Dennis)), Selena Anduze (Agent Rodriguez), Kate Forbes (Evanora Harkness), Lori Livingston (Skrull Agent), Chase Yi (EMT), Christine Renaud (Darcy Double), Jackson Robert Scott (Billy Reference)
Dir: Matt Shakman; **Writer:** Jac Schaeffer; **Ed:** Zene Baker, Michael A Webber

Notes: The series was announced in 2019 as one of the forthcoming MCU television series that were planned to interact more with the movies, and would be made by Marvel Studios, having absorbed Marvel Television. Olsen and Bettany swap top billing each episode. The first episode was indeed filmed before a live studio audience, and the first three episodes are – for the most part – broadcast in a 4:3 ratio (and the first two in black and white) to give the impression of the eras that they represent. Each episode has its own title sequence and theme which are directly inspired from sitcoms of their respective eras. Lighting and film style was also done to mimic those eras, while Dick Van Dyke was consulted as well. Some of the houses are recycled from other productions; Dottie's is the Murtagh house from **LETHAL WEAPON**, while Wanda's is the house from **NATIONAL LAMPOON'S CHRISTMAS VACATION**. Reputedly, the budget per episode was enormous and **WANDAVISION** is allegedly one of the most expensive television programs ever. The working title for the series was *Big Red*. Elizabeth Olsen's reading of "Previously on **WANDAVISION**..." gets progressively more tired over the series. Kat Dennings appearance in the finale was cut short as COVID prevented her from filming her scenes. The number plate of Wanda's car is 122822, which is the date of Stan Lee's birth (December 28, 1922). Slightly more curiously, after the release of the series Marvel Studios made some small changes to the post-credits sequence, changing the landscape slightly. The series gains the credit "A Kevin Feige Production" which all Marvel television series will bear going forward.

Should I Stay To The End? There are mid credit sequences in both episodes seven and nine, both of which are worth watching – the first moves the action forward, while the second hints at the return of the Skrulls and Monica being summoned, either by Nick Fury or Talos. There is a final post-credit sequence which presumably leads into **DOCTOR STRANGE IN THE MULTIVERSE OF MADNESS**.

It's All Connected: The series takes place about five weeks after **AVENGERS: ENDGAME**. From Wanda's perspective, she awoke and went to find Vision, who was taken by SWORD (the Sentient Weapon Observation and Response Division) and disassembled. Furious she tries to save him, but could not, and as such went to Westview where she and Vision had purchased a block of land to live happily ever after. Here, she used her magic to create a house and Vision, and then recreate Westview in the style of a 1950s sitcom, as well as place a barrier around the town that hid it. So devastated by her grief, she punished the citizens, locking away their children and hiding them from the rest of the world. From Monica Rambeau's perspective, she was at her dying mother's side when she was snapped away. When she returned, she discovered that Maria Rambeau had died three years earlier from cancer. Monica went back to SWORD where she worked, to discover Hayward had replaced Maria as the director of SWORD, and her first posting – grounded as she was – was to join Jimmy Woo of the FBI who was looking for a missing witness, and discovered a missing town. Monica entered Westview through the hex barrier and became part of the sitcom world that Wanda had created (now in the sixties). Monica helped Wanda give birth to her twins (now in the seventies), but when she mentioned the death of Pietro, Wanda expelled Monica from Westview. By this point Vision was beginning to suspect that something wasn't right. Everything that was happening in Westview was being sent to the outside world, and Hayward brought in a series of experts including Dr Darcy Lewis who picked up the signals of Wanda's broadcast, and they watched the various sitcoms. When Monica rejoined them, Darcy realised she had been altered in some way by moving through the barrier twice. When Monica went through the barrier a third time, she found her genetic structure altered, giving her certain abilities, including that of intangibility. Wanda encountered Pietro, who looked visually different to her brother, but was apparently the same person, and her children – Billy and Tommy – both aged themselves up to ten, but she stopped them getting any older after they lost their dog, Sparky. Throughout this entire situation, she was helped by her next-door neighbour Agnes. Agnes, however, turned out to be Agatha Harkness, a witch from four hundred years earlier, who was curious about Wanda's powers and wanted them for herself, believing those powers to be witchcraft. Agatha has, in her possession, the Darkhold, though it looks different to when it was held by Morgan Le Fey in *RUNAWAYS*. The Darkhold has a chapter on the Scarlet Witch, which Wanda is – indeed, going through Wanda's memories, revealed she had always had her powers, even before she was touched by the mind stone. Quite what this means about Pietro is never explained. Meanwhile, Hayward had rebuilt the Vision – though he was now white – and white Vision crossed the barrier, along with Hayward. There was a battle, with Agatha ultimately losing and having her mind wiped and sentenced to live in Westview as an average neighbour, while the white Vision was given access to his memories by Wanda's Vision, and he left. Wanda's decision to remove the hex and release Westview also meant she lost her Vision and her children. Monica, as noted above, is approached by a Skrull who says she is needed in space (presumably by Nick Fury or Talos), while Wanda ends up alone, living peacefully, though studying the Darkhold in her astral form. When she does, though, she hears the voices of her children.

There are several advertisements scattered throughout the series, all in some way tying into Wanda's past. The first is for a brand of Stark toasters, which has the same noise as the bomb which crashed into the Maximoff home. The second is for a Strucker timepiece. The third offers a bath in Hydra soak, if you want to get away without actually going anywhere The fourth ad is for Lagos paper towels, in case you make a mess you didn't mean to (Lagos being the city where Wanda accidentally killed a number of people while trying to stop Crossbones – the inference being obvious). The fifth and most curious is a boy stranded on an island, who cannot open the food brought for him by a shark, and as such withers away and dies. This appears to be less of a look at Wanda's past, and more about what Agatha's plan for her is. The sixth advertisement is an ad for Nexus anti-depressants – possibly the most on the nose advertisement as it points directly to Wanda's depression and the need to move as the world doesn't revolve around her.

Comic Notes: *Agatha Harkness:* is considerably different to her comic book counterpart. Aside from being physically much younger (the comic book version is an elderly grey-haired lady), she was Wanda's mentor and guided Wanda into using her magic to give birth to her twins. First appearing in *Fantastic Four #94 (Jan, '70)* and created by Stan Lee and Jack Kirby, Agatha was initially the governess of Franklin Richards, the son of Reed and Sue Richards. Agatha helped them defeat Annihilus during this time. Her son was the villainous Nicholas Scratch, and revealed Agatha belonged to a coven of witches called New Salem. She was again by the side of the Fanastic Four as they stopped Scratch and the Salem Seven. The Salem Seven took back control of New Salem and burnt Agatha at the stake, but she still existed on the astral plane. She was somehow resurrected around the time Billy and Tommy Maximoff were behaving oddly, to reveal they had parts of Mephisto's soul in them. When the demon absorbed them, Agatha wiped Wanda's memory of the boys. Later Nick Fury found Agatha's corpse and claimed she had been dead for some time. She remained in communication with Wanda, but was brought back to life when Wanda battled Chaos. She currently serves with the Daughters of Liberty.

Billy and Tommy Maximoff: first appear in *The Vision and the Scarlet Witch #12 (Sep, '86)* and were created by Steve Englehart and Richard Howell. There's a fair bit of difference between the comic book versions and the television versions, which is probably not surprising. As mentioned in Agatha's notes, Billy and Tommy were born thanks to Wanda Maximoff channeling a great source of magical energy. In truth, this source held the soul of Mephisto and as such the boys received some of this. Mephisto would take back these pieces wiping the boys out of existence. Allan Heinberg and Jim Cheung would resurrect the boys as Billy Kaplan in *Young Avengers #1 (Apr, '05)* and Tommy Shepherd in *Young Avengers #10 (Mar, '06).* The history of these two characters is significantly different to the twins, though both Billy and Tommy are identical, despite being born to different families, and as reincarnations of the Maximoff twins, Tommy has the power of super speed (going by the name Speed), while Billy has the powers of the Scarlet Witch, including magic, reality alteration, flight, teleportation, astral projection…it's quite a list (he goes by the name Wiccan). The boys would discover their previous identities and come to view Wanda as their mother. Wiccan is frequently praised as being one of the first prominent gay Marvel superheroes. Wiccan has served with the Guardians of the Galaxy and Avengers Idea Mechanics (an iteration of AIM), while Tommy has remained with the Young Avengers.

Sparky: does appear in the comics, surprisingly, though there he is green. He was actually a synthezoid built by Vision, using the brain of a dog who died when he dug up the Grim Reaper's corpse. Sparky was killed by a woman in a blind rage, but Tony Stark and Wanda reconstituted the dog. Created by Tom King and Gabriel Hernandez Walta, the pet first appeared in *Vision Vol 2 #6 (Apr, '16)*.

And There are a lot of little throwaway references, such as SWORD's drone being 57 (Vision first appears in *The Avengers #57*) and having Captain Marvel's costume colours and a jeep numbered 8512 – *The Vision and the Scarlet Witch* was a 12 issue series launched in 1985. And of course, in episode six, Wanda, Vision and Pietro wear versions of their comic book costumes at Halloween.

Ratings: *IMDB:* 8.3; *Rotten Tomatoes:* 92%; *Metacritic:* 77

Review: A brave launch for Marvel Studios' television series, delivering a program that is a slow burn, but benefits enormously from shorter episodes to play out an initial mystery that is finally explained, but continues to keep the audience guessing. The series is pretty much brilliant in so many ways, though arguably it drops the ball with the ending, as there are a couple of plot threads that remain unresolved. Some of the ideas seemed design to specifically cheat the viewer, but not in the usual Marvel way where the results are a surprise – Evan Peters casting being the best example of this. Nonetheless, it's great to see a series expand on two of the more interesting, but necessarily sidelined Avengers, and one that continues to push the MCU forward in an interesting new direction. More than that, to explore life and love between these two characters, and the price Wanda pays at the end gives a lot of depth that allows the viewer to forgive the cheats.

MARVEL LEGENDS

Before the first episode of **WandaVision** was released, Marvel began a series of 8-minute shorts that recapped specific characters in the Marvel Cinematic Universe, following the start of their journey up until where they currently were. The intention was that each episode would act as a catch up for a forthcoming series, and were effectively clip montages.

1.1	Wanda Maximoff (8/1/2021)
1.2	Vision (8/1/2021)
1.3	Falcon (5/3/2021)
1.4	The Winter Soldier (5/3/2021)
1.5	Zemo (12/3/2021)
1.6	Sharon Carter (12/3/2021)
1.7	Loki (4/6/2021)
1.8	The Tesseract (4/6/2021)
1.9	Black Widow (7/7/2021)
1.10	Peggy Carter (4/8/2021)
1.11	The Avengers Initiative (4/8/2021)
1.12	The Ravagers (4/8/2021)
1.13	The Ten Rings (1/9/2021)
1.14	Hawkeye (12/11/2021)
1.15	Doctor Strange (29/4/2022)
1.16	Wong (29/4/2022)
1.17	Scarlet Witch (29/4/2022)
1.18	Thor (1/7/2022)
1.19	Jane Foster (1/7/2022)
1.20	Valkyrie (1/7/2022)
1.21	Bruce Banner (10/8/2022)
1.22	King T'Challa (4/11/2022)
1.23	Princess Shuri (4/11/2022)
1.24	The Dora Milaje (4/11/2022)
1.25	Mantis (23/11/2022)
1.26	Drax (23/11/2022)

THE FALCON AND THE WINTER SOLDIER
[Season 1] *(Disney+)*

Regular Cast: *Sebastian Stan (Bucky Barnes/Winter Soldier), Anthony Mackie (Sam Wilson/Falcon), Emily VanCamp (Sharon Carter)[1.3-1.6], Wyatt Russell (John Walker), Erin Kellyman (Karli Morgenthau), Julia Louis-Dreyfus (Valentina Allegra de Fontaine)[1.5-1.6], Florence Kasumba (Ayo)[1.3-1.5], Danny Ramirez (Joaquin Torres)[1.1-1.3,1.5-1.6], Georges St-Pierre (Batroc)[1.1,1.5-1.6], Adepero Oduye (Sarah Wilson)[1.1,1.3-1.6] with Daniel Brühl (Baron Zemo)[1.2-1.6] and Don Cheadle (James Rhodes/Rhodey)[1.1]*

Prod: Ariella Blejer, Dawn Kamoche; **Music:** Henry Jackman; **Exec.Prod:** Kevin Feige, Louis D'Esposito, Victoria Alonso, Nate Moore, Kari Skogland, Malcolm Spellman; **Created by** Malcolm Spellman; **DOP:** PJ Dillon; **Prod.Des.:** Raymond Chan; **Costumes:** Michael Crow; **Marvel Studios**; 45

Episodes:

1.1 NEW WORLD ORDER *(19/3/2021)*

Both Sam and Bucky struggle to find their place in the new world, with Sam helping the air force in a number of operations, but giving up Captain America's shield, convinced he doesn't deserve it. Bucky tries to make amends for his past, but can't follow his psychiatrist's hopes, though he does try for a date. Meanwhile the government decide they need a new Captain America.

Cast: Desmond Chiam (Dovich), Dani Deetté (Gigi), Indya Bussey (DeeDee), Amy Aquino (Dr Raynor), Chase River McGhee (Cass), Aaron Haynes (AJ), Ken Takemoto (Yori), Ian Gregg (Unique), Miki Ishikawa (Leah), Gordon Danniels (Ancient Shop Owner), Vince Pisani (Loan Officer), Alphie Hyorth (Government Official), Rebecca Lines (Senator Atwood), Bryan Brendle (Crony), Jon Briddell (Major), Miles Brew (Colonel Vassant), Erik Bello (Kidnap Pilot), Tyler Merritt (Patron #1), Charles Black (Carlos), Ahmad Alhadi (Café Patron), Akie Kotabe (RJ), Wendy Rosas (RJ's Co-Worker)
Dir: Kari Skogland; **Writer:** Malcolm Spellman; **Ed:** Jeffrey Ford, Kelley Dixon

1.2 THE STAR-SPANGLED MAN *(26/3/2021)*

Sam sets off to find the Flag Smashers, following Torres' lead, but is joined by Bucky who is furious that he handed the shield over to the government and let John Walker become the new Captain America. They confront the Smashers, but take a heavy beating, before being joined by Walker and Lemar Hoskins, though this doesn't help. Walker suggests that the two pairs join forces, but Bucky has a better plan.

Cast: *Cle Bennett (Lemar), Carl Lumbly (Isaiah Bradley),* Desmond Chiam (Dovich), Dani Deetté (Gigi), Indya Bussey (DeeDee), Renes Rivera (Lennox), Tyler Dean Flores (Diego), Ness Bautista (Matias), Amy Aquino (Dr Raynor), *Elijah Richardson (Eli Bradley),* Noah Mills (Nico), Gabrielle Byndloss (Olivia Walker), Mike Ray (Alonso Barber), Neal Kodinsky (Rudy), Sara Haines (Herself), Scott Parks (Cop #1), Richard Christian Wooley (Cop #2), Ian Covell (Drunk), Jonathan Horne (Nervous Employee), Jecobi Swain (Neighborhood Kid), Rashaad Horne (Drumline Drum Major)
Dir: Kari Skogland; **Writer:** Michael Kastelein; **Ed:** Jeffrey Ford, Todd Desrosiers

1.3 POWER BROKER *(2/4/2021)*

Bucky breaks Zemo out of prison, and Zemo suggests that there is only one real person they can talk to about a new super soldier serum – the Power Broker on Madripoor. With Sam disguised as the Smiling Tiger, the trio meet with the Power Broker's agent, Selby, who realises they are not who they say they are. Forced to go on the run, the group meet Sharon Carter who agrees to help them if they get her a pardon. This brings them face to face with the man who has recreated the super soldier serum.

Cast: *Cle Bennett (Lemar),* Desmond Chiam (Dovich), Dani Deetté (Gigi), Indya Bussey (DeeDee), Renes Rivera (Lennox), Tyler Dean Flores (Diego), Noah Mills (Nico), Veronica Falcón (Mama Donya), Neal Kodinsky (Rudy), David Bowles (Base Commander), Nicholas Pryor (Oeznik), Forrest Conoly (The Bartender), Giovanni Rodriguez (Brass Monkey Goon), Imelda Corcoran (Selby), Robert Larriviere (Docent), *Olli Haaskivi (Dr Nagel),* Michael Macauley (The Warden), Meaghan Gillenwater (Sharon's Bodyguard)
Dir: Kari Skogland; **Writer:** Derek Kolstad; **Ed:** Jeffrey Ford, Rosanne Tan

1.4 THE WHOLE WORLD IS WATCHING *(9/4/2021)*

Ayo gives Bucky eight hours before the Dora Milaje retrieve Zemo for his crimes. Zemo, meanwhile, learns about where they will find Karli

Morganthau, and Sam opts to talk to her alone, though when Walker and Hoskins turn up, the pair are not happy with the arrangement. Sam almost gets through to Karli, until Walker bursts in and ruins the meet. Zemo is able to destroy the last of the super soldier serum except one vial, which Walker retrieves, and when Karli contacts them again, Walker is a different man.

Cast: *Cle Bennett (Lemar),* Desmond Chiam (Dovich), Dani Deetté (Gigi), Indya Bussey (DeeDee), Renes Rivera (Lennox), Tyler Dean Flores (Diego), Noah Mills (Nico), Janeshia Adams-Ginyard (Nomble (Dora #1)), Zola Williams (Yama (Dora #2)), Marie Martinová (Brave Girl), Veronica Falcón (Mama Donya), Adam Vacula (Teacher), Sinead Phelps (Latvian Fan), Antonie Formanová (Young Woman)
Dir: Kari Skogland; **Writer:** Derek Kolstad; **Ed:** Jeffrey Ford, Kelley Dixon

1.5 TRUTH *(16/4/2021)*

Between them, Falcon and the Winter Soldier are able to subdue Captain America and take his shield from him. Walker is consequently discharged from his position, but lies to Lemar's parents about who killed their son. Sam meets with Bradley and comes away less sure about the idea of taking the mantle of Captain America on, but he receives a visit from Bucky who has a present for him from Wakanda.

Cast: *Cle Bennett (Lemar), Carl Lumbly (Isaiah Bradley),* Desmond Chiam (Dovich), Dani Deetté (Gigi), Indya Bussey (DeeDee), Renes Rivera (Lennox), Tyler Dean Flores (Diego), Chase River McGhee (Cass), Aaron Haynes (AJ), Gabrielle Byndloss (Olivia Walker), Janeshia Adams-Ginyard (Nomble (Dora #1)), Zola Williams (Yama (Dora #2)), Gordon Daniels (Ancient Shop Manager), Alphie Hyorth (Government Official), *Elijah Richardson (Eli Bradley),* Tyler Merritt (Patron #1), Charles Black (Carlos), Antonio D Charity (Lemar's Dad), Tara Warren (Lemar's Mum), Shenai Hylton (Lemar's Sister), Demi Castro (GRC Leader #1), Salem Murphy (Prime Minster Lacont), Jane Rumbaua (Ayla), Noah Mills (Nico), Christian Brunetti (Secret Service Agent)
Dir: Kari Skogland; **Writer:** Dalan Musson; **Ed:** Jeffrey Ford, Todd Desrosiers

1.6 ONE WORLD, ONE PEOPLE *(23/4/2021)*

Having chosen to become Captain America, and equipped with a new suit, Sam leads Bucky and Sharon to the building where the GRC Conference is being held and Sam confronts Batroc while Bucky and Sharon go after the Flag Smashers, aided by Walker. During the confrontation, Batroc learns Sharon is the Power Broker, but she kills him. Sam is ultimately forced into fighting Karli, but he refuses, and Sharon ends it by killing her.

Cast: *Carl Lumbly (Isaiah Bradley),* Amy Aquino (Dr Raynor), Desmond Chiam (Dovich), Dani Deetté (Gigi), Indya Bussey (DeeDee), Renes Rivera (Lennox), Tyler Dean Flores (Diego), *Elijah Richardson (Eli Bradley),* Chase River McGhee (Cass), Aaron Haynes (AJ), Ken Takemoto (Yori), Miki Ishikawa (Leah), Gordon Daniels (Ancient Shop Manager), Vince Pisani (Loan Officer), Alphie Hyorth (Government Official), Rebecca Lines (Senator Atwood), Bryan Brendle (Crony), Jon Briddell (Major), Brad Brinkley (Secret Service Chief), Christian Brunetti (Secret Service Agent), Jane Rumbaua (Ayla), Jennifer Christa Palmer (Woman), Brian Sheppard (Middle-Aged Man), Nirvi Shah (Reporter #1), Regina Ting Chen (Reporter #2), Walt Elder (Older Man), Kevin Saunders (Older Man's Friend), Salem Murphy (Prime Minster Lacont), Demi Castro (GRC Official), Nicholas Pryor (Oeznik), Malachi Malik (Raft Guard Escort), Gabrielle Byndloss (Olivia)
Dir: Kari Skogland; **Writers:** Malcolm Spellman & Josef Sawyer; **Ed:** Jeffrey Ford, Rosanne Tan

Notes: In the closing title sequence of the last episode, the title is changed to *CAPTAIN AMERICA AND THE WINTER SOLDIER*. Valentina Allegra de Fontaine's first appearance was supposed to have been **BLACK WIDOW**, but because of the delays due to COVID, she appears here first. This series was also supposed to be the first MCU television series released, but again, COVID restrictions delayed filming and required *WANDAVISION* to be released first. Ironically, Wyatt Russell auditioned for the role of Steve Rogers in **CAPTAIN AMERICA: THE FIRST AVENGER**. Mackie and Stan swap top billing each episode. Henry Jackman reuses some of his music from **CAPTAIN AMERICA: THE WINTER SOLDIER** and **CAPTAIN AMERICA: CIVIL WAR**. Journalist Sara Haines appears as herself.

Should I Stay To The End? The last two episodes both have mid-credits sequences, and both are definitely worth staying for. 1.5's provides a link for what Walker is doing before the next episode, and 1.6's presumably will link into a forthcoming series, and features Sharon Carter.

It's All Connected: Set six months after the blip, we discover that Sam Wilson has been rebuilding his family roots, while also working with the US army and their liaison Joaquin Torres – someone who is very keen on working on Wilson's wings. Bucky has been in therapy, working to make amends for his dark past, but this includes meeting with an elderly man whose son Bucky killed many years earlier. This ultimately comes out, destroying the friendship. Wilson hands Rogers' shield to the Smithsonian, much to Bucky's chagrin, and even James Rhodes who attends the ceremony seems unimpressed. The government then appoint a new Captain America in the form of John Walker, a celebrated army officer, and he is given backup with Lemar Hoskins, codenamed Battlestar. Louisiana born, Sam is unable to get a bank loan for his sister's boat, and at one point is even accosted by police who think he is causing a problem with Bucky, thanks to racial intolerance. His associate, Torres, is investigating a group called the Flag Smashers, who have superhuman strength. They are led by Karli Morgenthau, a fanatic who wants the world to reopen all borders, as it did under the blip (it's worth noting the blip is a term that seems to describe both Thanos' snap and the return of everyone). Wilson and Bucky attempt to stop them, but fail, and though Walker and Hoskins offer an opportunity to work together, Wilson and Bucky refuse. Bucky takes Wilson to meet Isaiah Bradley, the man who inherited the mantle of Captain America after Steve disappeared, but this doesn't really help Wilson make a decision about being Captain America. They are forced to work with Baron Helmut Zemo (who turns out to be extraordinarily rich) and Sharon Carter (who turns out to have been very soured by her experiences with the US government, so much so she becomes the "Power Broker", the person who rules over the relatively lawless country of Madripoor). They also come into conflict with Ayo and the Dora Milaje. When the Flag Smashers strike again, they kill Battlestar, and Walker – in costume and on camera – brutally murders one of the Flag Smashers (not the one who killed Hoskins). He is subsequently discharged from the army and fired as Captain America. Wilson and Bucky are able to retrieve the shield, and Wilson decides it is time to step up. The Wakandans provide him with a new Captain America costume, which include wings (his old wings are given to Torres as a gift). As the Flag Smashers attempt to disrupt the GRC Conference in New York, assisted by Georges Batroc, Wilson, Bucky and a redeemed Walker attempt to stop them. They succeed, but Sharon Carter kills Morgenthau to stop her revealing the Power Broker's identity, while the rest are sent to the Raft. Walker is approached by Valentina Allegra de Fontaine, who has a new costume for him, a new codename (US Agent) and a job. Meanwhile Sharon Carter is granted a complete pardon, but intends to capitalise on this in her new position.

Comic Notes: *John Walker/US Agent:* Physically, John Walker looks very similar to the comic book version. In the comics, Walker was given super strength by the Power Broker Corporation and became the villain Super-Patriot, and fought Captain America. He then confronted the terrorist Warhead and stopped him, which brought him to the attention of Valerie Cooper. When Steve Rogers gave up the role of Captain America because the US government demanded he report directly to them, Cooper appointed Walker as the new Captain America. Similar to the series, after beating Professor Power to death, having his parents killed by extremists and then being captured by the Flag-Smashers, Walker had a mental breakdown. Walker then handed the title of Captain America back to Rogers. He later became US Agent and joined the West Coast Avengers, before reuniting with Battelstar, however his emotional instability meant he left the WC Avengers and became a solo vigilante, often coming into conflict with both heroes and villains. He has been a member of various Avengers groups, the Secret Defenders, the New Invaders and Omega Flight. He was later asked to briefly return as Captain America, joining Rogers and Sam Wilson in order to recover Captain America's shield. Most recently, as US Agent, he worked for Wilson Fisk as part of the Thunderbolts. He first appeared in *Captain America #323 (Nov, '86)*, becoming Captain America in *#333* and US Agent in *#354*, and he was created by Mark Gruenwald and Paul Neary.

Isaiah Bradley: Bradley shares a very similar back story to the television version. First appearing in *Truth: Red, White & Black #1 (Jan, '03)* and created by Alex Alonso, Robert Morales and Kyle Baker, it was revealed that Dr Josef Reinstein (a former pseudonym of Abraham Erskine) arranged Project: Rebirth to create a new Captain America. Horrifically, 300 black soldiers were experimented on, and only five survived the trials. The government then had the operation purged. Ultimately only Bradley survived, and he stole a Captain America costume and shield to fight Nazi super soldier efforts. He was court martialled for his actions, but pardoned by President Eisenhower. Sadly, in later life, the effects of the serum gave him Alzheimers, and when Steve Rogers met the man, he had little of his life open to him.

Karli Morgenthau: In the comics, the Flag Smasher is a supervillain (or two), the first being Karl Morgenthau, debuting in *Captain America #312 (Dec,'85)*, created by Gruenwald and Neary. Obviously, the gender swap means there is little physical similarity between the two characters, though the comic version also wanted to see country borders torn down. He created the ULTIMATUM society, and Captain America had a conversation with him not dissimilar to the one Sam has with Karli. Unlike the tv version, Karl had no super strength, but was a gifted hand-to-hand fighter. He was later killed by Domino, and succeeded by Guy Thierrault.

Valentina Allegra de Fontaine: or more accurately La Contessa Valentina Allegra de la Fontaine became Nick Fury's lover and was recruited to SHIELD. She shined in this position, but it was her unusual behaviour that led Fury to discover the Skrull secret invasion. However, when the real Valentina was released, it turned out she'd been working for Hydra, and she became the new Madame Hydra. She first appeared in *Strange Tales #159 (May, '68)* created by Jim Steranko and Joe Sinnott, but there's not a lot of similarity to the television version.

Joaquin Torres: made his comic book debut in *Captain America: Sam Wilson #3 (Nov, '15)*, created by Nick Spencer and Daniel Acuña, though a photograph of him appeared two issues earlier, and three issues later he took on the mantle of the Falcon, to Wilson's Cap. He looks not dissimilar to his television counterpart, but Karl Malus turned him into a falcon-human hybrid, which gave him the power of flight and regenerative abilities (so much so that after Cottonmouth bit his head off, it grew back). He also has a psychic link to Redwing, and as a consequence, a mild psychic connection to Sam Wilson. Torres was kidnapped by the Sons of the Serpent, but Captain America rescued him and Torres joined his fight against the Sons of the Serpent as Falcon. He was last seen as part of the Underground resistance to Hydra.

Eli Bradley: is also the grandson of Isaiah in the comics, and possesses super strength, agility and endurance. He is the second person to adopt the title Patriot, and first appeared in *Young Avengers #1 (Apr,'05)*, created by Allan Heinberg and Jim Cheung. Eli claimed he got his superpowers from a blood transfusion from his grandfather, but it was actually Mutant Growth Hormone that gave them to him. Iron Lad recruited him as a founding member of the Young Avengers, but he quit when the truth about his powers was revealed. Eli rejoined the Young Avengers and dated Kate Bishop, but he left again, guilty about his actions when he almost stopped Scarlet Witch from undoing the elimination of all mutants. Whether he continues to be of any significant part of the MCU remains to be seen…

Lemar: Lemar Hoskins first appeared in *Captain America #323 (Nov,'86)* as a token black member of the Bold Urban Commandoes (or Buckies). By issue #327 he was named Lemar, and #333 Lemar Hoskins. The following issue he became the new Bucky to John Walker's Captain America, but in #341 he gained the title Battlestar, and a new costume (which doesn't really look much like what is seen in the series). Like Walker he was given super-human strength by the Power Broker, but gave up his position when Steve Rogers took back the mantle of Captain America. He supported a number of superheroes, including Walker as the US Agent, but joined Captain America's side during Civil War. Most recently he was attacked and had his arm broken by a super soldier who felt Hoskins wasn't doing enough to promote racial equality. The decision to change Hoskins from Bucky to Battlestar came about when creators Mark Gruenwald and Paul Neary, were informed by writer Dwayne McDuffie, that the term "buck" was racially insensitive. Gruenwald was keen to do the right thing and with McDuffie's help they came up with a new codename, and made Hoskins more of a partner to Walker, rather than a sidekick.

Dr Nagel: is nothing like his comics counterpart, remotely, be it backstory or physical appearance. He first appeared in *Truth: Red, White & Black #1 (Jan, '03),* also created by Morales and Baker, and took Abraham Erskine's pseudonym, Josef Reinstein, to work for Project Rebirth. He was the man who created Isaiah's Captain America, but at the cost of an enormous number of black lives. What happened to him after World War II remains to be seen.

The Power Broker is a little complicated. The Power Broker first appeared in *The Thing #35 (May, '86)* – created by Roger Stern and Sal Buscema – and was later revealed to be Curtis Jackson. Jackson created the Power Broker Corporation and he hired Karl Malus to enhance people's strength. They would then get their subjects addicted to drugs and gain their dependence. Malus used the process on Jackson himself which backfired badly, and US Agent destroyed the equipment, leaving Jackson a grotesque super-muscled human. Happily, he lost his powers, but sadly was then killed by the Punisher. A second Power Broker surfaced later, equipped with a battle suit, who created an app for villains to get hold of henchmen quickly. This version of Power Broker came into conflict with Ant-Man and Stinger on a number of occasions. He was last seen on an island trying to create an app where supervillains could book their travel plans.

And Sam Wilson did indeed become Captain America in *Captain America Vol 7 #25 (Dec,'14)* at the request of an elderly Steve Rogers. But this being comics, Steve became young again and took it back and Sam became the Falcon again. However, it turned out there were a few people posing as Captain America, so Sam took the opportunity to do so again. Some of the series storyline was borrowed from 2003's *Truth: Red, White & Black* comic arc.

Ratings: *IMDB:* 8.3; *Rotten Tomatoes:* 92%; *Metacritic:* 77

Review: More a straightforward Marvel tale, ***THE FALCON AND THE WINTER SOLDIER*** feels like it could have been edited down into a two-and-a-half-hour movie, with a compelling storyline and impressive action sequences. The decision to open it up into a television series means that the viewers are given the chance to learn more about the characters and more importantly the motivations driving them. If it had been a movie, I suspect Isaiah Bradley would have been the first character cut out, and that would be a crying shame. There is a feeling that Marvel Studios is giving its second-tier characters a chance to shine, and a series like this demonstrates why it's such a good idea – everyone is on top form here, and the ties to the overall MCU, including the return of Baron Zemo, feel like earlier plot threads haven't been ignored and are now being tied up. A great series, and a great use of Sam Wilson and Bucky Barnes, but more importantly one that feels very steeped in the "now" of today, and the issues that go with it.

MARVEL ASSEMBLED

When *WandaVision* ended, there were rumours of a secret tenth episode that turned out to be totally untrue. However, Marvel did have something to broadcast; effectively a making of documentary for the series, which was the first of a new series called *Marvel Assembled*. A similar thing took place after *The Falcon And The Winter Soldier*, continuing the tradition.

1.1 WandaVision (12/3/2021)
1.2 The Falcon And The Winter Soldier (30/4/2021)
1.3 Loki (21/7/2021)
1.4 Black Widow (20/10/2021)
1.5 What If...? (27/10/2021)
1.6 Shang-Chi and the Legend of the Ten Rings (12/11/2021)
1.7 Hawkeye (9/2/2022)
1.8 The Eternals (16/2/2022)
1.9 Moon Knight (25/5/2022)
1.10 Doctor Strange in the Multiverse of Madness (8/7/2022)
1.11 Ms Marvel (3/8/2022)
1.12 Thor: Love and Thunder (8/9/2022)
1.13 She-Hulk: Attorney at Law (3/11/2022)

LOKI
[Season 1]*(Disney+)*

Regular Cast: *Tom Hiddleston (Loki), Sophia Di Martino (*The Variant/*Sylvie)* [1.2-1.6], Gugu Mbatha-Raw (Ravonna Renslayer),* Wunmi Mosaku (Hunter B-15)[1.1-1.2,1.4-1.6], *Jack Veal (Kid Loki)[1.4-1.5],* DeObia Oparei (Boastful Loki) [1.4-1.5], Eugene Cordero (Casey/Hunter K-5E)[1.1-1.2,1.6], Sasha Lane (Hunter C-20)[1.2-1.4], Tara Strong as Miss Minutes [1.1-1.2,1.5-1.6] special guest star Richard E Grant (Classic Loki)[1.4-1.5], *Jonathan Majors (He Who Remains)[1.6] and Owen Wilson (Mobius)[1.1-1.2,1.4-1.6]*
Super.Prod: Jess Dweck, Tom Kauffman; **Music:** Natalie Holt; **Exec.Prod:** Kevin Feige, Louis D'Esposito, Victoria Alonso, Tom Hiddleston, Kate Herron, Michael Waldron; **Created by** Michael Waldron; **DOP:** Autumn Durald Arkapaw; **Prod.Des.:** Kasra Farahani; **Costumes:** Christine Wada; **Marvel Studios**; 45

Episodes:

1.1 GLORIOUS PURPOSE *(9/6/2021)*
Having escaped the Avengers, Loki is arrested by the Time Variance Authority and brought before Ravonna Renslayer who informs him he has committed the crime of being a variant – acting outside the established timeline. However one of the TVA detectives – Mobius – thinks he can use Loki in tracking down a very dangerous variant.

Cast: Derek Russo (Hunter U-92), Erika Coleman (Flight Attendant), Munkhshur Bolbaatar (Gobi Villager), Josh Fadem (Martin), Raphael Luce (French Boy), Jon Levine (Paperwork Clerk), Aaron Beelner (Scanner Clerk), Philip Fornah (Minuteman #1), Dave Macdonald (Minuteman #2), Michelle Rose (Minuteman #3), Eric Jepson (Minuteman #4), Hannah Asleen (Minuteman #5), Daniel Newman (Minuteman #18), Ravi Naidu (Analyst #3), Lauren Revard (Miss Minutes On-Set Reader)
Dir: Kate Herron; **Writer:** Michael Waldron; **Ed:** Paul Zucker

1.2 THE VARIANT *(16/6/2021)*
Loki joins Mobius and B-15 as they set out to investigate a site the Variant has recently attacked, only to discover that C-20 has been taken. Loki's attempt to gain access to the Time Keepers fails and Ravonna later reprimands Mobius for failing to keep the Asgardian

under control. However, Loki discovers that the Variant is probably hiding in a natural disaster where any changes to the timeline would be immediately wiped out. With this information, he and Mobius are able to track down their target.

Cast: Neil Ellice (Hunter D-90), Kate Berlant (Ren Faire Woman), Philip Fornah (Minuteman #1), Dave Macdonald (Minuteman #2), Michelle Rose (Minuteman #3), Sarafina King (Minuteman #9), Alvin Chon (Minuteman #10), Ilan Muallem (Minuteman #11), Jesse Garvin (Analyst #1), Jordan Woods-Robinson (Analyst #2), Lucius Baston (Male Shopper), Austin Freeman (Randy), Ricky Muse (Warehouse Employee), Hawk Walts (Country Hoss), Zele Avradopoulos (Archives Susher), Dayna Beilenson (Archivist), Lauren Revard (Miss Minutes On-Set Reader)
Dir: Kate Herron; **Writer:** Elissa Karasik; **Ed:** Paul Zucker

1.3 LAMENTIS *(23/6/2021)*
Loki confronts his alternate self as she attempts to gain access to the Time Keepers, but the arrival of Renslayer means the pair have to flee, and find themselves on Lamentis-1, a planet facing imminent destruction. They are forced to work together and decide to travel to the ark which is going to escape the planet, though Sylvie knows the ark will never make it. Loki, however, thinks they should change the timeline by saving the ship.

Cast: Susan Gallagher (Lamentian Homesteader), Alex Van (Patrice), Ben Vandermey (PVT Hudson), Jon Collin Barclay (Corporal Hicks), Jwaundace Candece (Lamentian Mother), Malerie Grady (Lamentian Bartender), Michael Rose (Wealthy Man), Anya Ruoss (Wealthy Woman)
Dir: Kate Herron; **Writer:** Bisha K Ali; **Ed:** Calum Ross

1.4 THE NEXUS EVENT *(30/6/2021)*
Loki and Sylive's predicament trigger a deviation that allows the TVA to arrive and arrest them, but once inside the pair are reluctant to respond to anything, though Loki tells Mobius the TVA has lied to him, which bothers the agent, particularly in regard to Renslayer's attitude towards C-20's death. B-15 is also bothered by what Sylvie's possession of her revealed, and as Renslayer prepares to take the variants to the Time Keepers, a small revolution begins.

Cast: Cailey Fleming (Kid Sylvie), Neil Ellice (Hunter D-90), Jon Levine (Paperwork Clerk), Aaron Beelner (Scanner Clerk), Philip Fornah (Minuteman #1), Dave Macdonald (Minuteman #2), Michelle Rose (Minuteman #3), Sarafina King (Minuteman #9), Alvin Chon (Minuteman #10), Ilan Muallem (Minuteman #11), Isabelle Pierre (Analyst #4), Lauren Halperin (Alanlyst #5), Nicholas Zarrillo (Screaming Man), Matthew Gannon (Judge), Lauren Revard, Robert Pralgo (Time Keepers On-Set Readers)
Dir: Kate Herron; **Writer:** Eric Martin; **Ed:** Emma McCleave

1.5 JOURNEY INTO MYSTERY *(7/7/2021)*
As Loki acquaints himself with his alternate selves, Sylvie forms an uneasy alliance with Renslayer which quickly ends and she prunes herself, having learnt that all pruned timelines are sent to a void at the end of time. But Renslayer is still concerned about what is happening with the TVA, and when Sylvie meets her alternate selves, she comes up with a plan to go beyond the time they are currently in and learn precisely who has manipulated them into where they are now.

Cast: Neil Ellice (Hunter D-90), Sarafina King (Minuteman #9), Alvin Chon (Minuteman #10), Ilan Muallem (Minuteman #11), Lauren Revard (Miss Minutes On-Set Reader), Alec James Zais (USS Eldridge Sailor)
Dir: Kate Herron; **Writer:** Tom Kauffman; **Ed:** Calum Ross

1.6 FOR ALL TIME. ALWAYS. *(14/7/2021)*
Loki and Sylvie are initially met by Miss Minutes at the Citadel at the end of time, before they are introduced to He Who Remains, who explains to them that he is the one curtailing free will in order to prevent other versions of himself from starting another multiversal war. He offers them the chance to take his place, but Sylvie is only interested in destroying him. Meanwhile, Mobius confronts Renslayer about the truth, as the Hunters turn against her.

Cast: Neil Ellice (Hunter D-90), Sarafina King (Minuteman #9), Ilan Muallem (Minuteman #11), Lauren Revard (Miss Minutes On-Set Reader)
Dir: Kate Herron; **Writers:** Michael Waldron and Eric Martin; **Ed:** Emma McCleave

Notes: Jaime Alexander makes an uncredited cameo in 1.4 as Lady Sif (though bizarrely her stunt double is credited). Chris Hemsworth also makes an uncredited cameo as the voice of Throg (Frog Thor). At the end of time, there are a number of references to a wide variety of sources, including Helicarrier 42 (the Hydra Insight Helicarrier), the actual USS Eldridge and Ronan's ship. Also, rather neatly, in Kid Loki's headquarters is the computer game Polybius, famously an urban legend about a game allegedly developed by the FBI.

Stan Spotting: One of the portraits in the TVA hall shows a very seventies Stan Lee.

Should I Stay To The End? Episode 1.4 has a post-credits sequence that leads into the following episode, and explains what happened to Loki.

It's All Connected: Well, it is all connected, but *LOKI* opens up a whole web of possibilities…
The series technically takes place immediately after **THE AVENGERS**, but in an alternate timeline where Loki escaped using the Tesseract (as spun off from **AVENGERS: ENDGAME** – for the sake of clarity, "Loki" is the alternate version that this series centers around, while Prime Loki is the version from the MCU who was ultimately killed by Thanos). We're introduced to the Time Variance Authority, apparently ruled by the Time-Keepers, enforced by the Hunters who are supervised by Agents and Judges. We meet a number of Hunters, but B-15 is the most notable, while Agent Mobius M Mobius Is Loki's primary contact, and he reports directly to Judge Ravonna Renslayer. Mobius, it transpires, is hunting another variant of Loki – a woman named Sylvie, who is ruthlessly efficient in what she does – and hopes that the Loki variant they've recovered from **THE AVENGERS** timeline can help them (it gets more confusing, so hold on…).

Sylvie is one of a number of variants of Loki we meet along the way including a child version, another version that looks like the prime Loki but seems to think he is the President, a crocodile version, a boastful version who looks nothing like the Prime Loki, and an older version who dresses exactly like the 1960's comic book version. By the end of the series, a number of these work with Loki and Sylvie to help them achieve their common goal, which is the downfall of the Time-Keepers and the TVA.

At this point the TVA is curtailing the multiverse by removing variants and cutting off alternate timelines to keep the prime timeline in place. Loki notes that Sylvie works in timelines that have imminent disasters, because it's hard to create a new timeline when everyone is dying anyway. Similarly, he also realises that when the TVA "prune" people, rather than kill them, they are sent to the Void: essentially the end of time, and it is here that Loki and Sylvie meet the other Loki variants, and also Alioth who protects what is beyond the Void.

It turns out that the Time-Keepers are merely androids, and virtually everyone in the TVA is a variant who has been mind wiped and now works to stamp out other timelines. Mobius learns of this and confronts Renslayer with the truth, which seems to overwhelm her, so she sets off to find "free will". Behind the Time-Keeper is He Who Remains…

It is probably here where the series will strongly reconnect with the rest of the MCU, as He Who Remains is a scientist from the 31st century who has wiped out many other variants of himself as when they existed, they engaged in a war for multiversal dominance. Though powerful, he is also deceptive, and Sylvie finally kills him, but this opens the door for the Multiverse to exist once again, and when Loki returns to the TVA, he discovers that Mobius has no memory of him and it is ruled by a helmeted figure…

It's probably worth mentioning that there are aspects of this situation that are not really explained. For instance, it's not clear if killing He Who Remains restored the original multiverse, or simply allowed a new one to be created (did all the previous timelines that were pruned return?) It seems likely, based on later MCU properties, that killing He Who Remains was indeed retroactive and so perhaps the multiversal war was won by another of his variants (the helmeted one?) or did it simply peter out?

Comic Notes: *Sylvie* is actually a mix of two different characters. There has been a straight forward female version of Loki who first appeared in *Thor Vol 3 #5 (Jan, '08)* where Loki's spirit took over a body intended for Sif. This version of Loki essentially dresses like Loki and is every way a literal female version of the character. Sylvie Lushton, on the other hand, was a young lady given powers by Loki, who then modelled herself on the Enchantress, and went on to call herself that. The ***LOKI*** version of Sylvie is actually most like this version, both in look and power (given that Sylvie is indeed able to enchant people, though the costume is more like Lady Loki's, including the broken crown). Sylvie would become a Young Avenger, though this brought her into conflict with Loki and the Dark Avengers. Most recently she came into conflict with the original Enchantress who banished her to an unknown realm. She first appeared in *Dark Reign: Young Avengers #1 (Jul, '09)* created by Paul Cornell and Mark Brooks.

Mobius M Mobius first appeared in *Fantastic Four #353 (Jun, '91)*, created by Walt Simonson. The comics version doesn't look too far removed from the television version, though he is rarely grey in the comics (the mustache is always present – in fact his physical appearance is based on editor Mark

Gruenwald, whose writing often involved resolving continuity issues). His first appearance as is middle management in the TVA, but he obviously started lower than this, though when he was a junior, he was known as Mr Tesseract (due to the nature of time travel, Tesseract is Mobius' subordinate as they both exist at the same time). Rather than be demoted after attempting to put the Fantastic Four on trial, he went to work for Kang in Chronopolis.

Ravonna Renslayer: is quite different to her comic book counterpart, not least because the comics version is a white, blonde woman, who tends to wear a yellow skintight costume with an impressive tiara. She first appeared in *Avengers #23 (Dec, '65)*, created by Stan Lee and Don Heck, and is a Princess (Ravonna Lexus Renslayer) whose world is about to be annexed by Kang. Kang opts against this because he has fallen in love with her, and surprisingly she feels the same after a time. Like Kang there are different versions of her, and they have various relationships to other versions of Kang (one, for instance, is a confidante of Immortus). The Grandmaster gave Kang the opportunity to save Ravonna or kill the Avengers, and he chose the latter, which the Grandmaster revealed to Ravonna, setting her on a path that wasn't really by Kang's side. As the Temptress, and later Terminatrix, she invaded Kang's Chronopolis and fought him, won and took control, but she later revived him and they became lovers again. She was last seen still in his company.

Kid Loki: In the comics, Lock is a young boy who Loki is reborn as, without the memories of his adult self, until Thor convinces him otherwise. Thor took him back to Asgard where he was confronted by an echo of his other self, but the younger Loki turned it into a magpie named Ikol. He spent a surprising amount of time by Thor's side, believing in his brother even after Thor appeared to have died and been replaced. However, ultimately, Ikol waited patiently until it could take over the boy and once again the real Loki would be seen. He was briefly resurrected by Loki, though once the spell faded away, so did he. He first appeared in *Thor #617 (Nov, '10)* and was created by Matt Fraction and Pasqual Ferry.

He Who Remains: first appeared in *Thor #245 (Dec, '75)* created by Lee Wein, John Buscema and Joe Sinnott. He looks nothing like the MCU version – rather a very old man, but he is the director of the Time Variance Authority (the final director as well). He was the creator of the Time Keepers (or Twisters) who destroyed the universe as they were keen to get to the next one. Thor ultimately convinced him to avert the Time Keepers creation. The MCU version, however, is clearly meant to be a variant of Kang the Conqueror, who we will get to at some point in the future. But as such, the MCU He Who

Remains is a little more like Immortus (which ties in with Renslayer). Immortus first appears in *Avengers #10 (Sep, '64)* created by Lee and Heck, and is a future version of Nathaniel Richards, and is a descendant of Reed Richards (or possibly Victor Von Doom...or possibly both). This version has fought Kang the Conqueror (and is aware that they are different versions of each other), and has encountered the Time Keepers. Immortus was one of Nathaniel's identities who was taught by the Time Keepers, though he was aware that the future held enslavement for them, but he was careful to ensure that this version became the version to master time. Immortus has fought the Avengers – Thor in particular – on a number of occasions, and has been involved in numerous incidents, but ultimately married Ravonna Renslayer, and adopted Marcus Kang, an alternate Kang's son (to an alternate Ravonna). In order to die together, Ravonna and Immortus found an alternate Ravonna who killed them. He has never been resurrected, but due to the nature of time travel, doesn't really need to be...after all, characters can encounter earlier versions of Immortus at any point in time.

Alioth: surprisingly, looks almost identical to his comic book counterpart, who is also basically a purple cloud. He is the first being who ever escaped the constraints of time, and he has an empire bigger than Kang's. Kang had actually created a barrier to stop Alioth from taking his empire, but after he died, Ravonna Renslayer released Alioth who tried to conquer Kang's domain. A resurrected Kang and the Avengers stopped him, though later Kang used Alioth to try to destroy Tempus (an agent of Immortus...who is also Nathaniel Richards who is also Kang...it's very confusing...). Alioth was created by Mark Gruenwald and Mike Gustovich and first appeared in *Avengers: The Terminatrix Objective #1 (Jul, '93)*.

And there are a lot of impressive references in this series, especially towards the end when the Lokis are all united in the void. In a jar we get to see Throg – a variant of Thor who is a frog (first appeared in *Thor #364 (Feb, '86)*, another character Walter Simonson is to blame for), while the number plate on Mobius' car is an obvious reference to Mark Gruenwald. Thanos' helicopter (*Spidey Super Stories #39 (Dec, '78)*) and Qeng Tower (*Avengers: Ultron Forever #1 (Apr, '15)*) are both in the void, along with a lot of other junk. But the most interesting thing in the void would appear to be the head of the Living Tribunal, a character who first appeared in *Strange Tales #157 (Mar, '67)* – more a cameo, the being appears proper in the following issue) and was created by Stan Lee and Marie Severin. The Tribunal appears to be the supreme being in the Marvel multiverse, and keeps the it in balance (though does in turn serve One Above All). The Tribunal's powers seemed limitless, but it was killed by the

Beyonders when they fought over the multiverse.

Ratings: *IMDB:* 8.3; *Rotten Tomatoes:* 92%; *Metacritic:* 77

Review: Giving Loki his own television series seems an obvious choice, but it's also an interesting one, as it gets to focus on a character who isn't a hero, but has to face exactly what he is and why he does it. The series is at its most interesting when Loki is confronted, either by Mobius or by Sylvie, to look at himself in a different light, or via a different personality, and this makes the character both more relatable and more interesting. Loki has always worked not just because of his multiple appearances (and a performance by Tom Hiddleston which is never not outstanding), but because he flitters back and forth between being a selfish villain to a reluctant ally. Here Loki has to confront the reasons behind that, and it's fascinating. Ultimately what happens between him and his female alternate (again, another brilliant performance by Sophia Di Martino) sort of seems completely logical – and its both consequences that make sense. There's an outstanding cast (Gugu Mbatha-Raw is one of the UK's hidden gems, while Richard E Grant constantly entertains), probably topped by Owen Wilson's amazing Mobius, and of course a clever set up for future elements of the MCU, both on the small and big screen. Definitely worth the time to watch.

BLACK WIDOW
(8/7/2021)

On the run from Ross and his team, Natasha goes to ground until she receives a package from Budapest. When an armoured person attacks her for the package, Natasha takes the contents to Budapest and encounters her sister, Yelena Belova, another Black Widow from the Red Room. The package was an antidote to the chemical indoctrination Dreykov was using in the Red Room to control the widows. Shocked to discover Dreykov is alive, Natasha joins forces with Yelena and Alexei Shostakov, the famed Red Guardian, to bring Dreykov down permanently.

Cast: *Scarlett Johansson (Natasha Romanoff/Black Widow), Florence Pugh (Yelena Belova), David Harbour (Alexei), O-T Fagbenle (Mason), Olga Kurylenko* (Antonia /Taskmaster) *with William Hurt (Secretary Ross)* with Ray Winstone (Dreykov) *and Rachel Weisz (Melina)*
Dir: Cate Shortland; **Writers:** Eric Pearson, Jac Shaeffer, Ned Benson; **Prod:**

Kevin Feige; **Music:** Lorne Balfe; **Exec.Prod:** Scarlett Johansson, Brad Winderbaum, Nigel Gostelow, Victoria Alonso, Louis D'Esposito; **DOP:** Gabriel Beristain; **Prod.Des.:** Charles Wood; **Ed:** Leigh Folsom Boyd, Matthew Schmidt; **Costumes:** Jany Temime, Lisa Lovaas; **Marvel Studios;** 134; $200m; $379.8m

Notes: Jeremy Renner provides an uncredited voice cameo as Clint Barton, and Julia Louis-Dreyfus appears in the post-credits sequence as Valentina Allegra de Fontaine. Olivier Ricthers character, Ursa, is a nod to the mutant Ursa Major, a member of the Winter Guard, of which Red Guardian is also a member. Ever Anderson and Violet McGraw are the younger versions of Natasha and Yelena respectively. The film was originally to be released on the 1st May, 2020, but COVID-19 caused a delay, to November 6th, then May 7th 2021. It was delayed one more time with the decision to release it on Disney+ at the same time. Unusually the film has a title sequence, the first MCU film to do so since **THE INCREDIBLE HULK**.

Should I Stay To The End? It's not absolutely essential, but there's a rather nice contemporary scene that sets up the *HAWKEYE* series.

It's All Connected: The film is set not long after **CAPTAIN AMERICA: CIVIL WAR** with Natasha on the run from Secretary of State Thaddeus Ross, who seems to be taking her disappearance personally. Ross indicates they have Clint Barton, Sam Wilson and Scott Lang in prison (oddly, he doesn't mention Wanda Maximoff). Natasha is revealed to have lived in Ohio in 1995 with Alexei and Melina, both working for Dreykov, acting as her parents, and Yelena Belova her sister. On their return to Russia (via Cuba) the girls are taken to the Red Room to be trained as Widows (though Natasha has already been through the room once). We discover that the incident in Budapest, oft-mentioned by both Natasha and Clint Barton, involved Natasha completing her defection to the US by assassinating Dreykov (though she discovers this did not happen). Loki's mention of Dreykov's daughter in **THE AVENGERS** is explained by the fact Antonia Dreykov entered the building just before Natasha authorised its bombing to kill Dreykov. Antonia, like Dreykov, survived, though she was badly scarred and cybernetically enhanced. Dreykov, rather cruelly, turned her into Taskmaster, his personal hitman when the Widows fail. Taskmaster has photographic reflexes that allow her to mimic her opponent's fighting style, though it's unclear if this was a gift Antonia always possessed, or the result of the cybernetic enhancements. Melina developed the chemicals that Dreykov used to indoctrinate the Widows – a process that Natasha did not go through, but Yelena did. Natasha has a regular contact in the form of

Mason, and though he sees her as a friend, she initially does not. Alexei is a super soldier, though it's unclear how this happened. He was formerly known as Red Guardian, but he suggests he has been in prison since 1995. By the end of the movie, Natasha has destroyed the Red Room and Dreykov, and the Widows are free, now being led by Yelena, and including Antonia in their number. Natasha dyes her hair blonde, in line with **AVENGERS: INFINITY WAR** and states that she is about to rescue her friends from prison. Yelena also gives Natasha the vest she bought, which has a lot of pockets.

The post-credit sequence suggests that Yelena is now working for Valentina Allegra de Fontaine, and she gives Yelena her next target: Clint Barton, the man who murdered Natasha.

Comic Notes: *Yelena Belova*: shares a fair bit in common with her comic counterpart, including her physical appearance. She first appeared in *Inhumans #5 (Mar, '99)* created by Devin Grayson and JG Jones, and was effectively the replacement Black Widow for Natasha Romanova after Natasha defected. Like the movie version she trained in the Red Room, but after the death of her trainer, she volunteered to go to America to kill Romanova. Romanova, however, convinced her to be herself, and Belova went to Cuba to become a model and business woman. SHIELD brings Belova back to the world of espionage, but HYRDRA then mutated her into Super-Adaptoid, where she gained the powers to mimic other people's powers. Yelena was later kept in statis while Natasha was hypnotised into believing that she was actually Belova, but Natasha dealt with that, and Yelena was freed, and joined AIM. Those powers seem to have gone, as of late, and after the death of Natasha, Yelena became the Black Widow once again to honor her predecessor's legacy.

Alexei Shostakov/Red Guardian: Alexei first appeared in *The Avengers #43 (Aug, '67)*, created by Roy Thomas and John Buscema as, effectively, the Russian Captain America. His backstory is notably different to the movie – in the comics he was Natasha Romanova's husband, and a pilot. His death was faked and he was trained to be a "super soldier", whereupon he joined Colonel Ling to fight Captain America and Black Widow, who recognised her former husband. Alexei protected his wife from Ling, but was killed in the process. A life model decoy of Alexei appeared later to cause problems for Hawkeye, Mockingbird and Black Widow, now going by the name Ronin. He was beaten, but returned to cause more problems for Daredevil. The Red Guardian mantle was subsequently handed over to Aleksey Lebedev, Tania Belinksy (also known as Starlight), Jooof Petkus, Krassno Granitsky, a man known only as Anton, and finally Nikolai Krylenko.

Taskmaster: the character of Taskmaster is radically different to the comic version, and that's not even taking into account the gender swap. The comic Taskmaster is Anthony "Tony" Masters (Antonia being a nod to that name), and like the movie version has the ability to mimic the physical movements of anyone he witnesses. It's unclear if this is a superpower as such, or simply an extremely impressive skill. Taskmaster first appears in *The Avengers #195 (May, '80)* and was created by David Michelinie and George Pérez. He decided to use this skill for crime, and created a costume which had a skull mask and a long cloak. Despite confronting a number of Marvel heroes with varying degrees of success (depending on how much of his opponent's fighting style he has seen), Taskmaster actually spends a lot of time training others to combat super-powered heroes, including the likes of Crossbones and US Agent. He has also been employed, on occasion, to mimic superheroes in order to disgrace them (though this rarely lasts long). Taskmaster later joined the Thuderbolts when Civil War occurred, and then developed a strange friendship with Deadpool, which led to him fighting the Thunderbolts. Later he is confronted by Finesse, who believes him to be her father, but he reveals that the constant accumulation of fighting styles actually results in him losing other memories, including whether he has children. Most recently he rejoined the Thunderbolts, now working for Wilson Fisk.

Mason: Though not given a first name, in the comics Rick Mason is better known as the Agent anyway. Physically the two versions aren't too far apart (if you use the image on the cover of his first appearance), and indeed he is a covert operations specialist working for any number of governments. Interestingly, he is also the son of the villain The Tinkerer (Phineas Mason) – as that character appeared in **SPIDER-MAN: HOMECOMING**, it will be interesting to see if that relationship exists in the MCU. He has worked for SHIELD, been kidnapped to blackmail the Tinkerer and teamed up with Carol Danvers against Norman Osborne. He first appeared in *Marvel Graphic Novel: Rick Mason, The Agent #1 (Dec, '89)* and was created by James Hudnall and John Ridgway.

Melina: Again, though we're not given a second name in the movie, this is Melina Vostokova, or Vostokoff (or even Van Vostokoff), depending on your take on the character. She made her first comic appearance in *Marvel Fanfare #11 (Nov, '83)*, created by Karate Kid Ralph Macchio and George Pérez. Better known as the Iron Maiden (she wears a suit of armour with a purple cloak), she was an assassin for Russia, and sent to kill Black Widow. During Civil War she became a member of the Thunderbolts, and later joined the Soviet Revolutionaries Remont Six, where she fought Red Guardian.

And: In prison Alexei arm wrestles a bear of a man (pardon the pun) named Ursa. This is probably a reference to Ursa Major, or Mikhail Uriokovitch Ursus, another member of the Winter Guard alongside Red Guardian. Another member of the Guard was Crimson Dynamo, which Yelena calls Alexei at one point during the movie, and who was Anton Vanko in the comics (the father of Ivan, who appears in **IRON MAN 2**).

Ratings: *IMDB:* 6.9; *Rotten Tomatoes:* 79%; *Metacritic:* 67

Review: It's funny how this movie has been met with a lukewarm reception, as it's really good. Many of Marvel's movies feel like they are borrowing the style of other films, and this particularly feels like the MCU doing James Bond. The action sequences are brilliant and the fights between the Black Widows are always well done. There is a lot of continuity tied up with this movie, but whether you love it or not will probably depend on your feeling towards spy films. If they're your bag, this will definitely appeal.

WHAT IF…?
[Season 1]*(Disney+)*

Regular Cast: *Jeffrey Wright (Uatu, the Watcher)*
Prod: Carrie Wassenaar; **Music:** Laura Karpman; **Exec.Prod:** A C Bradley, Bryan Andrews, Victoria Alonso, Louis D'Esposito, Kevin Feige, Brad Winderbaum; **Animation Supervisor:** Stephan Franck; **Prod.Des.:** Paul Lasaine; **Marvel Studios;** 30

Episodes:

1.1 WHAT IF…CAPTAIN CARTER WERE THE FIRST AVENGER? *(11/8/2021)*
When Heinz Kruger activates his bomb, Colonel Phillips and Erskine are killed, and Steve is shot, forcing Peggy to step up and take the super soldier serum, which appears to work perfectly. Despite being sidelined by Colonel Flynn, Peggy finds an ally in Howard Stark, who gives her a costume and suit, while also building a huge armour for Steve to use. Together Captain Carter and the Hydra Stomper go into action against the Red Skull, who plans to bring a demon to Earth through the use of the Tesseract.

Cast: *Hayley Atwell (Peggy Carter/Captain Carter), Josh Keaton (Skinny Steve Rogers), Samuel L Jackson (Nick Fury), Jeremy Renner (Clint Barton/Hawkeye), Stanley Tucci (Dr Erskine), Dominic Cooper (Howard Stark),* Bradley Whitford (Colonel Flynn), *Ross Marquand (Johann Schmidt/Red Skull), Neal McDonough (Dum Dum Dugan), Sebastian Stan (Bucky Barnes), Toby Jones (Arnim Zola),* Darrell Hammond (Nazi General), Isaac Robinson-Smith (Brick), Andreas Beckett, David Cowgill, Terri Douglas, Matthew Lindquist, Arthur Ortiz, Helen Sadler, Shane Sweet, Matthew Wood (Additional Voices)
Dir: Bryan Andrews; **Writer:** A C Bradley; **Ed:** Graham Fisher

1.2 WHAT IF…T'CHALLA WAS A STAR LORD? *(18/8/2021)*
DEDICATED TO OUR FRIEND, OUR INSPIRATION AND OUR HERO, CHADWICK BOSEMAN
Kraglin and Taserface secure T'Challa instead of Peter Quill, and Yondu offers to show the boy the universe. Years later, T'Challa has been a powerful influence on the Ravagers, turning them into a Robin Hood style group, and even recruiting Thanos. However, when Nebula approaches them with an offer to steal from the Collector something that could benefit millions of people, T'Challa finds it hard to say no. Yondu, though, is unconvinced that crossing that Collector would be a good thing.

Cast: *Chadwick Boseman(Star Lord T'Challa), Karen Gillan (Nebula), Michael Rooker (Yondu), Djimon Hounsou (Korath), John Kani (T'Chaka), Josh Brolin (Thanos), Benicio Del Toro (The Collector), Kurt Russell (Ego),* Sean Gunn (Kraglin), *Chris Sullivan (Taserface), Seth Green (Howard the Duck), Danai Gurira (Okoye), Ophelia Lovibond (Carina), Carrie Coon (Proxima Midnight), Tom Vaughan-Lawlor (Ebony Maw), Fred Tatasciore (Drax & Corvus Glaive), Maddix Robinson (Young T'Challa), Brian T Delaney (Peter Quill),* Tanya Wheelock (Female Ravager), Dave Boat, Terri Douglas, Don Fullilove, Piotr Michael, Michael Ralph, David Sobolov, Debra Wilson, Matthew Wood, Michael Woodley (Additional Voices)
Dir: Bryan Andrews; **Writer:** Matthew Chauncey; **Ed:** Graham Fisher

1.3 WHAT IF…THE WORLD LOST ITS MIGHTIEST HEROES? *(25/8/2021)*
When Fury and Romanoff confront Stark, the injection to help his disease kills him. Romanoff is arrested, but the following day Barton murders Thor, though later in prison, Barton is also killed. Romanoff

tracks down Betty Ross in the hope of finding Bruce Banner and learning what killed Stark, and she soon realises someone is targeting the list of Avengers candidates.

Cast: *Samuel L Jackson (Nick Fury), Michael Douglas (Hank Pym/ Yellow Jacket), Lake Bell (Natasha Romanoff/Black Widow), Mick Wingert (Tony Stark/Iron Man), Clark Gregg (Agent Coulson), Frank Grillo (Brock Rumlow), Jeremy Renner (Clint Barton/Hawkeye), Stephanie Panisello (Betty Ross), Mark Ruffalo (Bruce Banner/Hulk), Tom Hiddleston (Loki), Mike McGill (General Ross), Jaimie Alexander (Lady Sif), Alexandra Daniels (Carol Danvers/Captain Marvel),* Terri Douglas, Elisa Gabriella, Piotr Michael, David Michie, Arthur Ortiz, Shane Sweet, Matthew Wood, Shelby Young (Additional Voices)
Dir: Bryan Andrews; **Writers:** AC Bradley & Matthew Chauncey; **Ed:** Joel Fisher

1.4 WHAT IF…DOCTOR STRANGE LOST HIS HEART INSTEAD OF HIS HANDS? *(1/9/2021)*
While travelling to an awards ceremony, a car accident costs the life of Christine Palmer, and Stephen Strange goes to Kamar-Taj to bring her back. Years later he decides to alter time, but the Ancient One confronts him after he tries repeatedly, each time Christine dying in some fashion. When the Ancient One tells him that her death is absolute, he decides to absorb the powers of other-dimensional beings in order to get enough power to save his love.

Cast: *Benedict Cumberbatch (Doctor Strange), Rachel McAdams (Christine Palmer), Benedict Wong (Wong), Tilda Swinton (The Ancient One),* Ike Amadi (O'Bengh), *Leslie Bibb (Christine Everhart),* Chuck Billy, Robin Atkin Downes, Fred Tatasciore (Additional Voices)
Dir: Bryan Andrews; **Writer:** AC Bradley; **Ed:** Joel Fisher

1.5 WHAT IF…ZOMBIES?! *(8/9/2021)*
After bringing back Janet Van Dyne from the Quantum Realm, Hope and Scott Lang unwittingly unleash a zombie virus on the planet, one which the microscopic Lang is able to pass on to the Avengers and consequently much of the world. Bruce Banner's return to Earth fortunately brings him into contact with Okoye and some other survivors who have found a signal from someone that may have found a cure to the virus.

Cast: *Mark Ruffalo (Bruce Banner/Hulk), Chadwick Boseman (T'Challa/Black Panther), Paul Bettany (Vision), Sebastian Stan (Bucky Barnes), Evangeline Lilly (Hope Van Dyne/Wasp), Paul Rudd (Scott Lang/Ant-Man), Jon Favreau (Happy Hogan/Zombie Happy), Danai Gurira (Okoye), Emily Vancamp (Sharon Carter),* David Dastmalchian *(Kurt), Hudson Thames (Peter Parker/Spider-Man), Tom Vaughan-Lawlor (Ebony Maw), Josh Keaton (Steve Rogers/Captain America),* Ashley Adler, Piotr Michael, Fred Tatasciore, Michael Ralph, Robin Atkin Downes, Matthew Wood, Matt Yang King, Mike Vaughn, Terri Douglas, Debra Wilson, Kari Wahlgren, Ashley Peldon, Dave Boat (Additional Voices)
Dir: Bryan Andrews; **Writer:** Matthew Chauncey; **Ed:** Graham Fisher

1.6 WHAT IF...KILLMONGER RESCUED TONY STARK? *(15/9/2021)*
Tony is almost killed while demonstrating weapons to the Army, but is rescued by Erik Killmonger. Tony immediately embraces the man, appointing him Obadiah Stane's replacement when Stane's treachery is exposed, but both Pepper and Happy are concerned at Killmonger's sudden rise to power. Tony is also keen to take on Killmonger's idea of an armoured soldier powered by Vibranium, but when James Rhodes confronts Killmonger, Killmonger kills him, revealing his true nature.

Cast: *Michael B Jordan (Killmonger), Jon Favreau (Happy Hogan), Chadwick Boseman (T'Challa/Black Panther), Angela Bassett (Queen Ramonda), Danai Gurira (Okoye), Andy Serkis (Ulysses Klaue), Don Cheadle (Rhodey), Paul Bettany (Jarvis), Leslie Bibb (Christine Everhart), John Kani (T'Chaka), Mick Wingert (Tony Stark/Iron Man), Kiff Vandenheuvel (Obadiah Stane), Beth Hoyt (Pepper Potts), Mike McGill (General Ross), Ozioma Akagha (Shuri),* Kimberly Bailey, June Christopher, Terri Douglas, Robin Atkin Downes, Don Fullilove, Khanya Mkhize, Michael Ralph, Justin Shaw, Debra Wilson, Matthew Wood (Additional Voices)
Dir: Bryan Andrews; **Writer:** Matthew Chauncey; **Ed:** Graham Fisher

1.7 WHAT IF...THOR WERE AN ONLY CHILD? *(22/9/2021)*
Without Loki to temper his behaviour, Thor grows up spoiled and restless, and as Odin enters the Odinsleep and Frigga goes to visit her family, Thor goes to Earth with Sif and the Warriors Three to party. Everything is fine until Korg puts Fury into a coma, and Hill summons Captain Marvel to deal with Thor. The fight becomes something impressive, but Jane Foster knows there is really only one person who

can deal with Thor, which means going to Asgard while Darcy marries Howard the Duck.

Cast: *Chris Hemsworth (Thor), Natalie Portman (Jane Foster), Tom Hiddleston (Loki),* Kat Dennings (Darcy), *Samuel L Jackson (Nick Fury), Jeff Goldblum (Grandmaster), Cobie Smulders (Maria Hill), Clark Gregg (Agent Coulson), Frank Grillo (Brock Rumlow), Taika Waititi (Korg), Karen Gillan (Nebula), Jaimie Alexander (Lady Sif), Seth Green (Howard the Duck), Alexandra Daniels (Carol Danvers/Captain Marvel), Rachel House (Topaz), Josette Eales (Frigga), David Chen (Hogun), Fred Tatasciore (Volstagg & Drax), Max Mittelman (Fandral), Clancy Brown (Surtur),* Kimberly Bailey, David Jordan Chen, June Christopher, Terri Douglas, Robin Atkin Downes, Max Mittelman, Michael Ralph, Kaitlyn Robrock, Fred Tatasciore, Kari Wahlgreen, Matthew Wood, Shelby Young (Additional Voices)
Dir: Bryan Andrews; **Writer:** AC Bradley; **Ed:** Joel Fisher

1.8 WHAT IF…ULTRON WON? *(29/9/2021)*
Ultron is successful in gaining his new form, and with it he is able to create war, bringing the human race to its knees. Though Hawkeye and Black Widow remain to fight him, Ultron encounters Thanos and is able to take the Infinity Stones. These give him a new insight into the multiverse and he makes contact with the Watcher. As he crosses the Multiverse, he confronts the Watcher, forcing the alien to make a choice he does not want to.

Cast: Jeremy Renner (Clint Barton/Hawkeye), Benedict Cumberbatch (Doctor Strange/Strange Supreme), Lake Bell (Natasha Romanoff/ Black Widow), Toby Jones (Arnim Zola), Ross Marquand (Ultron/Sub-Ultron Sentries), Josh Keaton (Steve Rogers/Captain America), Mick Wingert (Tony Stark/Iron Man), Alexandra Daniels (Carol Danvers/ Captain Marvel), Terri Douglas, Robin Atkin Downes, Piotr Michael, Dave B Mitchell, Arthur Ortiz, Ashley Peldon, Matthew Wood, Shelby Young (Additional Voices)
Dir: Bryan Andrews; **Writer:** Matthew Chauncey; **Ed:** Graham Fisher, Joel Fisher

1.9 WHAT IF…THE WATCHER BROKE HIS OATH? *(6/10/2021)*
At the behest of the Stephen Strange who lost his heart, the Watcher assembles a team to fight Ultron from across the multiverse. One of these is Gamora who has a machine that can crush the Infinity Stones,

but the group need a plan to confront Ultron and take the stones, leading them back to Ultron's own universe. Here they meet Black Widow who agrees to help them, still carrying the Zola virus that can wipe Ultron from his systems.

Cast: Samuel L Jackson (Nick Fury), Hayley Atwell (Peggy Carter/ Captain Carter), Lake Bell (Natasha Romanoff/Black Widow), Frank Grillo (Brock Rumlow), Georges St-Pierre (Batroc), Chadwick Boseman (Star-Lord T'Challa), Brian T Delaney (Peter Quill), Mick Wingert (Tony Stark/Iron Man), Cynthia McWilliams (Gamora), Michael B Jordan (Killmonger), Ozioma Akagha (Shuri), Chris Hemsworth (Thor), Benedict Cumberbatch (Doctor Strange/Strange Supreme), Ross Marquand (Ultron), Toby Jones (Arnim Zola), Tom Hiddleston (Loki), Kurt Russell (Ego), Chuck Billy, Arthur Ortiz, Helen Sadler, Justin Shaw, Kari Wahlgren, Matthew Wood, Robin Atkin Downes, Fred Tatasciore, Shondalia White, Terri Douglas (Additional Voices)
Dir: Bryan Andrews; **Writer:** AC Bradley; **Ed:** Graham Fisher, Joel Fisher

Notes: Announced in April, 2019, *WHAT IF…?* was originally talked about as a series that would have an episode for each of the 23 movies in the Infinity Saga. This was then changed, and the series became two seasons of ten episodes each. Unfortunately, the COVID pandemic reduced this to nine episodes. Although the episode length sits at around thirty minutes, they were originally to be longer, but again the pandemic necessitated a shorter running time. The episode that was dropped for the season revolved around Gamora killing Thanos – this episode would have fed into the finale, as that version of Gamora does appear (ironically, this episode was also one that Lego made a set for). There appears to be some miscommunication regarding casting as it was stated that some recasts occurred because the original actors were unavailable and the production team didn't want to limit their characters to just the actors they could get. Despite this Dave Bautista claims he was never asked to appear. Brad Winderbaum suggested the miscommunication as he claimed the actors were approached via their agents. Chadwick Boseman was one of the first to sign on, and tragically this became his final performance. Josh Keaton voiced Scott Lang in the *ANT-MAN* animated series. Fred Tatasciore has voiced the Hulk in an enormous number of projects since 2008. Lake Bell previously voiced Black Widow for *ROBOT CHICKEN*, but is perhaps better known as voicing Poison Ivy in *HARLEY QUINN*. Mick Wingert has voiced Tony Stark in a variety of projects since 2015.

Should I Stay To The End? There is a post credits sequence in the final episode that insinuates that Skinny Steve Rogers possibly remained entombed in the Hydra Stomper to the modern day. Whether this will be resolved or not remains to be seen.

It's All Connected: Well, sort of. The inherent concept, of course, is that it presents various universes in the multiverse where a change took place resulting in a totally different universe. As such, it ties in to a degree with *LOKI*, though more on that a little later. The final episode does tie the previous episodes together after a fashion – Captain Carter from the universe where Peggy took the serum unites with the Killmonger who saved Tony Stark's life, Thor the only child, Star-Lord T'Challa, Gamora from a universe which is slightly unclear and Black Widow from the universe where Ultron won; all of whom are brought together by Supreme Strange who lost Christine Palmer at the behest of the Watcher himself. They fight the Ultron from Black Widow's universe and are ultimately successful in defeating him, before they are all returned to their own universes. Sort of. Black Widow is actually returned to the universe where the Avengers were murdered by Hank Pym, though Nick Fury seems to have no objection to her appearance.

It's probably worth noting that the Loki who appears in the universe where Thor is an only child, looks like a Frost Giant, and not dissimilar to one of Mobius displays in *LOKI*.

Comic Notes: Most of the references to other characters in this series have already been explored in previous movies from which the episodes spin-off from, with two exceptions. The first are the zombies that appear in *What If… Zombies?!* There is a Marvel series called *Marvel Zombies* which has been surprisingly successful and had eight different series, including one with **ARMY OF DARKNESS**.

The second reference may not be a reference at all, but for the sake of completeness, the many tentacled monster that appears in a few episodes *might* be…

Shuma-Gorath: There's a complicated history to this character as it's technically not an original Marvel character. It was first mentioned in a short story called *The Curse of the Golden Skull* by Robert E Howard as part of his *Kull* series, and this reference may even in turn be a reference to H P Lovecraft's Shub-Niggurath. In the comics it is mentioned in *Journey Into Mystery Vol 2 #1 (Oct, '72)* where it replaces Yog-Sothoth and Kathulos. In *Marvel Premiere #10 (Sep, '73)*, it makes its first appearance, created by Steve Englehart and Frank Brunner. For a long time Shuma-Gorath ruled the world, demanding blood sacrifice, but a sorcerer banished it. Various people, such as Nicholas Scratch, have freed it or summoned it back to Earth, and it has been bested, invariably needing Dr Strange to do so. The most recent appearance of the ancient demon was when Strange banished Dormammu into it, wounding the creature which now sought revenge. It has enormous power, moreso than Dormammu or even Mephisto.

Ratings: *IMDB:* 8.3; *Rotten Tomatoes:* 92%; *Metacritic:* 77

Review: There's a sense of expectation with this series that doesn't always manifest. Equally a missing episode means that the last two episodes don't quite pay off as well as they should. Some episodes, such as the first, seems to be nothing more than a slightly different version of the movie it was based on. The real problem with the series is that at thirty minutes the episodes don't seem to have the time to explore the new universe it creates in as much depth as the viewer might want. Again, the first episode becomes a victim of this, with Captain Carter's future Avengers being of far more interest than her retreading Steve Rogers' path. It's unfortunate as the animation is quite good, and the reuse of original voice actors really helps (though when the original actors are alongside new voice actors, it does feel jarring). In all, ***WHAT IF...?*** Is disappointing because it doesn't quite meet its potential.

SHANG-CHI AND THE LEGEND OF THE TEN RINGS
(3/9/2021)

When travelling on a bus, Shaun is attacked by a group of men with impressive martial arts skills. His friend Katy is astonished that Shaun can not only hold his own, but actually beat back his opponents. He confesses to her he is actually Shang-Chi, the son of Wenwu, leader of the Ten Rings terrorist organisation. Concerned that his sister is in danger, Shang-Chi, with Katy, travels to Macow only to find his father is one step ahead of them. For Wenwu knows the pendants his children have reveal the pathway to Ta Lo, where he believes his late wife is being held prisoner.

Cast: *Simu Liu (Shang-Chi/*Shaun*),* Awkwafina (Katy), Meng'er Zhang (Xialing)*, Bendict Wong (Wong),* Fala Chen (Li), Wah Yuen (Guang Bo), *Florian Munteanu (Razor Fist), Andy Le (Death Dealer)* with Michelle Yeoh (Ying Nan) with Ben Kingsley (Trevor Slattery) and Tony Leung (Xu Wenwu) **Dir:** Destin Daniel Cretton; **Writers:** Dave Callaham, Destin Daniel Cretton, Andrew Lanham; **Prod:** Kevin Feige, Jonathan Schwartz; **Music:** Joel P West;

Exec.Prod: Charles Newirth, Victoria Alonso, Louis D'Esposito; **DOP:** William Pope; **Prod.Des.:** Sue Chan; **Ed:** Nat Sanders, Elisabet Ronalddóttir, Harry Yoon; **Costumes:** Kym Barrett; **Marvel Studios**; 132; c $175m; $430m

Notes: The idea of a Shang-Chi movie was first mooted in 2001, and Stephen Norrington was intended to direct, with Ang Lee producing. By 2005 Woo-Ping Yuen was signed to direct, but ultimately the movie fell through. The Abomination makes an appearance, voiced uncredited by Tim Roth. Mark Ruffalo and Brie Larson also appear uncredited as Bruce Banner and Carol Danvers. Jade Xu plays the Black Widow she portrayed in **BLACK WIDOW**. In December 2018 Liu actually tweeted Marvel asking for the role of Shang-Chi; he retweeted this a year later with a thank you. Filming was paused for four months in 2020 to accommodate the COVID-19 pandemic. This is Tony Leung's first American film, first English-speaking role and first time ever playing a villain. The film is dedicated to stunt supervisor Brad Allan (a member of Jackie Chan's stunt team), who died a month before the film opened. The symbols in the Ten Rings represent authority, power, strong, extraordinary, outstanding, influential, grand, mighty, strength and dominant. At one point there was talk of Paul Rudd appearing in the film (due to the fact it takes place in San Francisco), but it was decided this was largely unnecessary. The film was mostly shot in Australia amd did not open in China.

Should I Stay To The End? Absolutely. The mid-credits sequence opens up a potential sequel, as the rings have caused Wong to be concerned enough to seek Bruce Banner and Captain Marvel's help. The post-credits sequence shows that Xialing has taken control of the Ten Rings.

It's All Connected: There are a number of things in the movie that seem to contradict the placement of the film as taking place after **AVENGERS: ENDGAME**, but most have since gone on to be explained in later stories. It's certainly after the Blip because there are posters dedicated to those who need help because of what happened. Wong is based at Kamar-Taj but there is no sign of Dr Strange. Wenwu seeks out Ta Lo in 1996, and the film is described as being set in "present day", though it is ten years since the fourteen-year-old Shang-Chi was sent on his mission. Xialing waited six years before leaving her father after Shang-Chi left, having realised she could survive without her brother. Katy clarifies that Xialing was 16 when she left, and so would be 20 in present day (as it's been four years since she left). Assuming that the "present day" is 2024, Xialing was born in 2004, and Shang-Chi (who is 24) was born in 2000.

Wenwu marries Ying Li after fighting her at Ta Lo in 1996, and they have two children. He gives up leading the Ten Rings, something he has done for thousands of years, thanks to the titular rings. It's unclear how he obtained these, but they increase his strength and extend his lifespan. A gang that Wenwu once attacked sought revenge by killing Li. Wenwu then returned to the Ten Rings, and had his minion, Death Dealer, train Shang-Chi to avenge his mother. Xialing was also keen to be trained, but her father took no interest in her. Shang-Chi killed the man who killed Li, but disgusted with himself he went to America, changed his name to Shaun, met Katy and started a new life. Six years later his sister also left to China, where she started an underground fighting competition. Fighting in this competition are Wong and the Abomination, though Wong appears to be working with Abomination to help him. Trevor Slattery was brought before Wenwu to be killed for taking on the name of the Mandarin, but he was funny enough to have his life spared. The Dweller-in-Darkness is trapped behind a gate in Ta Lo, which exists in another dimension. Wenwu releases it, thinking it will free Li, but instead, the Dweller kills him. When those of Ta Lo and the Ten Rings defeat the Dweller, Xialing returns to take control of the Ten Rings, while Shang Chi goes back to New York, keeping the physical ten rings. Later Wong examines the rings, along with Bruce Banner and Carol Danvers, and they find that the rings are sending out a signal, though to whom, they cannot tell.

During the impressive train fight, Klev films the fight for his blog – it was he who asked Spidey to do a flip in **SPIDER-MAN: HOMECOMING**. A Black Widow from the eponymous movie also makes an appearance.

Comic Notes: *Shang-Chi*: first appeared in *Special Marvel Edition #15 (Dec, '73)*, created by Steve Englehart and Jim Starlin. Pitched as adapting the television series *KUNG FU* into a comic book, it was the editor Roy Thomas who requested that Sax Rohmer's characters (Dr Fu Manchu, Dr James Petrie, etc) were included, and that Shang-Chi himself would be half-white. Originally, he was the son of Fu Manchu and a woman that Fu Manchu specifically chose to be the mother of his child, and he was trained by Death Dealer to kill Dr James Petrie (which isn't a million miles from what we see in the movie). After completing his mission, he is convinced by Sir Denis Nayland Smith of his father's true nature, and opts to stay in London, where he becomes allies of Smith and MI6. Shang-Chi would fight several members of his family before seeing his father die. As time went on, Shang-Chi became more integrated into the Marvel universe, teaming up with the likes of Iron Fist and the Daughters of the Dragon, while continuing to fight surprise new siblings and the return of his father. He is later met by his half-siblings Brother Sabre and Sister Dagger who reveal to him that he was designated Brother Hand, and the spirit of Zheng Zu (the renamed Fu Manchu) had chosen him to take over the Five Weapons Society. Interestingly, Shang-Chi does indeed do this, with Sister Dagger at his side, though part of this is to ensure that Zheng Zu's influence is never felt on the organisation again. Most recently he united with the five champions of the Five Weapons Society to rescue his mother from the negative zone and stop his grandfather, Xin.

Shang-Chi's family: All of Shang-Chi's family have appeared in the comics in some form or another, but for a variety of reasons, none of them have translated directly across to the big screen. It's worth having a quick look at them, however, because the big screen versions do come from interesting places. *Ying Li*, Shang-Chi's mother, actually originated in the film, and her comic book version – named Jiang Li, as that was the original name for the movie character before she was changed – first appeared in *Shang-Chi Vol 2 #4 (Sep, '21)*, this version created by Gene Yuen Yang and Dike Ruan. There was a character in the comics before this who was Shang-Chi's mother, but we'll get back to her. Jiang Li also lives in Ta-Lo, and rescued Zheng Zu from a shipwreck, falling in love with him and having two children with him – Shang-Chi and Shi-Hua. Her story is not dissimilar to the movie version, though Zheng Zu rules the Five Weapons Society, and becomes distant when Hydra attacks and he thinks his family weak. Jiang Li fought Zu, but ended up in the negative zone. Curiously she has an affinity with insects, and is able to psychically bond with her children. *Xu Wenwu*, Shang-Chi's father, has quite the history. The character of the Mandarin was looked at in the entry for **IRON MAN THREE**, but in the comics Shang-Chi's actual father was Fu Manchu, the Marvel version of Sax Rohmer's supervillain Dr Fu Manchu, who first appeared in the novel *The Mystery Of Dr Fu-Manchu*, and would then go onto appear in 13 more Rohmer novels, several more novels by other authors and copious films. In the comics he first appears in *Special Marvel Edition #15 (Dec, '73)* created by Steve Englehart, Al Milgrom and Jim Starlin. Here he is a powerful sorcerer who creates the Five Weapons Society to protect China, befriending the Ancient One and battling Fin Fang Foom. He was later granted immortality by his brother, but became bitter and started building a criminal empire. He had a daughter, Fah Lo Suee, and then took a woman to bear him the child that was Shang-Chi. This history was revised when Marvel opted not to renew their licence to keep Fu Manchu, and the character was renamed Zheng Zu (Fah Lo Suee would be renamed Zheng Bao Yu), and the story of him gaining Shang-Chi (and Shi-Hua) was altered as above. Zheng Zu would go onto battle many heroes, but he was ultimately defeated by the Secret Avengers, who were able to kill him. Zu still exists on the astral plane where he has battled Shang-Chi. As such he has very little in common with Xu Wenwu. *Xu Xialing* on the other hand, is based on several characters. One is Zheng Bao Yu, one is Shi-Hua and the other is Sister Dagger – all of whom are daughters of Zheng Zu. Sister Dagger's loyalties lie with Shang-Chi, and she asked him to help her and their half-brother Brother Sabre to stop Sister Hammer, their older half-sister. Sister Dagger is a highly skilled fighter, particularly with daggers. She first appears in *Shang-Chi #1 (Nov, '20)* also created by Yang, Ruan and Philip Tan, and the only other name she is ever given is Esme. Zheng Bao Yu first appeared in *Master of Kung-Fu #26 (Mar, '75)* created by Doug Moench and Keith Pollard (though again, the original character first appeared in the Sax Rohmer novels), and here she is very much her father's daughter, growing up to be a sorceress and create her own criminal organisation. It is unclear, though, if Zheng Bao Yu still exists in Marvel continuity, due to the new backstory for Shang-Chi. Consequently, the three characters are a mix of different sources to create the movie versions.

Razor Fist: actually, doesn't look that different to his comic book version – though the comic version wears a black helmet and doesn't sport a beard. In the comics, there have been three Razor Fists, though none of them were named Mattias. William Young was the first, a bodyguard for Carlton Velcro who was shot by Velcro's guards while fighting Shang-Chi. William Scott was the second; he also worked for Velcro and was also shot to death, though by Velcro himself, accidentally. His brother, Douglas, was the third – though William and Douglas would pretend to be the same Razor Fist – and actually lost his hand in a fight with Colleen Wing. This is the longest serving version of the character, and is usually a thug for hire, fighting a variety of heroes; Shang-Chi being at the top of that list. He was most recently seen joining a group to fight Shang-Chi on his date with Domino. Razor First first appeared in *Master of Kung-Fu #29 (Jun, '75)*, created by Doug Moench and Paul Gulacy, while the latter two versions didn't appear until *#105 (Oct, '81)*, created by Moench and Gene Day.

Death Dealer: who, in the comics, is named Li Ching-Lin, is an MI6 agent, secretly also working for Dr Fu Manchu. It's probably worth mentioning that MI6 surprisingly turns up a lot in Shang-Chi's stories over the years (indeed at one point his sister was the head of MI6). When MI6 learns of Li's duplicity, he flees to Manchu and gets his costume and new name. Although he is tasked with killing Shang-Chi, he fails. He is later killed by Shang-Chi, and still later, his son Huo Li attempts to avenge him, unsuccessfully. Death Dealer first appears in *Master of Kung-Fu #115 (Aug, '82)* created by Moench and Day.

And: Xialing runs the Golden Daggers club; in the comics, the Golden Daggers are a criminal organisation run by Zheng Bao Yu.

Ratings: *IMDB:* 8.1; *Rotten Tomatoes:* 92%; *Metacritic:* 71

Review: Shang-Chi is an odd character to make a movie around; as a hero he has no "super" powers as such, he's simply an amazing martial arts expert (and indeed his sister Xialing is pretty much on par). But the story is really all about a family falling apart, and a man unable to move beyond the loss of his wife. That the story is tied into the MCU so tightly (the return of the Ten Rings, the introduction of the real Mandarin and the surprising return of Trevor Slattery) is an added bonus. The martial acts action is outstanding, and Simu Liu has an easy charisma which makes it difficult to dislike him. The MCU additions sometimes seem a little forced (Wong and the Abomination are fun to see, but seem unnecessary) as the rest of the movie is good enough to stand on its own feet.

THE TEN RINGS WILL RETURN

ETERNALS
(18/10/2021)

Having spent a great time on Earth after wiping out the Deviants, two of the Eternals – Sersi and Sprite – are shocked to be attacked by a Deviant. This leads the pair to reunite the rest of their group, as the Deviant menace they were sworn to destroy clearly still remains on the planet Earth. However, Sersi discovers that their leader Ajak has been murdered, apparently by Deviants, but this leads them to learn precisely why they were sent to Earth in the first place.

Cast: *Gemma Chan (Sersi), Richard Madden (Ikaris), Kumail Nanjiani (Kingo), Lia McHugh (Sprite), Brian Tyree Henry (Phastos), Lauren Ridloff (Makkari), Barry Keoghan (Druig), Don Lee (Gilgamesh),* Harish Patel (Karun) *with Kit Harrington (Dane Whitman) with Salma Hayek (Ajak) and Angelina Jolie (Thena), Bill Skarsgård (Deviant Kro), David Kaye (Arishem)*
Dir/Writer: Chloé Zhao; **Writers:** Patrick Burleigh, Ryan Firpo, Kaz Firpo; **Prod:** Kevin Feige, Nate Moore; **Music:** Ramin Djawadi; **Exec.Prod:** Kevin de la Noy, Victoria Alonso, Louis D'Esposito; **DOP:** Ben Davis; **Prod.Des.:** Eve Stewart; **Ed:** Dylan Tichenor, Craig Wood; **Costumes:** Sammy Sheldon Differ; **Marvel Studios**; 156; $200m; $402m

Notes: ETERNALS was originally envisioned as a television series, due to the many characters involved, but the decision was taken to make a movie instead. This film sees the reappearance of two actors who have previously appeared in the MCU – Gemma Chan, formerly Minn Erva in **CAPTAIN MARVEL** appears as Sersi, while Mahershala Ali voices Blade, having been Cottonmouth in the first season of *LUKE CAGE* (Patton Oswalt, who had a recurring role in *AGENTS OF SHIELD* also has a cameo voice role). The film firmly tries to embrace diversity, something which superhero films have struggled with in the past, and it was this vision by Chloé Zhao that convinced Jolie to join the cast. A number of other Eternals – Vampiro, Virako, Zuras and Valkin – were also planned for the film, but it was decided this would make the group unworkable. The film was banned in a number of countries, starting with China because of Zhao's criticism of the government, and several Middle Eastern countries when Disney refused to remove the scenes of Phastos and his husband. BTS is mentioned by Kingo at one point, and their song *Friends* appears. The original ending of the film would have had the Eternals' minds wiped as they were sent on another mission by the Celestials, though it was decided the ending was too bleak and so the new one was devised.

Should I Stay To The End? There's a lot going on, so most definitely. The first sequence introduces a new Eternal in the form of Harry Styles as Eros/Starfox, along with his troll, Pip (voiced by Patton Oswalt). The second sequence surrounds Dane Whitman about to use the Ebony Blade, before a mystery voice speaks to him…the uncredited voice of Mahershala Ali, the future Blade…

It's All Connected: There aren't any appearances by characters from the other films, but this certainly is connected to the wider MCU as at one point Dane Whitman specifically asks Sersi why they didn't interfere with Thanos' plan, placing it firmly after the Blip. Sersi, rather conveniently, says they were told not to…

This movie introduces us to a group of Eternals, led by Ajak, and consisting of Sersi, Ikaris, Kingo, Sprite, Phastos, Makkari, Druig, Gilgamesh and Thena. Dispatched to Earth by the Celestials to defend the natives from the vicious Deviants, when their mission is completed, they are simply told to wait around until the time comes for them to return. The Celestials look not dissimilar to the Celestial we see in **GUARDIANS OF THE GALAXY** when the Collector talks about the Infinity Stones, but for some this might lead to question whether Ego was telling the truth about being a Celestial. Ajak knows that the Eternals are actually on Earth to watch over the birth of a new Celestial, but when she realises that this will destroy the planet, she opts to try to stop it, earning herself a quick death from Ikaris, who then confronts the other Eternals when Sersi – having become the new leader – decides to follow in Ikaris' footsteps. Both Kingo and Sprite agree with Ikaris in blindly obeying the Celestials, but Kingo chooses to step out of the fight, rather than join a side. Ajak and Sersi both commune with the Celestial Arishem throughout the film, and at the end he opts to judge the Earth based on what Sersi, Phastos and Kingo believe of humans. He picks these three as, having stopped the rising of the Celestial Tiamut, they opted to stay on Earth with their new families. Sprite also remains, but Sersi changes her from an Eternal to a human. As the film goes on the Eternals discover that they are actually highly advanced robots built by the Celestials to kill the Deviants, who were also sent by the Celestials to destroy the apex predators of the planet and allow for a smoother emergence of the Celestials. Gilgamesh also dies, killed by the Deviant leader Kro, and ultimately Ikaris flies into the sun, guilt ridden for his actions towards Sersi, who he loved. Makkari, Druig and Thena take their ship, the Dojo, into space, to search for other Eternals, apparently finding one in the end – Eros. Sersi's lover is Dane Whitman, a man with apparently a strange family history, including ownership of the Ebony Blade, which he is reluctant to wield, and which attracts the attention of the vampire hunter Blade. Interestingly, Arishem appears in the sky, quite visible to most of the humans on Earth, though this would seem to be something fairly common place for humans now.

Comic Notes: *Eternals:* It's probably worth noting that a lot of leeway has been taken with the characters of the Eternals. The entire concept was created by Jack Kirby for *The Eternals #1 (Jul, '76)* and came from his interest in what he called "high concept science fiction" which he began with *New Gods* for DC, but was cancelled. Indeed, initially the comic would have been called "Return of the Gods", but legal reasons forced the change to Eternals. The series was cancelled and plot points would go onto be resolved in other series, by other authors, while the characters continued to show up from time to time, particularly the Celestials. Additionally, Jim Starlin's Titanians (one of whom was Thanos) and Stan Lee's Uranians were retconned into being Eternals. In the comics the Celestials created the Eternals and the Deviants, genetically engineered from humans (and Earth wasn't the only planet this happened to). The Eternals defend humanity from the Deviants, and though longer lived, with considerably more power (thanks to the cosmic energy that flows through them), they have a quite close bond with humans. A civil war led by two Eternal brothers – Kronos and Uranos – broke out over how the Eternals would treat humanity; as their defenders or rulers. Uranos lost and travelled to Uranus where they set up a colony. When some tried to return to Earth, they were shot down over Titan by a Kree ship (the Kree experimented on a captured Eternal, and used this science on humanity to create the Inhumans). Over time, some

Eternals have been assumed to be gods by humanity, while others have taken on the role of superheroes. Neil Gaiman's 2006 storyline retconned some of this to a degree, changing the age of the Eternals from tens of thousands to millions of years old, and limiting their power, as well as hardwiring them so they couldn't attack the Celestials. They were effectively the caretakers of humanity, keeping the Earth ready for judgement by the Celestials. Still later, it was revealed that the Celestials lied, and that humanity was being bred by the Celestials as a pathogen against the Horde, with the Eternals simply there to defend the creation and evolution of humanity until they were needed. This droves all the Eternals to commit suicide. They have all since been resurrected, because…well, because a movie was coming out.

There are *a lot* of Eternals in the comics. They can be split into different generations, so for the sake of completeness, the movie Eternals fall into the following generations –

First Generation (born before the fall of the city Titanos): well, er, none. But this was Kronos and Uranos' generation.

Second Generation (alive during the experiments of Chronus): Gilgamesh (aka the Forgotten One)

Third Generation (after the second but before the fourth generations): Ajak, Ikaris, Phastos, Thanos, Thena, Eros

Fourth Generation (born after the coming of the second Host): Druig, Makkari, Sersi, Kingo Sunen

Fifth Generation (born after the coming of the third Host): Sprite

Sersi: is not totally removed from her comic book counterpart – they broadly have similar appearances and both versions dress in green. The comic version first appeared in *Strange Tales #109 (Jun, '63)* though went by the name Circe, and was created by Stan Lee and Robert Bernstein. She was renamed Sersi in *The Eternals #3 (sep, '76),* and later comics retconned the two versions as the same person. Like all Eternals, Sersi has a range of powers, but does specialise in the transmutation of objects. She was the daughter of Helios and Perse, and did indeed enjoy living among humans, unlike the other Eternals. She has lived in a variety of places as a dancer, actress and adventurer, including ancient Greece, Nero's Rome and the court of King Arthur. She has a close association with the Avengers, joining them at Steve Rogers request, and then also had a relationship with Dane Whiteman. After forming a uni-mind with Thane Ector, Sersi became more aggressive. Initially it was thought Sersi was suffering from mahd w'yry, but in fact was possessed by Proctor. Sersi decided to go into exile as a consequence of this, and Whitman joined her. After being possessed by the Ego Gem, she and Whitman decided to spend time apart. Later, when Sprite tries to become human and reveals that the

Eternals' past is much greater than they thought (and that Sersi was in a relationship with Makkari), Sersi opts to leave the Eternals and the Avengers and retires. When the Final Host arrives to reveal the truth of the Eternals' purpose, Sersi was one of the many that committed suicide.

Ajak: is one of the gender-swapped characters, though the character has been retconned such that he has been both male and female in the comics. He lived in Polaria, away from the other Eternals (not unlike the movie). He rejoined the Eternals when Ikaris summoned his help on the arrival of the Fourth Host. Later, Ajak was killed when he joined Hercules' God Squad to battle the Skrulls. He was revived and had a bitter feud with Makkari, though saved the latter's life. Like the other Eternals, Ajak committeed suicide when the Eternals' true purpose was revealed. She was created by Kirby, and appears relatively early, debuting in *The Eternals #2 (Aug, '76)*.

Ikaris: like Ajak is a Polar Eternal, and would later appear to be Daedalus, who with a human gave birth to Icarus. When Icarus died, Ikaris took the name to honour his son. He awakened Ajak to deal with the Fourth Host, and then became a superhero to the people of Earth, working with a number of Earth's heroes, including Thor, Iron Man and the West Coas Avengers. He had a strong rivalry with Thena, beating her to become the Prime Eternal. When the Eternals all killed themselves, Ikaris was the last to do so, giving him time to explain to Dr Strange why they had done what they did. Unlike most of the Eternals, the movie and comic versions don't look too dissimilar. Ikaris first appeared in *The Eternals #1 (Jul, '76)*, created by Kirby.

Druig: is Ikaris' cousin in the comics, a bearded character who wears red, and is sometimes known as Ivan Druig. He was a particularly cruel character who joined the KGB because he enjoyed torture. In fact, he tortured Ikaris, who killed him as a result. The Celestials recovered his body, and he was somehow revived to become Deputy Prime Minister of Vorozheika. He used his powers to take control of the country, and used his country to try to take control of the Eternals. Created by Kirby, his didn't appear until *The Eternals #11 (May, '77)*.

Thena: first appeared in *The Eternals #5 (Nov, '76)*, but a later retcon revealed that she was also Minerva, who first appeared in *Red Raven Comics #1 (Aug, "40)* created by Martin A Burnstein. An Eternal of Olympia, born as Minerva, Zuras, her father, had her name changed to Thena (or Athena) in an effort to forge a bond between the Eternals and the Olympian Gods. The comic version looks quite similar to the movie version, though interestingly the comic version had a relationship with the Deviant Kro, even having twin children to him –

Donald and Deborah. Her relationship with Kro has been tempestuous, but ended when she realised what sort of rituals the Deviants engaged in. Over time she has joined the Heroes for Hire and befriended Thor and the Avengers. When Sprite wiped their minds, Thena believed she was a researcher at Stark Enterprises, and had a child named Joey, and when their memories returned, she chose not to rejoin the Eternals, but rather she stayed with Joey. However, like all the Eternals, she killed herself when she discovered the true purpose of the Eternals.

Makkari: is another example of an Eternal whose backstory retconned another character (or two!). In this case the Eternal first appeared in *The Eternals #5*, like Thena, but the retcon revealed that Mercury in *Red Raven Comics #1* and Hurricane in *Captain America Comics #1 (Mar, '41)* were both Makkari under different names (and both created by Martin A Burnstein). Hurricane formed the Monster Hunters (which we later found out was to seek out Deviants) while as Mercury he joined the First Line. As you can guess from the pronouns, Makkari has been gender swapped for the movie, though unlike other movie Eternals he has not been gender swapped in the comics. Additionally, the comic version is not a person of colour, nor is he hearing impaired. Makkari is known for his speed, and would appear to be faster than the likes of Quicksilver. Initially an Olympian Eternal, he spent time in a number of Earth eras, helping them (including, obscurely, Elvis Presley), and has fought alongside the Avengers and Thor. When Sprite wiped the Eternal's memories, Makkari believed himself to be medical student Jack Curry, and as he rediscovered his powers, Sprite tricked him into exposing the Dreaming Celestial. The Celestial spoke to him, and Makkari became his prophet, believing he had been personally created by the Celestial. Like the other Eternals, he killed himself when the Eternals' true purpose was revealed.

Sprite: The child of the Eternals in the comics, she is also a male there, though recently Sprite has changed genders. Whereas a lot of Eternals were mistaken as gods by humans, Sprite has often given rise to fictional characters such as Puck or Peter Pan. Though the movie version seems to be playful, the comic Sprite is malicious and has little interest in the consequence of his actions. This was taken to a new extreme when he was responsible for the Eternals loss of memory and powers as punishment for being treated as a child. Zuras killed him as punishment for what he did. When the Eternals were resurrected after their mass suicide, Sprite was as well, now a girl, and though lacking memories of her former life, is intrigued when she learns of it. She first appeared in *The Eternals #9 (Mar, '77)*, another Kirby creation.

Phastos: has some similarities to the comic version, in that they are both black, and both the master technicians of the group. The comic version, however, remains on Earth not because of love but because of a desire to find something. He is also anti-war for the most part. Curiously, he is much younger than the other Eternals, and actually has a specific weapon he uses (an energy hammer). He first appeared in *The Eternals Vol 2 #1 (Oct, '85)*, created by Peter B Gillis and Sal Buscema.

Kingo Sunen (as is his full name), is more Japanese influenced in the comics than Indian influenced. He is an actor in Japan, but before that he spent centuries learning the ways of the samurai. Kingo is actually one of the best swordsmen on the planet. Like Druig, he didn't appear until *The Eternals #11*.

Gilgamesh: is probably better known in the comics as The Forgotten One, though he was created by Jack Kirby, like the majority of the other Eternals, and first appeared in *The Eternals #13 (Jul, '77)*. He's significantly different in the comics to how he is the movie; here he is sometimes also known as simply Hero and has been assumed to be Gilgamesh or Hercules, and was actually exiled from the Eternals for meddling with humans too much. Sprite convinced him to leave this exile and join the fight against the Deviants. As Gilgamesh he joined the Avengers, notably fighting during the *Inferno* saga, but was later killed by Neut, working for Immortus. Like the other Eternals, he succumbed to Sprite's mind wipe, and was tricked by Ajak into killing Makkari.

Dane Whitman: aside from a superficial physical appearance, Dane Whitman's backstory is quite different in the comics to how it appears to be in the movies – he's not English for a start. Dane had an ancestor, Sir Percy of Scandia, who was the Black Knight, and after his death at the hands of Mordred, Sir Percy's descendants would take on the mantle. One such descendant, Nathan Garrett became the Black Knight, but was a villain rather than a hero, and when he was badly wounded by Iron Man, he bequeathed the role to his nephew, Dane Whitman. Whitman became the Black Knight, but proved to the Avengers he was going to be a hero, and when he later visited Castle Garrett, he encountered the spirit of Sir Percy and was given the Ebony Blade – a sword many of the previous Black Knights had used. Whitman would join the Avengers subsequent to this, as well as the Defenders. He has travelled in time and across space, but after returning to modern times, he was forced to briefly step down from the Avengers when he learnt that using the Ebony Blade drove him closer to madness with each kill. Freeing Sir Percy's spirit from the sword appeared to stop the curse, but when Namor used it to kill his wife, the curse returned and Whitman was actually slowly turned into a metal statue. Sir

Percy joined with Dr Strange, and when the former was merged with the sword it ended the curse and restored Whitman. He had a relationship with Crystal, the Inhuman, and then Sersi, the Eternal, and because of Sersi's mental instability, he joined minds with her, but this resulted in the pair leaving the Avengers and attempting to find a solution to Sersi's issues. In the Ultraverse, Whitman took control of the Ultraforce and turned them into a better team (while allowing him a quick fling with Topaz – take a look at **THOR: RAGNAROK** for more information on her), and then he found Sersi again and they returned to the proper universe. Since then, he has been involved with Excalibur, MI-13, joined the Euroforce (after being excluded from The Avengers, because he started to lose his mind again), went to Weirdworld, joined the Secret Avengers, was killed by the Obsidian Dagger and then resurrected because the Ebony Blade possesses King Arthur's power of self-revival. Given his brief appearance in the movie, and his reluctance to touch the Ebony Blade, one might imagine the movie version has a lot more to explore than what we saw in this film.

Kro: looks almost nothing like his comic book original (though the Deviants have been altered significantly for the movie – in the comics they are grotesque humanoids rather than the animalistic versions in the movie). He appeared first in *The Eternals #1 (Jul, '76)*, created by Kirby, and is the Warlord of the Deviants. He is a shape-shifter, and immortal, and as noted above, was in a relationship with Thena which bore two children. When the Deviants were in a position to potentially destroy the Eternals, Kro tried to save Thena (though she refused), and then later when the situation was reversed, Thena did save Kro, who became the only survivor of the Deviant invasion. Kro took control of the Deviants, snatching it from the priest Ghuar, but his attachment to Thena saw him abdicate his position out of depression. From this point, Kro and Ghuar have often split the Deviants into two antagonistic factions, but his children tend to be his greatest priority. Later when Ghuar led the Deviants against the Eternals and was beaten by Thor, Kro took power again, and promised the Avenger that he had no interest in using his people to attack the Eternals again. (Well, until he changes his mind in the future, of course. This is Marvel comics after all…)

Arishem: though the Celestials have been examined in previous volumes, Arishem is a new face to the movies. He first appears in *The Eternals #2* (created by Kirby, obviously), and was part of the Fourth Celestial Host. He judges species to determine if they are worthy of life, and spent fifty years judging humanity (though he probably won't take as long in the movies). Little else is known about him, though he did lead a war against the Watchers. His appearance in the movie is different to how he appears in the comics – the movie version is more inspired by the Celestial Eson.

Tiamut: is another Celestial, though he is also known as The Dreaming Celestial. He personally created Makkari and was part of the Second Host that arrived on Earth to judge it, but was exiled as he turned against his fellow Celestials. He judged humanity unworthy, but was overruled by Arishem and fought the Judge. He claims to have defeated Arishem but was brought down by other Celestials, though this could be a lie. Created by Kirby, he first appeared in *The Eternals #18 (Dec, '77)*.

Domo: the spaceship, does have a comic book counterpart. In fact, there is an Eternal named Domo, who was Duras' right-hand man. Domo assisted Thanos, but tried to betray him, which resulted in Thanos killing him. He first appeared in *The Eternals #5 (Aug, '76)*, created by Kirby.

Starfox: is actually Eros of Titan, an Eternal and the brother of Thanos. He does look very similar to the movie version, and was good friends with Mar-Vell before joining the Avengers, where he gained his Starfox codename. However, Eros has a tendency towards a hedonistic lifestyle and would often abandon the Avengers to pursue that. Starfox's abilities to influence others led to him being placed on trial for sexual assault, and though he wasn't completely to blame for what had happened around him, it was determined that he had influenced others in an inappropriate fashion and as such he agreed to Moondragon removing those powers from him. Thanos attempted a rebirth in Starfox, and Gamora killed him to prevent this, though it wasn't successful. He was resurrected and imprisoned subsequently, before being rescued by Sersi who needed his help. Whether the movies progress down this dark path remains to be seen. Regardless, his first appearance was in *The Invincible Iron Man #55 (Feb, '73)* and he was created by Jim Starlin.

Pip the Troll: goes by the name Pip Gofern in the comics and sort of looks like the version seen in the movie. He first appeared in *Strange Tales #179 (Jan, '75)* created by Jim Starlin, and is broadly Laxidazian royalty. He wasn't actually a troll – that transformation came as a consequence of drinking with Laxidazian trolls, and resulted in his exile. He allied himself with Adam Warlock, and was placed in the Soul Gem when Thanos destroyed his mind, and later worked for X-Factor Investigations. Most recently he allied himself with Yondu's Ravagers and settled with them on Ego.

And: Isaac and Sylvia, the names that Phastos uses to introduce Ikaris and Sersi, are the comic book secret identities of those Eternals.

Ratings: *IMDB:* 6.8; *Rotten Tomatoes:* 92%; *Metacritic:* 53

Review: It's not so much that **ETERNALS** is a bad film…it's very well directed and beautifully shot, and the location work makes the whole thing look spectacular. But there's an inevitable problem with anything that's going to introduce a lot of superheroes in it, and that's the need to develop those heroes to give them a personality. The film starts well, but then grinds to a crawl as we learn about what the Eternals have been doing over the past centuries. And though it looks wonderful and is interesting, the audience is screaming "let's get back to the actual plot!!!" By the time it does, the film returns to surer footing, but it's not enough to wipe away the length of boredom in the middle of the movie. I hope it gets a sequel in order to show us the characters in a pacier film, but sadly this one feels like a lot of wasted potential.
ETERNALS WILL RETURN…

HAWKEYE
[Season 1]*(Disney+)*

Regular Cast: *Jeremy Renner (Clint Barton), Hailee Steinfeld (Kate Bishop), Florence Pugh (Yelena)*[1.4-1.6], *Tony Dalton (Jack Duquesne), Alaqua Cox (Maya Lopez), Fra Fee (Kazi), Vincent D'Onofrio (Kingpin)*[1.5-1.6], *Brian D'arcy James (Derek Bishop)*[1.1], *Aleks Paunovic (Ivan),* Piotr Adamczyk (Tomas), Zahn McClarnon (William Lopez)[1.3], special guest star Linda Cardellini (Laura Barton)[1.1-1.2,1.4-1.6] with Simon Callow (Armand III)[1.1-1.2] and *Vera Farmiga (Eleanor Bishop)*
Line Prod: Leeann Stonebreaker; **Music:** Christophe Beck & Michael Paraskevas; **Exec.Prod:** Jonathan Igla, Rhys Thomas, Brad Winderbaum, Trinh Tran, Victoria Alonso, Louis D'Esposito, Kevin Feige; **Created by** Jonathan Igla; **DOP:** Eric Steelberg [1.1-1.2,1.6], James Whitaker [1.3-1.5]; **Prod.Des.:** Maya Shimoguchi; **Costumes:** Michael Crow; **Marvel Studios**; 45 - 60

Episodes:

1.1 NEVER MEET YOUR HEROES *(24/11/2021)*
While Clint Barton enjoys time with his children at Christmas, Kate

Bishop discovers some disturbing secrets about her mother's fiancé and a connection to Armand Duqesne III, a man who later turns up dead after a secret auction. When the auction is interrupted by the Tracksuit Mafia, Kate steals the Ronin costume and when she rescues a dog, hits the news, ending Clint's holiday.

Cast: Carlos Navarro (Enrique), Ben Sakamoto (Cooper Barton), Ava Russo (Lila Barton), Cade Woodward (Nathaniel Barton), Clara Stack (Little Kate Bishop), Nichele Lambert (Greer), Regina Bryant (Franny), Brian Troxell (Catering Captain Gary), Barry Ratcliffe (Auctioneer), Milo Wesley (Auction Waiter), Katelyn Farrugia (Waitress), Noah Artis (Waiter), Shaun Lynch (Campus Security Guard), Jonathan Bergman (Armand VII), Annalise Bergen (Little Girl in Theater), Nick Caruso (Guy in Theater Men's Room), Yoon Jae Kim (Chinese Restaurant Waiter), Adam Pascal (Lead New Yorker #1), Ty Taylor (Lead New Yorker #2), Aaron Nedrick (Musical Iron Man), Avery Gillham (Musical Hawkeye), Harris Turner (Musical Hulk), Jason Scott Macdonald (Musical Thor), Meghan Manning (Musical Black Widow), Nico DeJesus (Musical Ant-Man), Tom Feeney (Musical Captain America), Jordan Chin (Musical Loki), Gino Cosculluela, Bernard Bell, Brittany Nicholas, Gabrielle Mouchakkaa, Keith Nedd, Kimo Lowery Kepano, Kristen Yancy, Marissa Milele (Musical New Yorkers), Anthony Burrell, Ehizoje Azeke, Graham Michael Dobbs, Ricardo Zayas (Musical Chitauri), Pat Kiernan (Himself)
Dir: Rhys Thomas; **Writer:** Jonathan Igla; **Ed:** Terel Gibson

1.2 HIDE AND SEEK *(24/11/2021)*
Clint gets Kate to safety and tells her to remain safe while he tracks down the Ronin costume, though it becomes clear this is not as easy as first seems given the Tracksuit Mafia are now well aware of who she is. They take cover in another home, and Clint sends his kids home while he goes after the costume, now in a LARPing event. Meanwhile Kate confronts her mother and Jack Duqesne to learn more.

Cast: Ava Russo (Lila Barton), Ben Sakamoto (Cooper Barton), Cade Woodward (Nathaniel Barton), Clayton English (Grills), Carlos Navarro (Enrique), Ivan Mbakop (Detective Caudle), Tinashe Kajese (Dee), Adetinpo Thomas (Wendy), Robert Walker-Branchaud (Orville), Adelle Drahos (Missy), Ashley Ames (Eleanor's Assistant), Monisha Shiva (Mother), Rhys Bhatia (Child), Candy McLellan (Samurai), Pat Kiernan (Himself)

Dir: Rhys Thomas; **Writer:** Elisa Clement; **Ed:** Terel Gibson

1.3 ECHOES *(1/12/2021)*
Prisoners of the Track Suit Mafia, Clint and Kate are confronted by their leader, Maya, who seems sympathetic to Clint's deafness, but is determined to find Ronin – the person who killed her father some years earlier. Clint and Kate are able to escape, though Maya is questioned about her obsession with Ronin. Kate suggests they break into her mother's home to investigate Bishop's files on the Track Suit Mafia, but Clint is confronted by Jack.

Cast: Carlos Navarro (Enrique), Cade Woodward (Nathaniel Barton), Darnell Besaw (Little Maya), Phoenix Crepin (Little Kazi), Sissi Kal (Maya's Teacher), John Crow (Karate Teacher), Derick Kown (Cranky Pete's Waiter), Nina Zoie Lam (Audiologist), Bryan Terry Snell (MMA Fighter), Malachi Everett (Bigger Karate Kid), Taylor Rogers (Kid in Car)
Dir: Bert & Bertie; **Writers:** Katrina Matthewson & Tanner Bean; **Ed:** Roseanne Tan

1.4 PARTNERS, AM I RIGHT? *(8/12/2021)*
Though warned away from involving Kate in his activities, Clint contacts her when Laura reveals that Jack would appear to be the person running the tracksuit mafia. The Bartons have a more pressing issue, however, and that is the fact someone has stolen a very important watch. Upon tracking it down, they discover Maya has it, and when Clint, Kate and Maya engage in a fight, they are joined by a Black Widow.

Cast: Ava Russo (Lila Barton), Ben Sakamoto (Cooper Barton), Cade Woodward (Nathaniel Barton), *Clayton English (Grills),* Carlos Navarro (Enrique), *Adetinpo Thomas (Wendy),* Robert Walker-Branchaud (Orville), Adelle Drahos (Missy), Richard Dedomenico (Little Old Man), Chris Romrell (Larper #1), Theo Kypri (Track Suit Mafia in Suit)
Dir: Bert & Bertie; **Writers:** Erin Cancino & Heather Quinn; **Ed:** Tim Roche

1.5 RONIN *(15/12/2021)*
With the situation spiralling out of control, Clint finds himself forced to don the Ronin guise one more time and confront Maya, and while it ends awkwardly, Maya wonders why Kazi abandoned her father the

night he was killed. Meanwhile Yelena confronts Kate in regards to Clint, and makes it clear she intends to kill him, though when Yelena seeks out who employed her, she finds something unexpected.

Cast: *Clayton English (Grills),* Ivan Mbakop (Detective Caudle), Franco Castan (Detective Rivera), Yssa Mei Panganiban (Sonya), Annie Hamilton (Ana), Michael Silberblatt (Man with Ana), Gabrielle Lahoz Thomas (4-year-old with Ana), Keon Rahzeem Mitchell (Uber Driver)
Dir: Bert & Bertie; **Writer:** Jenna Noel Frazier; **Ed:** Rosanne Tan

1.6 SO THIS IS CHRISTMAS? *(22/12/2021)*
Maya requests some time away, but the Kingpin is aware that she is turning against them, and orders Kazi to deal with both her and Eleanor Bishop. Clint vows to stand by Kate until the end, and they prepare a plan to take care of business at Eleanor's Christmas party. When the pair arrive, the Kingpin and his Tracksuit Mafia are close behind, and both Yelena Belova and Maya Lopez are also ready to exact their revenge as well.

Cast: Ava Russo (Lila Barton), Ben Sakamoto (Cooper Barton), Cade Woodward (Nathaniel Barton), *Clayton English (Grills),* Carlos Navarro (Enrique), Ivan Mbakop (Detective Caudle), *Franco Castan (Detective Rivera), Adetinpo Thomas (Wendy),* Robert Walker-Branchaud (Orville), Adelle Drahos (Missy), Brian Troxell (Catering Captain Gary), Jonathan Bergman (Armand VII), Aaron Nedrick (Musical Iron Man), Avery Gillham (Musical Hawkeye), Harris Turner (Musical Hulk), Jason Scott Macdonald (Musical Thor), Meghan Manning (Musical Black Widow), Nico DeJesus (Musical Ant-Man), Tom Feeney (Musical Captain America), Jordan Chin (Musical Loki), Adam Pascal (Lead New Yorker #1), Ty Taylor (Lead New Yorker #2), Gino Cosculluela, Bernard Bell, Brittany Nicholas, Gabrielle Mouchakkaa, Keith Nedd, Kimo Lowery Kepano, Kristen Yancy, Marissa Milele (Musical New Yorkers), Anthony Burrell, Ehizoje Azeke, Graham Michael Dobbs, Ricardo Zayas (Musical Chitauri)
Dir: Rhys Thomas; **Writers:** Jonathan Igla & Elisa Clement; **Ed:** Tim Roche

Notes: This was originally going to be a movie (one that Renner was under contract for), but Feige felt a television series would be a better fit for it. Cox's audition was so good, it was decided to change the character of Maya to incorporate the fact Cox is an amputee, rather than find a way to hide it. This

88

was Cox's first television performance. Both Renner and Steinfeld learnt American Sign Language to make Cox feel welcome. Feige encouraged the idea of *Rogers: The Musical*, and as such, the production team approached Marc Shaiman and Scott Wittman, the writers of *Hairspray* to write a full sequence that could be filmed. Shaiman then appeared as the orchestra conductor for filming.

Should I Stay To The End? That very much depends on whether you like musicals or not. The mid credits sequence in 1.6 is the full-length version of "I Can Do This All Day" from *Rogers: The Musical*. It's fun, but not remotely relevant to anything.

It's All Connected: As usual, the timing of these series is always a little hard to accurately pinpoint. It's definitely after the blip (obviously), and we're told Tony sold Avengers Tower a few years ago. The first we know of the sale of the tower is in **SPIDER-MAN: HOMECOMING** which was 2017 (probably...). It's Christmas and we know that Kate was 10 in 2012, and she survived the snap. She's currently 22, so we can say that it takes place in December, 2024. The series reintroduces us to Clint Barton and his family – his wife Laura and their children Lila, Cooper and Nathaniel – and we see that Clint has very much retired from his previous life, and has developed a hearing impairment thanks to the sheer number of explosions he has been in. Clint's involvement in this story comes about through a number of things – the first being someone wearing the Ronin costume, while the second is the appearance of a watch that we later learn belonged to Laura, who is revealed to have been formerly Agent 19 of SHIELD, neatly confirming Tony's guess back in **AVENGERS: AGE OF ULTRON**.

On the other side of things, we meet Kate Bishop, daughter of Eleanor and the deceased Derek. Eleanor is now dating Jack Duquesne, and when Jack's uncle Armand is killed, Kate gets hold of the Ronin suit and uses it. Jack, it transpires, is a sword enthusiast who is keen to get hold of Ronin's sword (which came with the costume). At the age of 12, Kate's father was killed in the Chitauri Invasion, but she saw Hawkeye fighting with nothing more than a bow and arrow, and this inspired her to follow in his footsteps. She is keen to join Clint, who is not so keen because of the guilt associated with the death of Natasha Romanov. Nonetheless, by the end of the series, Clint has bequeathed his code name to her. Kate's mother runs Bishop Security, which was formerly run by her husband, and one of their staff is Michael Kemp – last seen in prison in **DAREDEVIL**, helping Matt Murdock to get out.

Yelena Belova is after Clint to avenge Natasha's death, having been sent by Valentina Allegra de Fontaine. Eleanor and her late husband, it transpires, were working for Wilson Fisk. The Kingpin retains his cufflinks from his previous appearances, but is no longer as wealthy as he once was, his new headquarters appearing to be in a café (or, at least, that's where he chooses to conduct business with Eleanor. It maybe that this is where he runs things when dealing with the Tracksuit Mafia). Fisk also appears to be considerably more powerful than he was previously, having possibly even developed super strength. It's unclear how this has happened, but stranger things have happened in jail, haven't they Luke Cage? Fisk has a paternal relationship with Maya Lopez, going so far as to describe her as family. She feels the same way, though this comes to an end when she learns that Fisk had Kazi kill her father. For some time, she seemed to have a romantic relationship with Kazi, though Kazi's loyalty to Fisk brings that to an end. Maya is an extremely accomplished fighter, often using her prosthetic legs as weapons. Ultimately, Maya shoots Fisk in the face.

Comic Notes: *Kate Bishop:* first appeared in *Young Avengers #1 (Apr, '05)* created by Allan Heinberg and Jim Cheung. Given that the live action version's roots are based firmly in the Chitaurai Invasion, it's no surprise that they are quite different characters (though physically they are a close match). In the comics, Katherine Elizabeth Bishop was attacked in Central Park and this was what inspired her to engage in combat training (she has only ever told her therapist and Jessica Jones the exact nature of the attack). On meeting the Young Avengers, she tracked them down and helped them against Kang, which led to her joining the team. She has a very close relationship to both Stature and Patriot, but it was Captain America who gave her the codename Hawkeye, while Jessica Jones gave her the bow and arrow Barton once used. She refused to register as a superhero during Civil War, and was later part of Barton's Young Avengers. She and Clint joined forces to clean up the streets and deal with Madame Masque, before Clint sent her away and she moved to Los Angeles, though her father cut her off from their wealth. Since then, she has supported various heroes, including Iron Man, America Chavez, Spider-Man, Ghost Rider and Gwenpool.

Jack Duquesne: looks not dissimilar to the comic version, thanks to the particularly impressive mustache. He lived in Siancong as a child, but a group of rebels killed his father, and he joined a travelling circus as a result, specialising in sword mastery. At this point it's obvious that the live action and comic versions are very different. Notably, in the comics, he actually trained Clint Barton, but when Barton found Duquesne stealing money, the latter again fled, but this time became the villain Swordsman. He tried to join the Avengers, but his criminal history and Hawkeye made that impossible. He was later accepted, but was working for the Mandarin at the time, though curiously he betrayed the Mandarin to the Avengers. He has continued to fight the Avengers, working for a variety of villains including the Mandarin again, the Red Skull and Batroc. Curiously he fell in love with Mantis and rejoined the Avengers, sacrificing his life to save them. He was briefly resurrected, and he and Mantis had a daughter, Sequoia, but since then his body has merely been a vessel for the Cotati (a race of telepathic plants). He first appeared in *The Avengers #19 (Aug, '65)* created by Stan Lee and Don Heck.

Maya Lopez: goes by the codename Echo in the comics, and while she physically looks similar to the television version (and is Native American), she is notable for the white hand print on her face as Echo. She is indeed deaf, but does not have prosthetics. She first appeared in *Daredevil Vol 2 #9 (Dec, '99)*, created by David Mack and Joe Quesada, but would actually use the Ronin identity a few years later. The backstories are quite similar for both versions – in each their father is William (or Willie) – and he was killed by the Kingpin, who then raised Maya as his own. She is sent to deal with Matt Murdock, but falls in love with him. She is able to defeat Daredevil, but Murdock reveals the truth about Kingpin and Maya shoots him in the face. This causes a great deal of anguish for her, and discovering Murdock has moved on and the Kingpin is still alive, Maya turns to Wolverine for help. His Japanese teachings allow her to become the Ronin, and Daredevil introduces her to the Avengers. She is later killed by Elektra, though resurrected by the Hand (sound familiar?), and has gone onto helping a number of superheroes. She was again killed, this time by Count Nefaria, but is resurrected again…though this time no excuse is given. Most recently she has absorbed the Phoenix Force and become the new Thunderbird.

Laura Barton: is a comic character from the *Ultimate Marvel* universe. Here she is a blonde, the long-time girlfriend of Clint, who she later married. Like the live action version, they have three kids (though they are named Callum, Lewis and Nicole), but unlike the live action version she was never a member of SHIELD. She and her children were murdered by Black Widow, who was a traitor to the US. Hawkeye would later kill Black Widow to avenge his family. She first appeared in *Ultimates 2 #2 (Mar, '05)*, created by Mark Millar and Bryan Hitch.

Kazimierz "Kazi" Kazimierczak: in the comics he is better known as the Clown, due to wearing clown makeup, and he became a killer after his friend died in a subway accident. He was employed by the Kingpin and the Tracksuit Mafia to kill Hawkeye, killing Grills in the process. When he, Ivan Banionis and the

Tracksuit Mafia attempted to take Hawkeye's building, they were defeated by Hawkeye's resistance. He first appears in *Hawkeye Vol 4 #8 (Feb, '13)*, created by Matt Fraction and David Aja.

Eleanor & Derek Bishop: the backstory of the Bishops is a little different in the comics. Derek first appears in *Young Avengers #2 (Mar, '05)*, created by Allan Heinberg and Jim Cheung. We learn he is Kate's father (and also Susan's), that he was once married to Eleanor, but is now married to Heather – whom his daughters dislikes. Aside from being rich, that's pretty much the extent of what we learn of him. Eleanor, on the other hand, is revealed not to have died, and full of furious anger, she is the mastermind behind Madam Masque. She makes her first appearance in *Hawkeye Vol 5 #7 (Jun,'17)*, created by Heinberg, Kelly Thompson and Leonardo Romero.

Grills: like a number of other characters here, first appeared in *Hawkeye Vol 4 #1 (Aug, '12)*, created by Fraction and Aja. He's a very different character from the television version – an overweight white guy who is one of Clint Barton's neighbours in the building Barton buys. He tends to call Barton "Hawkguy" and was probably nicknamed Grills because he ran the BBQ for building gatherings. Sadly, he was killed by the Clown.

Wendy Conrad: is actually a villain known as Bombshell who first appeared in *Hawkeye #3 (Aug, '83)* created by Mark Gruenwald and Eliot Brown. Unlike the television version, this woman is a white, blonde woman who was a mercenary and expert juggler, employed by a number of people including Crossfire who wanted her to kill Hawkeye. From there she bounced around before working for Crossfire again in London, and coming up against Union Jack, who convinced her to surrender in order to save her life. When she next appeared, she was a reformed character and worked for Misty Knight and her Heroes for Hire.

Detective Rivera: has a comic book counterpart who first appears in *Hawkeye Vol 5 #9 (Aug, '17)*, created by Thompson and Romero. It's one of the very rare occasions when a black female character in the comics has been swapped to a Hispanic male. Her appearances have been largely to help Kate Bishop when she has been in legal difficulty.

The Tracksuit Mafia: first appeared in *Hawkeye Vol 4 #1 (Aug, '12)*, created by Fraction and Aja, and their television appearance is very faithful to the comic version – even down to referring to each other as Bro. They are sometimes known as the Tracksuit Bros (Hawkeye himself dubbed them the Tracksuit

Draculas), and Ivan Banionis is indeed one of their members. They serve much the same purpose in the comics as they did in the show – the Kingpin's thugs for hire – though in the comics they employ Kazi Kazimierczak to kill Hawkeye, rather than Kazi being a member. They haven't been seen outside the *Hawkeye* series.

And the entire series is based loosely on Matt Fraction's *Hawkeye Vol 4* run, which is why a number of characters from that series appear. Lucky the Pizza Dog is also a character from *Hawkeye Vol 4 #1*, though the comic lucky belonged to Ivan of the Track Suit Mafia. He was originally named Arrow, and tried to protect Clint Barton from the Mafia's attack, but the Mafia repaid the dog with a vicious mauling. Barton rescued it and adopted it, though Kate Bishop took him on after Barton left the building he bought. In the comics Mockingbird is Agent 19, and of course in the comics Hawkeye married Mockingbird. The house that Clint and Kate break into belongs to actress Moria Brandon (allegedly Kate's aunt). In the comics Moira Brandon's estate was turned into the Avengers Compound.

Ratings: *IMDB:* 8.3; *Rotten Tomatoes:* 92%; *Metacritic:* 77

Review: This is enormous fun. Giving Clint Barton (and Jeremy Renner) the chance to really come to life on screen has been a long time coming, and it really shows Hawkeye in a new light; a guy who is considered the lowliest of the Avengers, but who doesn't care because it's not what he's about. He's just a spy doing a job, and the fact that he unwittingly has an impact on people is what he has to learn. Kate Bishop, the person who that impact was on, also has to learn, and Steinfeld brings her to life fantastically. It's hard to know who to praise, as aside from the two leads, Tony Dalton and Alaqua Cox try to steal every scene they're in, and then Forence Pugh and Vincent D'Onofrio turn up and the game completely changes. It's a rare treat, and should justifiably be celebrated. Top notch.

SPIDER-MAN: NO WAY HOME
(16/12/2021)

The consequences of J Jonah Jameson's revelations of Spider-Man's identity results in Peter and his friends not getting any college acceptances. Deciding he has only one option, Peter asks Dr Strange to create a spell which will cause the world to forget he is Spider-Man. However, as he makes more and more changes to the spell, Strange is unable to contain it, and the spell allows those who know Peter is Spider-Man across the multiverse to cross over. This results in Doctor Otto Octavius, Norman Osborn, Flint Marko, Dr Curt Connors and Max Dillon confronting Spider-Man – just not the Spider-Man the five know. As the multiverse threatens to collapse, Strange sets out to send the five back, but when Peter discovers they will die if they return, he decides to change the plan.

Cast: *Tom Holland (Peter Parker/Spider-Man)*, Zendaya (MJ), *Benedict Cumberbatch (Dr Strange), Jacob Batalan (Ned Leeds), Jon Favreau (Happy Hogan),* Jamie Foxx (Max Dillon/Electro), *Willem Dafoe (Norman Osborn/The Green Goblin), Alfred Molina (Otto Octavius/Dr Octopus), Benedict Wong (Wong), Tony Revolori (Flash Thompson), with Marisa Tomei (May Parker)* and *Andrew Garfield (Peter Parker/Spider-Man)* and *Tobey Maguire (Peter Parker/Spider-Man), Angourie Rice (Betty Brant), Arian Moayed (Agent Cleary),* Paula Newsome (MIT Vice Chancellor), Hannibal Buress (Coach Wilson), *Martin Starr (Mr Harrington),* JB Smoove (Mr Dell), *J K Simmons (J Jonah Jameson), Rhys Ifans (Dr Curtis Connors/The Lizard), Charlie Cox (Matt Murdock), Thomas Hayden Church (Flint Marko/Sandman)*
Dir: Jon Watts; **Writers:** Chris McKenna, Erik Sommers; **Prod:** Kevin Feige, Amy Pascal; **Music:** Michael Giacchino; **Exec.Prod:** Victoria Alonso, Avi Arad, Louis D'Esposito, Rachel O'Connor, JoAnn Perritano, Matt Tolmach; **DOP:** Mauro Fiore; **Prod.Des.:** Darren Gilford; **Ed:** Jeffrey Ford, Leigh Folsom Boyd; **Costumes:** Sanja Milkovic Hays; **Marvel Studios/Colombia Pictures/Pascal Productions**; 148; $200m; $1.916b

Notes: The build up to this film was quite tumultuous. Negotiations between Disney and Sony broke down and Sony withdrew the rights for Marvel to use Spider-Man in the MCU, thanks to the companies all wanting different things, but unwilling to compromise. The story was put around that Tom Holland drunkenly called the studio bosses and convinced them to work together, but this seems a little unlikely to have been what resolved the issue. Disney wanted a larger return on the distribution profits while Sony wanted Venom to be incorporated into the MCU. Sony was unwilling to give Disney more profit, while Marvel weren't keen on using Venom. A compromise, however, was reached and Venom's appearance in the film seemed to give the compensation Sony required, however the use of the five villains and alternate Spider-Men was probably what gave Sony what they really wanted – a degree of legitimacy. Giacchino makes use of his score for **DOCTOR STRANGE**, but also uses Danny Elfman's themes from **SPIDER-MAN** and **SPIDER-MAN 2**, along with James Horner's theme from **THE AMAZING SPIDER-MAN**, and Electro's theme from **THE AMAZING SPIDER-MAN 2**, composed by Hans

Zimmer. A large number of comic book writers are thanked, as a lot of threads from comic stories appear in the film, notably *One More Day* by J Michael Straczynski and Joe Quesada. Flash Thompson has a book called Flashpoint which is probably a thinly veiled reference to the DC comic in which multiple universes collided. Both Lexi Rabe (the young Morgan Stark in **AVENGERS: ENDGAME**) and Tom Holland's brother Harry, filmed appearances that were later cut. To celebrate the sixtieth anniversary of Spider-Man in comics, and twentieth in film, **SPIDER-MAN: NO WAY HOME – THE MORE FUN STUFF VERSION** was released in June, 2020. It includes an extra thirteen minutes of material (including the scene that features Harry Holland) and a new post-credits sequence. A new poster was also released, which actually featured Maguire and Garfield as well.

Should I Stay To The End? Possibly not. The mid-credits sequence features Tom Hardy as Eddie Brock and the voice of Venom attempting to rationalise being in the MCU, before they are sent back to their own reality. There is the suggestion that a part of the symbiote is left behind, however. The post-credits sequence is a trailer for **DOCTOR STRANGE IN THE MULTIVERSE OF MADNESS**. The post-credits sequence on **THE MORE FUN STUFF VERSION**, however, is actually Betty Brant discussing the end of her peers time at school, though notably Peter is not in (or unidentifiable) in all the pictures.

It's All Connected: Well, yes it really is, and we're not just talking about the MCU!
There are a number of references to the MCU, of course, including a poster for *Rogers: The Musical* which appears in **HAWKEYE** and one of the many news chirons that appear in the movie reads "Turmoil in New Asgard", presumably a reference to the forthcoming **THOR: LOVE AND THUNDER**. Broadly speaking, however, this movie takes place almost immediately after **SPIDER-MAN: FAR FROM HOME**, as Peter reacts to J Jonah Jameson's reveal about his identity. From here time elapses as various events occur. Peter is arrested by the Department of Damage Control, which seems to have a much broader scope than it does in the comics. Agent Cleary leads the charge on Peter's arrest, though May secures the services of Matt Murdock – the same Matt Murdock from **DAREDEVIL**, presumably confirming that those Netflix series are indeed part of the MCU, as originally claimed – a *very* good lawyer who is able to get the charges dropped. However, they can't get into MIT, and it appears that Peter is either unable or unwilling to use his connection to Tony Stark to help. Happy has stolen a number of things from Stark Industries, including a fabricator, which is able to fabricate more than just a costume.

Peter's past contacts remain, including Betty and Flash, while his teachers are divided on discovering he is Spider-Man – Harrington and Dell are keen, but Coach Wilson is not a fan. It's worth noting that Erskine and Pym have been added to the montage in the school entrance hall. In order to make his life easier, Peter contacts Dr Strange, but the spell that is started keeps getting interrupted by Peter, which breaks open the multiverse, allowing those that know Peter is Spider-Man to cross over. Wong was against the casting of the spell, but not to the point where he stopped Strange – and as is made clear, Wong is now the Soceror Surpreme, so he has the authority to do so. This seems to be an interesting situation as there are two crossovers (Max Dillon and Eddie Brock) who didn't know that Spider-Man was Peter; though perhaps they did…

Two very specific universes cross over with the MCU, though from various different points in time, which is interesting. Norman Osborn crosses over from a point before his death in **SPIDER-MAN**, but after discovering Peter Parker is Spider-Man. Otto Octavius crosses over from the same universe, but at a later point (specifically in **SPIDER-MAN 2** just before he gets mental control back again from his arms). He is aware that Osborn died in battle with Spider-Man. Similarly, Flint Marko is aware of Ocatavius' death, but as he knows Peter's identity, he presumably comes from a point after **SPIDER-MAN 3**. Curt Connors crosses over from a different universe, but it's unclear at what point (it's certainly after **THE AMAZING SPIDER-MAN**). Max Dillon also crosses over from the same universe, during the final fight in **THE AMAZING SPIDER-MAN 2**. Dillon is one of the crossovers who didn't know that Peter was Spider-Man, but in the film there is the suggestion that maybe Dillon is downloading information as well as power, and as such learnt (or ascertained) from OsCorp records that Peter was Spidey. Eddie Brock also crosses over from a third universe (clearly not the version from the **SPIDER-MAN** universe), though he categorically has no idea who Spider-Man is, let alone Peter Parker. There is speculation, however, that Venom has this knowledge based on a connection to other symbiotes across the multiverse.

More importantly, of course, two versions of Peter Parker also cross over. It would appear that time runs roughly in synch across all three universes, so the two Peters that appear are both older than than the MCU version. The initial version to crossover (the Andrew Garfield Spider-Man) has never really recovered from the death of Gwen Stacy, and is also crippled with guilt at going too far in stopping his opponents. The second version to crossover (the Tobey Maguire Spider-Man) is still happily in a relationship with Mary-Jane Watson, though admits that it's not always easy to balance his life. Mention is made of the fact that the Maguire version produces webs naturally, while the Garfield version hasn't encountered aliens. Both the Maguire and

Garfield versions have never heard of the Avengers.

The multiverse continues to open after the MCU Peter refuses to send the five villains back to their timelines (and subsequently to their deaths), and when Dr Strange is finally released from the mirror dimension he attempts to put Peter into, he weaves a new spell. Peter convinces him to wipe everyone's memory of him in order to seal the universal breaches, which returns the villains to their timelines and also the alternate Peter Parkers. Before this, though, the three Peters are able to restore Octavius' sanity, and cure Connors, Marko, Dillon and Osborn of their mutations. Unfortunately, the side effect of this is that MJ and Ned (and indeed everyone) lose their memory of Peter Parker completely, requiring Peter to rebuild his life from scratch.

Comic Notes: Most of the new characters in this film have been covered in the companion guide to *It's All Connected – Excelsior*, which details all the Marvel movies outside the MCU. This covers the **SPIDER-MAN** and **THE AMAZING SPIDER-MAN** series. It would be a great purchase to make! However, for the sake of completeness, here's a brief overview of the six villains who appear in this film.

Green Goblin: Norman Osborn first appeared in *The Amazing Spider-Man #14 (Jul, '64)*, though he wouldn't appear as Osborn for another nine issues. He was created by Stan Lee and Steve Ditko, and his backstory is also quite similar to the movie. The costume not so much so, though the alternate green and purple costume he wears towards the end of the film is more in line with the comics.

Otto Octavius: first appeared in *The Amazing Spider-Man #3 (Jul, '63)*, and was another Stan Lee and Steve Ditko creation. The backstory for the comics' version is much the same as the movie version, though there are some differences – Octavius wasn't married in the comics, though he did get engaged to Mary Alice Anders, and called it off at his mother's insistence. When his mother died, Octavius become embittered and obsessed with his work. One explosion later and he was fused to the mechanical arms he used for research, and a life of crime followed. Octavius would go onto plague Spider-Man for most of his life, though interestingly, at one point his mind was placed in Peter Parker's body and he became Spider-Man.

The Lizard/Dr Curt Connors: would appear five issues later in #6 (Nov, '63) – again created by Lee and Ditko – where the one-armed scientist (having lost an arm during war) took a formula of reptilian DNA designed by himself and Ted Sallis (the Man-Thing) and transformed into the Lizard; a giant reptile creature that was slightly insane. The Lizard has often fought Spider-Man and other heroes (notably the X-Men), but Curt Connors remains a close friend and ally of Peter Parker's.

Eddie Brock: first appeared in *Web of Spider-Man #18 (Sep, '86),* created by David Michelinie and Marc Silvestri. Spider-Man gained a new costume in *The Amazing Spider-Man #252 (May, '84),* which was written by Tom DeFalco and Roger Stern, with art by Ron Frenz. However, the costume was actually created by fan Randy Schueller, and was designed, from Schueller's idea, by Mike Zeck. In *Secret Wars #8 (Dec, '84)* it was revealed that during this time, Peter Parker's costume was damaged and he was given a new, black costume, that was actually an alien symbiote. When Peter realised that the costume was a symbiote and was alive and susceptible to sound, he used a cathedral bell to get rid of it. Eddie Brock, on the other hand, was a journalist who disgraced himself by exposing a killer who was actually nothing more than a compulsive liar. Blaming Spider-Man, Brock goes to a church, and the symbiote attaches to him, creating the villain Venom – debuting in *The Amazing Spider-Man #299 (Apr, '88),* which was written by Michelinie, with art by Todd McFarlane.

Max Dillon: or Electro as he is better known, first appeared in *The Amazing Spider-Man #9 (Feb, '64),* created by Stan Lee and Steve Ditko. He was an electrical engineer in the comics, who was hit by lightning, which caused a mutation that turned him into, effectively, a capacitor. Though he has often fought many Marvel superheroes, his arch nemesis is Spider-Man, and he is often a member of the Sinister Six. His original appearance was a green costume with yellow lightning mask (which is what the altered version of his costume is based on), but the original version is based more on the cartoon version of Electro. Foxx's casting is against type for the character, who is not African American.

William Baker: who would later adopt the name Flint Marko, and then go onto become the Sandman – was one of the earliest Spider-Man villains, turning up in *The Amazing Spider-Man #4 (Sep, '63),* and if you guessed he was created by Lee and Ditko, you can claim a no prize. His background is broadly the same as the movie version; Marko strayed into a nuclear testing site, and his body bonded with irradiated sand. He was already a villain, so he simply used his new abilities to continue this line of work.

Cleary: first name Albert, first appears in *Damage Control #1 (Jan, '89),* created by Dwayne McDuffin and Eddie Colon. He doesn't have a huge backstory, short of joining the team after it was established, and ultimately being promoted to comptroller. Appearance wise, it's mildly interesting to note that in the comics he is black, while in the movies his background appears more Asian.

And: as mentioned above, the idea of Peter giving up his relationship with MJ comes from the comic *One Day More*, in which Peter makes a deal with Mephisto to give up the past in order to keep May alive.

Ratings: *IMDB:* 6.8; *Rotten Tomatoes:* 92%; *Metacritic*: 53

Review: Whether the plan was always to make this film, or if Marvel were forced into adapting to suit Sony and Disney, it's ultimately irrelevant. **NO WAY HOME** is a daring concept for a movie (and one that admittedly has already been done on television by CW's Arrow-verse), and it pays off completely, helped in no small part by Tobey Maguire and Andrew Garfield bringing their Spider-Men back to life so well. Holland remains the heart of the film, and May's fate will bring a tear to your eye, but the writing ensures that the additional Peter Parkers are there to help Holland on his journey. All this without addressing the brilliance of the returning cast and the amazing performances from Foxx, Molina and (of course) Dafoe. **NO WAY HOME** is a tour de force for the MCU, rounding off the creation of Holland's Spider-Man, and paving the way for the future of the character.

DOCTOR STRANGE WILL RETURN

HAS THE MULTIVERSE BEEN REWRITTEN?

The consequences of **SPIDER-MAN: NO WAY HOME** are never really explained and don't, on the face of it, make sense. After all, if the various villains are returned, now no longer villains, surely this means that they are going back to their deaths, only this time as good people? If they don't die, then wouldn't that change the history of those two timelines, and as such, the history of the Maguire and Garfield Peter Parkers?

As it's never actually explained, the only answer that can be provided is one that is purely speculative, but the probable solution is this: those two timelines aren't altered, rather new ones are created as a result. The two alternate Peter Parkers return to their timelines, and in those timelines, everything that happened in the Raimi and Webb movies still take place, creating the two Peter Parkers we saw.

But the saving of the five villains creates five new timelines, spinning off from the two established ones we know. In the first of these new timelines, Osborn is suddenly cured of his Goblin serum, and as such doesn't go after Peter, and doesn't die by his own stupidity. In this timeline, maybe that Otto Octavius never succumbed to his arms, as it would be Norman, rather than Harry, supervising Octavius.

The second timeline wouldn't be too far removed from the principal timeline. In fact, it may be the actual timeline, as in the established timeline Octavius gained his sanity at around the time he was taken to the MCU. Much of what happened would still play out and the timeline would probably be quite similar (sadly still resulting in Octavius' death).

The third timeline may also not be too far removed from the principal timeline either, as Flint Marko was taken after **SPIDER-MAN 3** and therefore his restoration may have played out as it was supposed to. A similar take could be had for the fourth timeline, as we're unaware of what happened to Connors post **THE AMAZING SPIDER-MAN**.

The fifth timeline is the one that would be significantly different, as Dillon would be returned at a point where he'd be unable to absorb electricity and therefore his entire menace would be gone. Presumably Dillon would flee, potentially with Gwen, leaving the Harry Osborn Green Goblin to fight Spider-Man. Assuming Spidey beats the Goblin, this might end with Gwen actually surviving the incident.

Finally, this leaves the MCU, and this is the one where the most confusion arises. With Peter being wiped from the memory of everyone, it's unclear how great an impact that would have. Everyone may have forgotten him, but it would appear the magic may have changed physical items like photographs in order to ensure that he has been forgotten (or perhaps people simply look at photos and wonder who the other guy is). Some records may have gone, but it's possible others remain (who exactly arranged for May's funeral, for instance?). Perhaps the saddest thing is the thought that Peter's impact wasn't great enough such that his removal from history makes little difference to the lives of those around him.

MOON KNIGHT
[Season 1]*(Disney+)*

Regular Cast: *Oscar Isaac (Marc Spector/Steven Grant/Jake Locklev/Moon Knight/Mr Knight),* May Calamawy (Layla El-Faouly), Khalid Abdalla (Selim) [1.3-1.4,1.6], Ann Akinjirin (Bobhi)[1.2-1.5], *Karim El Hakim (Khonshu performer) [1.1.-1.3 1.5 1.0],* David Ganly (Billy)[1.2-1.5], Fernanda Andrade (Wendy Spector) [1.5], Antonia Salib (Taweret)[1.4-1.6], *Rey Lucas (Elias Spector)[1.5],* Sofia Danu

(On-Set Ammit)[1.6], Saba Mubarak as the voice of Ammit [1.6], *F Murray Abraham as the voice of Khonshu [1.1.-1.3,1.5-1.6] special guest star Gaspard Ulliel (Anton Mogart)[1.3] and Ethan Hawke (Arthur Harrow)*
Prod: Peter Cameron; **Music:** Hesham Nazih; **Exec.Prod:** Kevin Feige, Louis D'Esposito, Victoria Alonso, Brad Winderbaum, Grant Curtis, Oscar Isaac, Mohamed Diab, Jeremy Slater; **Created by** Jeremy Slater; **DOP:** Gregory Middleton [1.1,1.3,1.5-1.6], Andrew Droz Palermo [1.2,1.4]; **Prod.Des.:** Stefania Cella; Costumes: Meghan Kasperlik; **Marvel Studios**; 45 - 60

Episodes:

1.1 THE GOLDFISH PROBLEM *(30/3/2022)*

Steven Grant goes about his daily life, sleeping at night tied to his bed because of his sleepwalking, and totally failing to remember inviting someone on a date. When he wakes up in a completely unknown place where the locals worship a cult leader, he starts to hear a strange voice in his head and continues to lose time. Waking up again in London, he has lost two days, but it becomes clear what he experienced wasn't a dream, and there is something within him that offers to help.

Cast: Lucy Thackeray (Donna), Saffron Hocking (Dylan), *Shaun Scott (Crawley),* Anouk Christiansen (Little Girl in Museum), Nina Mahiri (Female Photo Patron), István Mezei (Male Photo Patron), Alexander Cobb (JB), Gábor Szemán (Alpine Guard), András Korcsmáros (Alpine Man), Gabriella Csizmadia (Alpine Woman), James Bomalick (Cupcake Van Driver), Peyvand Sadeghian (Pet Shop Owner), Eric Colvin (Steakhouse Waiter), Anne Kavanagh (Elevator Lady), Marcell Szelle (Museum Disciple), Michael Benjamin Hernandez (Marc Spector/Steven Grant Double)
Dir: Mohamed Diab; **Writer:** Jeremy Slater; **Ed:** Cedric Nairn-Smith

1.2 SUMMON THE SUIT *(6/4/2022)*

Terrified by what is happening to him – and worse that he doesn't have any proof to back up his version of events – Steven faces the consequences of the jackal attack, which include him getting fired, and decides to track down his alter ego's lock up in the hope it gives him some answers. He finds a scarab and then meets Layla, who claims to be his wife, but the pair are approached by policeman working for Harrow, who informs him that the scarab will point him towards Ammit, something which the ghostly Khonshuu who haunts him definitely does not want.

Cast: *Shaun Scott (Crawley),* Alexander Cobb (JB), Darwin Shaw (Dornfeld), Terique Jarrett (Storage Employee), Miriam Nyarko (Jamila), Fiz Marcus (Female On-looker #1), Lorna Anders (Female On-looker #2), Michael Benjamin Hernandez (Marc Spector/Steven Grant Double)
Dir: Aaron Moorhead & Justin Benson; **Writer:** Michael Kastelein; **Ed:** Joan Sobel

1.3 THE FRIENDLY TYPE *(13/4/2022)*

In Egypt, Marc Spector tries to locate the scarab, but is foiled not only by Steven, who takes control of the body briefly, but also apparently by a time gap that neither he nor Steven can account for. Layla tracks him down in Cairo, but Khonshuu has a plan to summon the other gods to get their help – though they refuse and believe Harrow is doing no harm. Marc and Layla meet with an old friend of hers, only to be betrayed to Harrow who believes he has found Ammit.

Cast: Barbara Rosenblat (Forger), Diana Bermudez (Yatzil), Declan Hannigan (Horus's Avatar), Hayley Konadu (Tefnut's Avatar), Nagisa Morimoto (Isis's Avatar), Loic Mabanza (Bek), Jalil Naciri (Alpha), Mohamed El Achi (Beta), Ahmed Dash (Young Punk), Larz Nan (Taxi Driver), Amr Elkady (Juice Vendor), Mahmoud-Mohamed Sihem Soltan (Felucca Woman), Kristóf Nagy (Security Guard), Michael Benjamin Hernandez (Marc Spector/Steven Grant Double)
Dir: Mohamed Diab; **Writers:** Beau DeMayo and Peter Cameron & Sabir Pirzada; **Ed:** Ahmed Hafez

1.4 THE TOMB *(20/4/2022)*

Layla manages to protect the powerless Marc/Steven, and when he regains consciousness, Steven decides to remain in control, much to Marc's anger. Steven and Layla enter the tomb in search of Ammit, but are separated when one of the priest's that were buried alongside the Pharoah attacks them. Steven gets to the Pharoah's tomb and finds what they are looking for, but Harrow is right behind, and shoots him.

Cast: Lucy Thackeray (Donna), *Shaun Scott (Crawley),* Loic Mabanza (Bek), Thibault Chiron (Heka Priest #1), József Fodor (Heka Priest #2), Joseph Millson (Dr Grant), Bill Bekele (Rosser), Alex Martin (Disciple), Zizi Dagher (Psychiatric Ward Patient), Michael Benjamin Hernandez (Marc Spector/Steven Grant Double)
Dir: Justin Benson & Aaron Moorhead; **Writers:** Alex Meenehan and Peter Cameron & Sabir Pirzada; **Ed:** Ahmed Hafez

1.5 ASYLUM *(27/4/2022)*

Confronted unexpectedly by Taweret, Marc and Steven are told that they are essentially dead, but are unable to enter the Field of Reeds unless they are able to balance the scales of their souls. As Marc flips between two different realities, one in which Harrow is his psychologist, the other where he stands with Steven examining their past and how they got there, time runs out for him to reconcile his past life with his present.

Cast: *Claudio Fabian Contreras (Randall Spector),* Carlos Sanchez (Young Marc), David Jake Rodriguez (Teenage Marc), Usama Soliman (Abdallah El-Faouly), Michael Benjamin Hernandez (Marc Spector/ Steven Grant Double)
Dir: Mohamed Diab; **Writers:** Rebecca Kirsch and Matthew Orton; **Ed:** Joan Sobel

1.6 GODS AND MONSTERS *(4/5/2022)*

Layla frees Khonshuu but flatly refuses to become his avatar, happy to take on Harrow herself. Meanwhile in the land of the dead, Marc goes back for Steven and on finding him, Osiris grants them their life again. Khonshuu fights Ammit, but when he can sense Marc's return, he restores the Moon Knight to him and together they set out to stop Harrow and Ammit.

Cast: Diana Bermudez (Yatzil), Declan Hannigan (Horus's Avatar), Hayley Konadu (Tefnut's Avatar), Nagisa Morimoto (Isis's Avatar), Hazem Elessaway (Patrol Guard #1), Kimo Rady (Patrol Guard #2), Ahmed Said (Patrol Guard #3), Nicole Iskander (Young Egyptian Woman), Tassir Khalfallah (Female Nurse), Michael Benjamin Hernandez (Marc Spector/Steven Grant Double)
Dir: Mohamed Diab; **Writers:** Jeremy Slater and Peter Cameron & Sabir Pirzada, Danielle Iman; **Ed:** Cedric Nairn-Smith

Notes: The third episode, in which Gaspard Ulliel is the special guest star, is also dedicated to his memory – Ulliel sadly passing away after filming. There are various songs used over some of the titles. These include: "El Melouk" performed by Ahmed Saab featuring 3enba and Double Zuksh for episode 2; "Love and Revenge – Saat Saat" performed by Sabah for episode 5; "A Man Without Love" performed by Englebert Humperdinck for episode 6 (this song also features prominently in the first episode). For several scenes where Marc Spector interacts with Steven Grant, Oscar Isaac's brother Michael Benjamin

Hernandez stands in opposite Isaac. A QR code appears in each episode which link to various Marvel comics featuring Moon Knight. The hieroglyphics on Moon Knight's trousers read "Rise and live again as my fist of vengeance, my moon knight."

Should I Stay To The End? Most definitely. The mid-credits sequence in the final episode confirms that there is a third personality and essentially explains a number of moments in the series where it appears neither Marc nor Steven is aware of what is going on. It also gives us Harrow's fate.

It's All Connected: The timing of this series is another which isn't explicit. It certainly takes place after the return of everyone snapped away by Thanos – there aren't a lot of connections to the wider MCU, but one is indications of programs set up to help people affected by the blip – and it's probably set after *HAWKEYE*, so maybe 2025.

That is really the only connection to the wider MCU that we get. We are introduced to Marc Spector, initially through his alternate personality Steven Grant, and we discover that Spector is actually the avatar of the Egyptian god Khonshu, who can speak to both Spector and Grant. Khonshu not only saved Spector's life when he was a mercenary, he gave him powers and an Egyptian style suit, to become the Moon Knight. Spector is the son of Elias and Wendy, the latter of whom was abusive to him when he lost his brother. It was this abuse that caused Spector to create Steven Grant to better cope with his situation. Grant discovers he has access to Moon Knight as well, but his costume is a white suit with a hood, and is better identified as Mr Knight. Grant works at the London National History Museum, though is later fired, and also believes he sleepwalks, though in fact he later discovers that his alternate personalities sometime take over. A third personality, Jake Lockley – a vicious killer – also takes control at some points, though neither Spector nor Grant is aware of Lockley. Spector, as a mercenary under the control of Raoul Bushman, was involved in the murder of Abdallah El-Faouly, and he later met, fell in love with and married Layla El-Faouly. The El-Faouly's were both archaeologists, seeking out the truth behind the Egyptian gods. During the series, Layla is contacted by Khonshuu who hopes to have her replace Spector as his avatar, but it is to the goddess Taweret that she agrees, and gets her own superpowers and suit, as the Scarlet Scarab.

Spector is dogged by Arthur Harrow, the servant of the goddess Ammit, who seeks to realise Ammit's intention of wiping the world clean of evil by rooting it out before it happens. Harrow is a true believer, and genuinely shocked when Ammit chooses him as her avatar, as Harrow is aware of his own sins. Ultimately Harrow is beaten and imprisoned, but later shot dead by

Jack Lockley at Khonshuu's command. Harrow did lead a cult, including cops Bobbi and Billie, but it is unclear what happened to the cult after Ammit was beaten by Khonshuu.

Various other gods' avatars appear, including Osiris', Isis', Hathor's, Horus' and Tefnut's. It's never quite explained whether the Egyptian gods are real gods, or whether they are beings so powerful they are simply worshipped as gods. In this particular instance, they appear to be treated more as gods than simply advanced aliens.

By the end of the series, Spector and Grant are fully aware of each other and are comfortable with sharing their body, but have both stood down as being Khonshuu's avatar – though it appears Jake Lockley has not. Presumably Spector remains married to Layla.

Comic Notes: *Marc Spector:* is fairly faithful to the comics in appearance, though there are a few differences elsewhere. He first appeared in *Werewolf by Night #32 (Aug, '75)* created by Doug Moench and Don Perlin, and his backstory is roughly the same as the series – he was a mercenary who fought his boss, Bushman, getting virtually killed in the process, before Khonshu revives him to become the Fist of Khonshu, the Moon Knight. This took place in Egypt, and when he returns to the US, he uses his impressive fortune to set up three separate identities in order to infiltrate various aspects of society – billionaire Steven Grant, taxi driver Jake Lockley and the mysterious Mr Knight. This is later retconned so that the identities aren't simply covers, but part of Marc Spector's Disassociative Identity Disorder. In the comics it's hinted that perhaps Spector's DID is not part of a childhood trauma, but potentially the consequences of his psychic link to Khonshu. Spector has a number of other personalities in the comics, including many who believe themselves to be other heroes, and "Inner Child" who is a little red-haired girl. Various writers have written the character in different ways, with some eschewing the idea that Spector has any enhanced abilities, while others have killed the character and resurrected him, hinting that Spector may very well be immortal while under Khonshu's protection. Interestingly, Marc has had a long term on-off relationship with a woman named Marlene, and together the two have had a child named Diatrice Alraune. Most recently, Moon Knight was arrested by the Thunderbolts when Wilson Fisk outlawed superheroes.

Arthur Harrow: looks nothing like the MCU version, being a bearded redhead in the comics. Similarly, his backstory is radically different to the cult leader we meet on screen. In the comics, Harrow was a scientist who continued on the horrific experiments started by the Nazis in World War 2, but keeping it a secret, he was nominated for a Nobel prize, until he was outed. He was recruited by OMNIUM, and though Moon Knight shut down his US operations, OMNIUM relocated him. He first appeared in *Moon Knight Vol 2 #2 (Apr, '85)*, created by Alan Zelenetz and Chris Warner.

Randall Spector was indeed the younger brother of Marc, though he didn't die at a young age. He grew up resenting Marc's skills in various pursuits, but like Marc he joined the US military and then became a mercenary. After he killed Marc's girlfriend during a mission for the CIA a vengeful Marc almost killed Randall, but failed. As a result of this he became the serial killer known as the Hatchet Man. Randall would end up in Bushman's group, unknown to Marc, and discovered a parchment that suggested there were two Khonshus, and one would slay the other. He assumed that this meant he should kill his brother to gain the power of Moon Knight. With the help of a friend in the CIA they convinced Marc Randall really was dead. Randall gathered a number of people together to fight Moon Knight, but with the Punisher on his side, Moon Knight defeated them. Despite being technologically augmented to become the Shadow Knight, Randall was ultimately killed by the Punisher. When the resurrected Randall was convinced by the Hand he was the avatar of Khonshu, he again became the Shadow Knight, and killed many people before threatening to commit suicide using a bomb. Having made a deal with Khonshu regarding his powers, Moon Knight completed his side of the deal – killing his brother for good. Randall first appeared in *Hulk! #17 (Aug, '79)* and was created by Doug Moench and Mike Zeck.

Elias Spector: first appeared in *Moon Knight #37 (Jan,'84)* created by Alan Zelenetz and Bo Hampton. His backstory is skimmed over in the series, but in the comics he is a Rabbi. However, due to retconning there has been two backstories for Elias and Marc. In the original, Marc's desire for violence saw him become a boxer, which Elias begged him to stop. Marc joined the US Marines, followed by Randall, which caused Elias to have a heart attack. Having survived this, he took on Reuben Davis as a student, before passing away from cancer. More than a little crazy, Davis would resurrect Elias to use as a soldier against Moon Knight, though Moon Knight stopped him. The retconning saw Elias and his mother helped out of Czechoslovakia by Yitz Perlman, but it later transpired Perlman killed Jews in an effort to extend his life (this was the incident that appeared to cause Marc's DID). Perlman fled when Elias discovered the truth, but he had to put Marc into a psychiatric hospital to help his son. Elias was always disappointed with both of his sons' obsession with war, and sadly his death prevented him from healing wounds with his son

Anton Mogart: seems to bear little relation to his comicbook counterpart, though they do share an interest in owning great works of art, or unique treasures. While the television version enjoys his toys in Egypt, the comic version lived in New Jersey, and stole simply to own them. However, he did it under the guise of the Midnight Man and wore what was roughly a black version of Moon Knight's costume. He was stopped by Moon Knight, but the result saw him fall into a river and then the sewers where acidic waste deformed him and drove him insane. He and Bushman teamed up to fight Moon Knight, but failed. Later he was killed in another fight with Spector, only for his son to assume the mantle of the Midnight Man. He first appeared in *Moon Knight #3 (Jan, '81)* created by Moench and Bill Sienkiewicz.

Khonshu is of course a genuine Egyptian lunar god that has been adapted by Marvel, so it's the Marvel version that will be noted here. He first appears in *Moon Knight #1 (Nov, '80)*, created by Doug Moench and Bill Sienkiewicz, though he is mentioned much earlier when we learn more about Moon Knight's abilities. He is one of the Heliopolitan pantheon, which included Bast who would later become part of the Wakandan pantheon. There is some debate as to whether the Ennead (the Heliopolitan gods) are proper gods as such, as it seems clear they can be hurt, but they do possess enormous power. Khonshu starts out as apparently benevolent, but over time becomes increasingly antagonistic, resulting in Moon Knight going head-to-head with the god at one point. Khonshu appeared to choose Marc Spector as his avatar when the boy was very young, and resurrected him when he was killed by Bushman to serve him. Unlike the television series, Khonshu is often at odds with Anubis, with whom he has fought.

Bertrand Crawley: often known as Creepy Crawley, he first appeared in *Marvel Spotlight #28 (Mar, '76)* created by Moench and Don Perlin. He's certainly not an English living statue, rather he's a homeless informant for Moon Knight. Surprisingly, he doesn't look too dissimilar to his television counterpart (well, when the gold makeup is off…)

And: Layla's character, and her father's, while not specifically comic characters, are based off two characters each – Marlene Alraune and Mehemet Faoul for Layla, Abdoul Faoul and Peter Alraune for Abdallah. It's not stated on screen, but Layla becomes the Scarlet Scarab on assuming the avatarship of Tawaret. Two people have been the Scarlet Scarab in the comics; Abdul Faoul was the first Scarlet Scarab, appearing in *Invaders #23 (Sep, '77)*, and created by Roy Thomas, Frank Robbins and Frank Springer. He led the Sons of the Scarab in the forties and after finding the Ruby Scarab, gained the powers of the Scarlet Scarab. He initially fought against the Invaders, but joined them when he realised the Nazis were not going to help the Egyptian people. He remained Egypt's defender until he died, whereupon he gave the secret of the Ruby Scarab to his son. Mehemet had to actually find the thing, but on doing so adopted the mantle of the Ruby Scarab and set out to retrieve the Eye of Horus. This brought him into conflict with Thor, though the two reached a compromise. This version first appeared in *Thor #326 (Dec, '82)* and was created by Doug Moench and Alan Kupperberg. Additionally, as mentioned above, Marc was married to Marlene Alraune, whose archaeologist father Peter was murdered by Bushman, in the same way Abdallah was. She later discovers that Spector is Moon Knight, and also that Spector has DID, and encourages him to give up his Moon Knight identity and live a more peaceful life. Her relationship with Spector (and indeed Grant) was complicated, and when she met him as Jake Lockley, the two had a daughter together – Diatrice Alraune. Marlene first appeared in *Marvel Spotlight #28 (Mar, '76)*, created by Moench and Don Perlin. So while Layla El-Faouly is neither of those characters (nor Abdallah El-Faouly), the broad basis for the the two is pretty clear. One of the missed calls on the phone that Steven finds in episode one is from Duchamp. This is a reference to Jean-Paul "Frenchie" Duchamp, Spector's long time comic associate.

Ratings: *IMDB:* 7.4; *Rotten Tomatoes:* 86%; *Metacritic:* 69

Review: Marvel's leap into Moon Knight is very unexpected for both fans and general viewers, as the series takes the mythology, turns it upside down and produces something that is unusual for a number of episodes, before taking a right turn which makes you question the entire series. **MOON KNIGHT** keeps the viewer on their toes, but never ultimately gives in by allowing easy answers. By the end it's hard to tell if everything happened, or if some of it was genuinely all in Marc's clearly clouded head (did a giant Khonshu really fight a giant Amit near Cairo?). It's daring and Isaac's performance is brilliant. The only thing that is disappointing is the thought we might not get more of it.

DOCTOR STRANGE IN THE MULTIVERSE OF MADNESS
(6/5/2022)

While attending the wedding of Christine Palmer, a demonic creature appears in the streets of New York and Strango and Wong attempt to contain it, whilst rescuing a young woman. She later reveals herself to be America Chavez and the demon was sent by its master to track her down and take her abilities to jump through the multiverse. When Strange goes to Wanda for help, he realises that she is the person sending the demons; she needs America to get to a universe where her children are alive, and she is willing to stop at nothing to get what she wants.

Cast: *Benedict Cumberbatch (Dr Stephen Strange), Elizabeth Olsen (Wanda Maximoff/The Scarlet Witch), Chiwetel Ejiofor (Baron Mordo), Benedict Wong (Wong), Xochitl Gomez (America Chavez), Jett Klyne (Tommy Maximoff), Julian Hilliard (Bill Maximoff) with Michael Stühlbarg (Dr Nic West) and Rachel McAdams (Dr Christine Palmer), Hayley Atwell (Captain Carter), Anson Mount (Black Bolt), Lashana Lynch (Captain Marvel), John Krasinski (Reed Richards), Patrick Stewart (Professor Charles Xavier), Charlize Theron (Clea)* **Dir:** Sam Raimi; **Writers:** Michael Waldron; **Prod:** Kevin Feige; **Music:** Danny Elfman; **Exec.Prod:** Victoria Alonso, Louis D'Esposito, Jamie Christopher, Scott Derrickson; **DOP:** John Mathieson; **Prod.Des.:** Charles Wood; **Ed:** Bob Murawski, Tia Nolan; **Costumes:** Graham Churchyard; **Marvel Studios**

Notes: This film is credited as "A Kevin Feige Production", mimicking what the television series done since **WANDAVISION**. COVID created a number of problems with the movie industry, but for the MCU it made quite a few changes. The film was originally slated for release in May, 2021, with Scott Derrickson eagerly returning to write and direct, but as Kevin Feige talked about the introduction of America Chavez and the movie splitting the MCU apart, Derrickson described the film as a proper horror film, before Derrickson abruptly announced he was stepping down as director because of creative differences, though he would remain an executive producer. When Sam Raimi came on board to direct, it seemed McAdams wouldn't be returning. COVID meant that production on the film was delayed (which was a benefit as neither Raimi nor screenwriter Michael Waldron were ready for this), and further complications came up as Sony insisted on **SPIDER-MAN: NO WAY HOME** keeping its November 2021 release date, forcing other films to be pushed back after it. Elizabeth Olsen agreed to the film on the condition it didn't simply repeat **WANDAVISION**, and Benedict Cumberbatch's intended appearance in that series was removed, requiring some rewrites to the film. It was intended that the consequences of this film would result in the multiversal crossover of **NO WAY HOME**, but with the change in release dates, it was **DOCTOR STANGE** that would would feel the consequences of the third **SPIDER-MAN** film. COVID again caused filming problems as various cast members were required to isolate after coming into contact with positive cases, including Cumberbatch. Late reshoots were undertaken in order to play up the idea of the Illuminati, which was originally to have another member – Daniel Craig as Balder the Brave. Craig declined, reluctant to expose himself to COVID with a young child. It was made clear that the Illuminati that appear in the film are not the MCU Illuminati, rather a **WHAT IF…?** style version. The monstrous Gargantos is actually based on the character of Shuma-Gorath in the comics, but the name is owned by Robert E Howard's estate, so can't be used. The film was not released in China, and also banned in Saudi Arabia because of the LGBTQ content. Bruce Campbell makes a cameo appearance as the pizza ball vendor (Campbell has cameoed in most of Raimi's films, including his three **SPIDER-MAN** films). Raimi's 1973 Oldsmobile Delta 88 also makes an appearance. When Charles Xavier appears, he is in a yellow wheelchair and green suit, which is his appearance in **THE X-MEN** animated series from the 1990s. Suitably, a riff of the theme song is played as he enters as well. The statue that kills the alternate Captain Marvel is Xena, the Warrior Princess. The musical battle sees Dr Strange use Beethoven's "Symphony No 5 in C minor" while Sinister Strange uses Bach's "Toccata and Fugue in D minor". Interestingly, this is one of the very few movies where two captains from **STAR TREK** appear in the same scene together – Anson Mount and Sir Patrick Stewart. The Ultronbots are voiced by Ross Marquand, who voiced Ultron in **WHAT IF…?**. The prime Baron Mordo was to appear and be killed by Wanda in the movie, but this was dropped in order to preserve the surprise of Wanda being the villain (though as it was given away in the trailers…). Michael Stuhlbarg was to appear in more of the movie, including getting killed in the 838 universe, but was unable to due to scheduling conflicts.

Should I Stay To The End? The first one, yes, as it features Charlize Theron as Clea, asking Strange to help her in a new battle, which he is happy to do. The last one is more of a joke, and is somewhat typically Raimi in fashion, showing Bruce Campbell saying "It's ended!"

It's All Connected: Dr Strange, Wong, Mordo, Christine Palmer and Nic West are all back from the previous film (or films in some cases) with Christine getting married to someone who is a big fan of Strange's, while Wong seems mostly based in Kamar-Taj and Strange is the guardian of the Bleeker St mansion. Those around him are concerned about his general happiness which he dismisses for most of the film. Strange still wears the Eye of Agamotto, even though the time stone is no longer in it. We get a visit to Kamar-Taj where there are many magicians still there, including a large green yak like creature named Rintrah. We are never really given any explanation about him, so for now we shall just have to assume this is normal. Wanda Maximoff also appears, as do her two sons, though they aren't the real thing (not that there was a real thing…)

New to all of this, though, is America Chavez, a young girl from another universe who has the ability to cross the multiverse (an ability which inadvertently flung her two mothers into another universe). She doesn't have a huge amount of control over her power, and as such there are people who wish to take the power from her to ensure damage can't be done by the Scarlet Witch.

America's powers are sought after by Wanda, who wants to absorb them in order to be able to find her twin sons and then be able to preven them ever dying. Having read the Darkhold and heard her sons' voices, she is convinced that they exist – and she is right. America reveals that dreams are in actuality interpretations of parallel universes. However, the Darkhold corrupts those that use it, and Wanda is no exception. This isn't the first time we've seen the Darkhold in the MCU – it has turned up in both *AGENTS OF SHIELD* and *RUNAWAYS*, though in both cases it looked different. Wong notes that the actual book is just a copy of the writings on the wall at Wungadore. Wungadore is effectively the Darkhold, and the books are just transcriptions. Presumably we have therefore seen three of these transcriptions.

America's powers cause her to travel to several different universes, including one where Stephen Strange is a long-haired defender, who wants to take her powers to stop Wanda. Strange notes that they are aware of the Multiverse after the events of **NO WAY HOME**, leading to some confusion about the nature of Spider-Man. There are several universes that are briefly seen, including one where everyone is made of paint, one where everything is animated, one where dinosaurs still walk the Earth, one dominated by the Living Tribunal, one with what appear to be giant bees, one adversting Grindhouse Releasing on the taxis, one that seems ultra-futuristic with hovercars, one where everything is made of bone, another that has rather beautiful background music, one in which everyone is diced and a black and white one. Strange and America end up in the 838 universe, where Christine works for the Baxter Foundation, the Illuminati destroyed Thanos and consequently Strange himself, and cars go on a red signal. And this is where it gets really interesting…

The Illuminati are made up of several characters who are alternate versions of other characters. The first is Captain Peggy Carter, similar to the *WHAT IF…?* version. The second is Maria Rambeau, an alternate Captain Marvel who presumably went though what Carol went through. The third is Black Bolt, an alternate version of the one seen in *THE INHUMANS*. The fourth is Reed Richards, the head of the Fantastic Four and the Baxter Foundation, while the fifth is Charles Xavier, who looks like the Xavier seen in the Fox movies, but is dressed like the Xavier from the 1992 cartoon series. Of all the Illuminati, he is the most sympathetic to Strange's cause, though the entire Illuminati are killed by Scarlet Witch when she arrives. They also use versions of Ultron as their guards (or perhaps the Iron Legion would be a better explanation). These sound like the Ultron seen in **WHAT IF...?**

Strange is able to stop Wanda when she returns to Wungadore to steal America's powers (albeit using a dead alternate version of himself), but he does this after a battle with a more sinister version of himself who has been corrupted by the Darkhold, and can manifest a third eye in his forehead. At the end of the movie, Strange collapses and the third eye opens, and later when Clea appears, the Strange that goes with her has the third eye. It's not clear, however, what is going on here. On the face of it, it seems that prime Stephen Strange has been corrupted by the Darkhold, but there might be other alternatives. In the comics Strange has occasionally had the third eye but it doesn't mean corruption, so this might be an increase to Strange's magical abilities. Equally, this may not be prime Stephen Strange – it may be the Sinister version who escaped from his dimension. This may also be the version that goes with Clea at the end. Presumably all this will be explained in a third **DOCTOR STRANGE** film.

Comic Notes: *America Chavez:* is pretty close to the comic version, both in appearance, powers and backstory. She did indeed get raised in a Utopian reality by her two mothers, though in the comics her mothers sacrificed themselves to save that world. America decided to become a superhero to prove herself. She travelled to many realities, before finding the 616 universe where she joined the Teen Brigade. After various adventures she left them and got into a feud with an alternate kid Loki, before falling in love with an alternate Kate Bishop. The second *Secret Wars* storyline saw her arrested by Doom and and a member of A-Force, and she subsequently joined the Ultimates. More recently, however, America's sister Catalina has shown up to reveal that in fact America is not from a parallel universe, but from an island on Earth that her mothers took them to in order to try to cure Edges Syndrome. Their parents sacrificed themselves to save the girls, because their benefactor had disturbing plans for them, and America created the parallel universe backstory to cope with this. She first appeared in *Vengeance #1 (Sep, '11)* and was created by Joe Casey and Nick Dragotta.

Reed Richards: first appeared in *The Fantastic Four #1 (Nov, '61)*, and was created by Stan Lee and Jack Kirby. His powers are essentially what you see in the movie – the ability to elongate and reshape his body as if it were pliable plastic. As a member of Marvel's first family, he's been involved in a multitude of major Marvel comic arcs, but on a personal level he married Sue Storm (also a member of the Four), has two children (Franklin and Valeria), and is involved in a love triangle with Namor, the Sub-Mariner, and also, rather bizarrely, Dr Doom (indeed, Valeria's parentage is curiously questionable thanks to Valeria also being the child of Sue and Doom in the future). *Civil War* split the Fantastic Four in half, and then split Reed and Sue as they took different sides. Because of the 2015 failed movie, the Four has been kept to the background of the comics for a while, but hopefully that might all change.

Charles Xavier: made his first appearance in *The X-Men #1 (Sep, '63)*, created by Lee and Kirby as well. He born to a wealthy family and at a young age discovered his telepathic abilities and also went bald. He studied at Oxford – becoming a geneticist and psychologist – and met a woman named Moira Kinross, with whom he fell in love. She would call the engagement off during the Korean War, but he would go onto meet a number of people who would influence his life, and fight an alien named Lucifer, who crippled him. Later he formed the School for Gifted Youngsters – again coming into contact with people he had met earlier on – and from there would form the X-Men. From there, like Reed Richards, he's been involved in a variety of different plots, all of which have had a lesser or greater impact on the MCU, and like these characters has died and been brought back on several occasions. With the movies residing at FOX, Marvel comics have also sidelined the X-Men for quite some time, though a recent revival seemed initially to be without Xavier, until the mysterious masked man was revealed…

And: In the comics Wungadore is actually where Wanda was born.

Ratings: *IMDB:* 6.8; *Rotten Tomatoes:* 92%; *Metacritic*: 53

Review: There's a vague feeling that **MULTIVERSE OF MADNESS** doesn't quite live up to its name, in that we don't actually spend a huge amount of time across the multiverse, rather we concentrate on just a few. Equally while we get a few different Stranges and two Christine Palmers, that's about the extent of the alternate versions of characters we see. This is a good film, and its very entertaining, with everyone on top form, but you can't help escape the feeling that it's a beast that's had its claws blunted. Perhaps if the subtitle had been different, it wouldn't feel like we aren't getting what was promised, but as it is, as good as this film is, there's always a nagging feeling of what if…?

DOCTOR STRANGE WILL RETURN

HOW MUCH DOES THE GENERAL PUBLIC KNOW?

Nicodemus West talks to Stephen Strange about how much he lost during the Snap, and seems to blame Strange directly for what happened. Strange, of course, says he made the best decision that he could at the time, but West isn't particularly reassured. It does raise the question, though, was West blaming Strange as an Avenger, or because he specifically chose to hand over the time stone to Thanos? And if the latter…how did he know that?

There have been a few occasions in Phase 4 where people have shown a surprising amount of knowledge of what happened in the fight with Thanos, arguably more than they actively should. The events on Titan shouldn't really be known to the whole world, and broadly the fight in Wakanda should be relatively unknown as well, as neither of these events would have been widely reported. (The fight in Manhattan, on the other hand, was probably covered by the press). So from the outset, how much did the public actually know?

Knowledge of Captain America would be interesting. We know there were Captain America comics, and we also know that there were attempts to recreate Captain America (with varying degrees of success) after Steve Rogers disappeared. But the return of Captain America was celebrated, so clearly there was no actual public Captain America after Rogers. AvengerCon in *MS MARVEL* celebrates the birthplace of Captain America (Camp Lehigh) and there are cosplayers wearing the dancing girl outfits, and, of course, the Smithsonian has a display to him. The comics might therefore have continued and so the legend of Captain America is common knowledge.

Black Widow leaking SHIELD documents in **THE WINTER SOLDIER** would have brought much more of the adventures to the public knowledge, but it's probable that most people haven't read these, and the government and its agencies may have worked to discredit the leaks, meaning that while the details of the movies are out there, its possible many people don't believe them, or simply haven't read about them.

However, events that weren't part of SHIELD's mandate, such as Isiah Bradley, weren't among those documents, so any work that was done outside of SHIELD would still remain secret.

Clearly the Sokovian Accords prove that the public are aware of some of the more major incidents the Avengers have been involved in, especially the Lagos incident, and obviously Sokovia. What's also possible is that these incidents weren't reported in such a way as to make the Avengers look good. It's likely that Zemo has far more sympathy from the public than might be seen from the perspective of the Avengers. Coach Wilson suggests that Cap is a war criminal in **HOMECOMING** and given his distaste of Spider-

Man, he's probably one of many who have a dim view of the superhero community.

Also at AvengerCon in *MS MARVEL* is the blink-and-you'll-miss-it moment where someone is selling a novel called *I Was There*. There's a lot of information regarding this, but none of it was stated on screen; instead the series crew have given details, which accordingly might be overwritten. But at present, information suggests the book was written by a SHIELD agent who interviews Hawkeye and also claims first hand experience of Tony using the Infinity Stones – though apparently he was several thousand feet away. This might be one of the ways that people know what happened in the battle with Thanos, even though some of the details may be inaccurate.

Another book for sale at AvengerCon was *Carol – A Definitive Account of the Cosmic Avenger*. Interestingly, this book is more about trying to reveal who Captain Marvel actually is, and as such might have been written from the SHIELD data dump. It also presumably does work out who Captain Marvel is, based on the title.

It's probably worth noting there have been several movies within the MCU made about certain heroes, including *A Pay to All Planets: The Peter Quill Star-Boy Story*, though given that Rocket is referred to as Trash Panda, and Groot as Mr Tree, we can probably doubt the accuracy of any products talking about the Guardians.

Other movies that we've seen include *The Snap, Finding Wakanda, Hunting Hydra* and *Nova: Einstein Rosen Bridges*. The first three are movies directed by Paul Greengrass, while the last is a series presented by Erik Selvig, all seen in **FAR FROM HOME**. *Heart of Iron: The Tony Stark Story* is another documentary, obviously about Stark. Though a lot of independent research would have been done to put these documentaries together, some perhaps even with the help of certain important people, they aren't all necessarily reliable. Presumably all of these have a degree of truth to them, but how much of that truth is believed becomes the real question.

Big Me Little Me is a podcast by Scott Lang followed by Kamala Khan, among others, but the amount of detail Lang has provided seems considerable, and is certainly where Kamala got most of her understanding of the battle from. Ultimately this podcast seems to be the best source of information about the fight, even if it might be slightly biased.

With all that being said, however, it is possible that there are certain people who have a *very* good understanding of what took place. We know that may of Stark's suits had the ability to record, given that the Spider-Man suit did. As such, it's not unreasonable to assume that the Iron Man, Rescue, War Machine, Spider-Man and Hulk Buster suits all had recording capability, and given that all five of those suits were front and center in the battle with Thanos, a lot of the battle was consequently recorded. What happened to those recordings is the question. Pepper would presumably have custody of them, but she may have been obligated to hand them over to the US Government, if not the UN itself. While it's unlikely they were then disseminated, it does mean that certain high-level officials have detailed knowledge of what happened during that fight and accordingly may have leaked some of that information. In fact, it's possible that someone like Quentin Beck leaked the footage, if he were able to get hold of it (and given how vast his operation was, there's no reason to believe he didn't).

Ultimately, this means that actual non-biased and reliable information of the events that have taken place in the MCU could be obtainable. However, it's probably the sort of thing that would come from crazy, conspiracy theorists that are discredited at every opportunity by official sources. As such, even though the information would be relatively easy to come by, in the MCU it's probably not believed. Consequently, the general public in the MCU might have the ability to know a large amount of what's happened, but it's unlikely that they would believe it if they did the actual research.

MS MARVEL
[Season 1]*(Disney+)*

Regular Cast: *Iman Vellani (Kamala Khan), Matt Lintz (Bruno), Yasmeen Fletcher (Nakia)*[1.1-1.4,1.6], *Zenobia Shroff (Muneeba), Mohan Kapur (Yusuf)* [1.1-1.3,1.6], *Saagar Shaikh (Aamir)*[1.1-1.3,1.6], *Rish Shah (Kamran)*[1.2-1.6], *Laurel Marsden (Zoe)*[1.1-1.2,1.6], *Samina Ahmed (Sana)*[1.4-1.5], Fawad Khan (Hasan) [1.4-1.5], Adaku Ononogbo (Fariha)[1.3], Arian Moayed (Agent Cleary)[1.2,1.6], Alysia Reiner (DODC Agent Sadie Deever)[1.2-1.3,1.6], Laith Nakli (Sheik Abdullah)[1.2-1.3,1.6], Nimra Bucha (Najma)[1.2-1.5], Azhar Usman (Najaf)[1.1-1.3,1.6], *Travina Springer (Tyesha)*[1.2-1.3,1.6], *Mehwish Hayat (Aisha)*[1.4-1.5], Adaku Ononogbo (Fariha)[1.4-1.5] special guest star Farhan Akhtar (Waleed)[1.4] *with Aramis Knight (Red Dagger)*[1.4-1.6]
Super.Prod: Jenna Berger, Sabir Pirzada; **Music:** Laura Karpman;
Exec.Prod: Bisha K Ali, Adil & Bilall, Sana Amanat, Brad Winderbaum, Victoria Alonso, Louis D'Esposito, Kevin Feige; **Created by** Bisha K Ali; **DOP:** Robrecht Heyvaert [1.1,1.6], Carmen Cabana [1.2-1.3], Jules O'Loughlin [1.4-1.5]; **Prod.Des.:** Christopher Glass; **Costumes:** Arjun Bhasin; **Marvel Studios**; 45 - 60

Episodes:

1.1 GENERATION WHY *(7/6/2022)*

Kamala Kahn and her friend Bruno are keen to attend AvengersCon, but unfortunately her mother is less than enthused, though Kamala's brother convinces his parents to let his sister go. This falls apart when Kamala is determined to go as her idol, Captain Marvel, whom Mrs Kahn does not deem appropriate. With little choice, Kamala and Bruno come up with a new plan to get to the con, even as Kamala decides to add a curious bracelet to her costume.

Cast: Arian Moayed (Agent Cleary), Alysia Reiner (Agent Deever), Jordan Firstman (Mr Wilson), Anjali Bhimani (Auntie Ruby), Sophie Mahmud (Auntie Zara), Randy Havens (Driving Instructor), Ned Yousef (Other Captain Marvel), Jack Ha, Mason Mecartea, Rebecca Ray, Olaniyan Thurmon (Audience Members), Ryan Penagos (AvengerCon Announcer), Connor Jones (Shawn), Paul Kim (Paul), Joshua Starr (Korg Kid), Rakesh Gosain (Tailor), Philip Covin (Gym Teacher), Cheslee Duke, Jada Keche Howard (Students)
Dir: Adil & Bilall; **Writer:** Bisha K Ali; **Ed:** Nona Khodai, Sabrina Plisco

1.2 CRUSHED *(15/6/2022)*

While Kamala explores her new powers – Bruno believing that the bracelet actually activates a natural ability – she meets Kamran, a boy at the school who she develops a crush on. They go to Zoe's party and the pair become closer, though later Kamala has to lie to her brother and claim that Kamran is a long-lost cousin. Meanwhile Nakia decides to join the Mosque Council, but at the Eid celebrations, Kamala is forced to use her powers to rescue someone, even as Damage Control move in on them.

Cast: *Samina Ahmed (Sana),* Anjali Bhimani (Auntie Ruby), Matthew J Vasquez (Miguel), Jordan Firstman (Mr Wilson), Sophie Mahmud (Auntie Zara), Ishan Gandhi (Hameed), Sheila Awasthi (Snapchat Girls), Iyad Hajjaj (Uncle Rasheed), Nandina Minocha (Auntie Humaira), Yash Gajera, Rany Abu-Elniaj (Mosque Bros), Paul Kim (Paul), Connor Jones (Shawn), Vseant Nath, Shivani Persaud (Hameed's Parents), Chris Mayo (OnLooker), Philip Covin (Gym Teacher), Joseph Echavarria, Kelvin Hodge, Cheslee Duke (Guy Students), Jada Keche Howard (Girl Students)
Dir: Meera Menon; **Writer:** Kate Gritmon; **Ed:** Emma McCleave,

Sushila Love

1.3 DESTINED *(22/6/2022)*

Kamran's mother introduces Kamala to the rest of her group, revealing that they knew Kamala's great grandmother and that the bracelet is a way of potentially getting them back to their own dimension – they are actually Clandestines and not from Earth at all. Kamala starts to think about this, but Kamran's mother decides she cannot wait. As such, at Aamir's wedding, Kamran's family turn up to retrieve the bracelet.

Cast*: Samina Ahmed (Sana),* Ali Alsaleh (Aadam), Dan Carter (Saleem), Anjali Bhimani (Auntie Ruby), Sakina Jaffrey (Auntie Shirin), Sophie Mahmud (Auntie Zara), Jordan Preston Carter (Gabe), Nic Starr (Mr Hillman), Tonia Jackson (Mrs Hillman), Michelle Pokopac (Crying Bride), Tanweer Mian (Brown-Jovi Lead Singer)
Dir: Meera Menon; **Writers:** Freddy Syborn, AC Bradley & Matthew Chauncey; **Ed:** Emma McCleave, Sushila Love, Sabrina Plisco

1.4 SEEING RED *(29/6/2022)*

Kamala and Muneeba go to Karachi at Sana's request, and there Sana tells her granddaughter that the bangle is trying to send her a message. When Kamala goes exploring, she encounters the Red Daggers, a group of vigilantes sworn to keep watch to stop the Clandestines. Waleed, their leader, helps Kamala gain more control over her power, even as the Clandestines escape from Damage Control.

Cast: Ali Alsaleh (Aadam), Dan Carter (Saleem), Vardah Aziz (Zainab), Asfandyar Khan (Owais), Anjana Ghogar (Rukhsana Auntie), Zawar Jafri (Muadhin), Parmanand Mishra (Flight Passenger), Kashan Rana (Red Dagger's Friend), Rahul Mishra (Soda Man), Zion Usman (Young Sana), Om Narayan (Heritage Walk Photographer), Panjabi Yadav (Heritage Walk Shirt Vendor), Sukjyot Dahuja (Heritage Walk Sunglasses Vendor), Maryam Samuel, Sheez Jehan (Women at Partition), Kabita Mahadur (Mother at Partition), Munir Christo Masih (Father at Partition), Noman Arshad (Son at Partition), Stiash Usman (10-Year-Old-Girl at Partition), Ismail Bashey (Voice of Flight Passenger)
Dir: Sharmeen Obaid-Chinoy; **Writers:** Sabir Pirzada, AC Bradley & Matthew Chauncey; **Ed:** Nona Khodai

1.5 TIME AND AGAIN *(6/7/2022)*

Before Partition, Aisha goes on the run from the rest of the Clandestines, and encounters Hasan, a supporter of Indian Independence. The two fall in love and Sana is born, but later Najma finds her, demanding the bracelet so they can return home. Aisha takes her family on the run under cover of separation, but as Najma tracks her down, Kamala arrives to help her ancestors escape the Clandestines.

Cast: Vardah Aziz (Zainab), Asfandyar Khan (Owais), Zion Usman (Young Sana), Shyam Annabathula (Rohan), Bilal Dar (Voice of Rohan), Alastair Murden (Newsreel Narrator), Niel Dickson (Radio Announcer)
Dir: Sharmeen Obaid-Chinoy; **Writer:** Fatimah Asghar; **Ed:** Nona Khodai

1.6 NO NORMAL *(13/7/2022)*

Kamala and Muneeba return home, only for Kamala to be told of the destruction of Bruno's store. She tracks him and Kamran down, but Damage Control is close behind, and with Nakia, Zoe and Aamir's help, the group set out to find a way to get Kamran to Kareem without Damange Control getting him first. However, Agent Deever goes rogue even as Kamran's anger threatens to cause more destruction than ever.

Cast: Jordan Firstman (Mr Wilson), Anjali Bhimani (Auntie Ruby), Sophia Mahmud (Auntie Zara), Nic Starr (Mr Hillman), Tonia Jackson (Mrs Hillman), Matthew J Vasquez (Miguel), Sheila Awasthi (Snapchat Girl #1), Iyad Hajjaj (Uncle Rasheed), Ishan Gandhi (Hameed), Yash Gajera, Rany Abu-Elniaj (Mosque Bros), Paul Kim (Paul), Jesse James Locorriere (Richardson), Lex Lauletta (Blockhead), Ethan McDowell (Agent Barrie), Nicholas Dekay (DDOC Agent #1), Dev Acharya (Mosque Member), G Willow Wilson (Them/Self)
Dir: Adil & Bilall; **Writers:** Will Dunn and AC Bradley & Matthew Chauncey; **Ed:** Nona Khodai, Sabrina Plisco

Notes: Aside from The Weeknd's Blinding Lights, the closing credits feature a number of different songs, making use of the Pakistani origins of the show. These include: *Rozi* (Eva B), *Peechay Hutt* (Hassan Raheem, Justin Bibis & Talal Qureshi), *For Aisha* (Memba ft Evan Giia & Nooran Sisters), *Up Inna* (Cadenza, MIA & GuiltyBeatz), *Tu Jhoom* (Naseebo Lal & Abida Parveen) and

Aavegi (Ritviz). With that being said, perhaps the most surprising bit of music is the use of the animated nineties *X-Men* series theme when Bruno suggests Kamala is a mutant. The credits themselves change throughout the series, with the first three episodes using "New Jersey" credits (animated images of characters over a backdrop of New Jersey), the next two using "Karachi" credits (again, animated images over a backdrop of Karachi, following a similar sequence to the New Jersey collection). The final episode mixes the two titles, demonstrating the contrast between the two. "The Real GWW" online vlogger in the final episode is actually G Willow Wilson, one of the creators of Kamala Khan.

Should I Stay To The End? There is a mid credits sequence for the first episode which reintroduces us to Agent Cleary of Damage Control, and his partner Agent Deever, who become regular cast from the next episode, so it's probably worth it. The mid credits sequence for the last episode has a greater impact on the MCU as a whole, as it features a cameo from Brie Larson as Carol Danvers when she and Kamala make an unexpected swap in locations…though where Kamala has gone remains a mystery for now…

It's All Connected: The series centers around Kamala Khan who is mildly obsessed with Captain Marvel and wants to be very much like her. Kamala has a father, Yusuf, a mother Muneeba and an older brother Aamir, who is treated very differently due to his age and gender. They are, in many ways, a very typical Pakistani family. Kamala's fantasies are not approved of by her mother, though her father is a little more indulgent. However, Kamala decides to incorporate her grandmother Sana's bracelet into her Captain Marvel costume and this gives her surprising abilities – she is able to manipulate a sort of light-force, which she can use for a variety of things including allowing her to leap frog on light discs and increase her strength with oversized light fists.

Kamala confides in her best friend Bruno, who has a crush on her, but not in her friend Nakia, a teen with a desire to change the world and as such spends a lot of the season campaigning to get onto the Mosque board. Zoe is another girl who goes to the same school as Kamala, but the two are not particularly close friends, though ironically it is Zoe who Kamala rescues at AvengersCon when she is almost killed. She meets a young man named Kamran, with whom she becomes a little infatuated, but Kamran's mother, Najima, is connected to Kamala's own great-grandmother, Aisha, in that the two are Clandestines, aliens from another dimension – the Noor. In fact, Najima and her acolytes are desperate to return to the Noor, but need Aisha's bracelet and Kamala to do so. When Kamala and her mother travel to Pakistan at Sana's invitation, Kamala meets the Red Daggers, headed by Waleed, who exist to stop the Clandestines as Najima's plan will effectively cause the Noor to overwrite the prime dimension.

Kamala ends up time travelling (via the bracelet) to Pakistan during partition when Aisha and her husband were on the run from Najima, but though Kamala is able to save the young Sana, fulfilling the story that Sana always told, Aisha is killed by Najima. Returning to the present, Kamala is able to stop Najima as the Veil – the dimensional portal – grows too powerful. Kamran inherits his mother's powers, which are not dissimilar to Kamala's own, and Kamala manages to convince Kamran to go to the Red Daggers for help, knowing that Kareem, the new head of the Daggers, will help Kamran. All of this occurs as Kamala comes under the scrutiny of the Department of Damage Control. Here, Agent Cleary, who investigated Peter Parker when he was outed as Spider-Man, sends Agent Deever to retrieve Kamala, but Deever is hugely unsuccessful with her mission.

Ultimately Bruno sets off for college, but before he does so, he reveals that his investigation into Kamala's abilities showed that the bracelet didn't actually give her powers, rather it unlocked an ability already within her - a mutation of some description. Nakia learns the truth of Kamala and forgives her for not telling her immediately, while Zoe surprisingly confesses she knew all along Kamala was the one who rescued her, and she joins their little friendship group.

In the MCU timeline this is definitely set post March 2025, as that's when the Halal food caravan has a health certificate for. The drones that the DODC have are adapted from Stark Drones, as are the sonic weapons, which are similar to the ones General Ross used against the Hulk in 2008. There are now conventions for the Avengers, where people go in costume and buy merchandise surrounding the team. The convention also reveals a number of curious things, like movies and books written about the MCU, and that Scott Lang has his own podcast. When Kamala swaps places with Carol Danvers at the end of the series, it's unclear where Carol has been, though her costume looks different to previous versions.

Comic Notes: *Kamala Khan:* first appears in *Captain Marvel #14 (Aug, '13)*, created by Sana Amanat, Stephen Wacker, G Willow Wilson, Adrian Alphona and Jamie McKelvie. The concept came, curiously, from a desire for a new Ms Marvel (Carol Danvers officially becoming Captain Marvel), and Amanat and Wacker created a broad concept for the character, which Wilson then turned into a Desi girl from New Jersey, feeling that the character would be more interesting as a second-tier superhero from a second-tier city struggling with her own Muslim faith. Surprisingly the television version takes a lot from the comics, including her appearance, background and her love of Carol Danvers.

What is quite divergent though, is her powers. In the comics she is a polymorph with elastic and malleable abilities, along with superhuman strength, and a regenerative healing factor. Another notable difference is that in the comics she is an Inhuman, as opposed to the television series where she is a mutant (this stemmed from the fact that Marvel was reluctant to create new mutant characters at the time as Fox would immediately have the movie rights to them). Kamala's story has gotten bigger since she started, becoming an Avenger, joining the Champions (alongside the Miles Morales version of Spider-Man), the Secret Warrriors (also acting as a mentor to Moon Girl during this period) and notably developing a degree of friction between herself and Captain Marvel. One of the most interesting things to happen to her, was when she got critically injured during a fight between the Champions and Roxxon. As a consequence of this, the government created "Kamala's Law" or more accurately the Underage Superhuman Welfare Act, effectively banning those under twenty-one from becoming superheroes. This would have a knock-on effect resulting in Kamala choosing to violate the law and ultimately causing its repeal.

Muneeba, Yusuf & Aamir Khan: all first appeared in *All New Marvel NOW! Point One #1.NOW (Jan, '14)* created by G Willow Wilson and Adrian Alphona. All three look remarkably similar to their comic book counterparts and their personalities are quite similar as well. The only significant difference is that in the comics, Kamran exposes Aamir to what he thinks is Terrigen mist in an attempt to force him to gain powers like his sister. However, it wasn't Terrigen mist, but did gave him psychic forcefield projection powers; unlike his sister he is not an Inhuman.

Tyesha Hillman-Khan: is similar to her comic book version as well. The comics do give a little more backstory about her meeting with Aamir, the two meeting at the Islamic Masjid in Jersey City. She first appeared in *Ms Marvel Vol 4 #2 (Dec, '15)* created by Wilson and Takeshi Miyazawa.

Sana & Aisha: both characters have comic book counterparts, though Sana's is not as obvious. Muneeba's mother is simply referred to as Naani, and is the wife of Naana. She looks not dissimilar to her television version, but very little is known about her. Aisha is much the same, though she is named, and like we see on television, she did move from Bombay to Karachi – though that is the only thing she shares in common with the television version. Aisha first appeared in *Ms Marvel Vol 4 #8 (Jun, '16)* while her daughter appeared in the following issue, #9 *(Jul, '16),* and both were created by Wilson, Miyazawa and Alphona.

Kamran: looks very similar to the comic version, and they both grew up in Jersey City, though his mother was Bushra, and ordinary human being. Kamran, on the other hand, was an Inhuman and when he was exposed to Terrigen mist, he gained the ability to create biokinetic charges, which also makes him turn bluish-white. He and Kamala did have a romantic affair in the comics, but Kamran had been recruited by Lineage, and he kidnapped Kamala on learning she was Ms Marvel. Lineage's plan was to overthrow Black Bolt, but he failed. Kamran's current status remains unknown. He first appeared in *Ms Marvel Vol 3 #13 (Mar, '15)* created by Wilson and Miyazawa.

Bruno Carrelli: like Kamala, first appears in *Captain Marvel #14 (Aug, '13),* created by Wilson and Alphona, and is a close friend of Kamala's who works at Circle Q, which matches the television version quite closely. He is also the only one who knows who Ms Marvel secretly is, and creates Kamala's costume for her, utilising her mother's bangles. However, in the comics he has a brother Vick, and a mother with a drug problem.

Nakia Bahadir & Zoe Zimmer: Nakia, like her television version, attends Coles Academic High School with Kamala and Bruno, and is a very good physical and personal match for the other version. She is very much a social activist, and also a devout Muslim. Zoe, although not physically dissimilar in the comics, is slightly more of a bully towards Kamala, Bruno and Nakia due to their families being immigrants – though ironically Zoe is herself an immigrant, as she is French. Zoe would later address her approach to life, and confess to Nakia that she was secretly in love with the Muslim girl. Both girls first appear in *Ms Marvel Vol 3 #1 (Feb, '14)* created, of course, by Wilson and Alphona.

Red Dagger: or Kareem, first appeared in *Ms Marvel Vol 4 #12 (Oct, '16)* created by Wilson and Mirka Andolfo. He looks broadly like his tv counterpart, but his backstory is very different. His family are actually friends with the Khans, and he lives with Kamala's grandmother in Karachi. Here he is the Red Dagger, an expert marksman and protector of Pakistan, though there is no Red Dagger organisation in the comics. Rather sweetly he encounters Ms Marvel when Kamala visits Karachi, and later they meet again in Jersey when Kareem does a student exchange program, but goes out to do good as the Red Dagger. This leads the pair to suspect each other's secret identity, though neither outright confess it.

Ratings: *IMDB:* 6.2; *Rotten Tomatoes:* 97%; *Metacritic:* 78

Review: Initially the series feels very much like it is an extension of the style of

SPIDER-MAN: HOMECOMING and this works very well, but once it starts to move into the territory of Kamala's past, actual Pakistani cultural references start to dominate, giving the series a real sense of uniqueness. There's an awful lot to love here, especially Iman Vellani as Kamala, who is pitch perfect. However, the fact it explores a part of the world that the MCU has seen very little of is tremendously interesting. It's another well cast and wonderful Marvel series, from a company that now seems to embrace the diversity that the world offers it, and is all the better as a result.

MS MARVEL WILL RETURN IN THE MARVELS

DIMENSIONALLY TRANSCENDENTAL

With *LOKI* opening up the multiverse, and specific reference being made to the Noor dimension, it is now clear that ther are two different types of dimensions in the MCU, and it's probably clearer to say that one is a parallel dimension, while the other is a realm. The former ties into the multiverse, and initially it was believed that these were the result of branching timelines, but that may not always be the case. After all, in **MULTIVERSE OF MADNESS** Dr Strange and America Chavez pass through a number of different dimensions, including ones where the buildings are made of bone, they are literally composed of paint or they are animated. This would suggest that parallel universes are not simply branching timelines, but some actually have completely different physical properties.

The various realms we have seen, however, most definitely have different physical properties – the Noor dimension is composed of light, the Quantum realm is a place that exists in a microscopic environment, and the Dark Dimension is one where the dimension obeys the dark magic rules. As a result, however, it's not entirely clear what the difference between a universe and a realm is.

It may be that the universes are indeed only the result of a branch in the timeline. Where the universes seem to have different physical properties, perhaps this is because the timeline branch occurred at the Big Bang, such that when it happened, the result was different in some cases, creating universes that had different physical properties, but only because of the difference in the timeline.

Realms seem to exist "between" universes. At the end of **MULTIVERSE OF MADNESS**, Clea seems to hint that the Dark Dimension is accessible from a number of different dimensions. As such these realms are uncertain spaces that exist because of their unique physical makeup; a makeup that isn't the result of the Big Bang exploding in a different way. If we take one step further from what Clea has said, then these realms are accessible from every dimension; so no matter whether you leave from the MCU, or you leave from the Amazing Spider-Man universe, when you get to the Quantum Realm, you are in the same place.

This has a number of difference ramifications, not least the idea that you could use these realms to travel between dimensions, or even from place to place in the same dimension (which is not dissimilar to how Limbo is used by Magik in the comics). Additionally, as it's not clear what is considered a realm, should the Astral Plane also be considered a realm then perhaps the panthers that T'Challa saw when he went to the Astral Plane are not just the previous Black Panthers, but Black Panthers from across all the dimensions.

Finally, there is the question of incursions. Reed Richards suggested that an incursion was when two universes collided. However, in **MS MARVEL** the plan is to have the Noor dimension overlap the MCU, which would seem, on the face of it, to be an incursion as well. However, perhaps when realms collide with universes, this is not an incursion, but rather something more serious, as two dimensions with different physical properties are coming into contact.

The Red Daggers were only guessing that the Noor Dimension would overwrite the MCU. Perhaps it might actually have resulted in the destruction of both dimensions entirely?

THOR: LOVE AND THUNDER
(7/7/2022)

When Sif sends a distress signal to Thor, he parts ways with the Guardians of the Galaxy and heads to his friend only to be told that a being named Gorr is hunting down all gods to kill them. New Asgard is next on his agenda, and though Thor and Korg, along with Valkyrie and Jane Foster (who has also gained the power of Thor) are able to stop Gorr, the God Butcher steals their children. With little option, the team head to Omnipotence City to beg Zeus to raise an army to stop Gorr.

Cast: Chris Hemsworth (Thor), Christian Bale (Gorr), Tessa Thompson (Valkyrie), Taiki Waititi (Korg), Jaime Alexander (Sif) with Russell Crowe (Zeus) and Natalie Portman (Dr Jane Foster/The Mighty Thor) featuring The Guardians of the Galaxy – Chris Pratt (Peter Quill/Star Lord), Dave Bautista (Drax), Karen Gillan (Nebula), Pom Klementieff (Mantis), Sean Gunn (Kraglin/On-set Rocket) featuring Vin Diesel (Groot), Bradley Cooper (Rocket)
Dir/Writer: Taika Waititi; **Writer:** Jennifer Kaytin Robinson; **Prod:** Kevin Feige, Brad Winderbaum; **Music:** Michael Giacchino, Nami Melumad; **Exec.Prod:**

Victoria Alonso, Louis D'Esposito, Brian Chapek, Todd Hallowell, Chris Hemsworth; **DOP:** Barry Idoine; **Prod.Des.:** Nigel Phelps; **Ed:** Matthew Schmidt, Peter S Elliot, Tim Roche, Jennifer Vecchiarello; **Costumes:** Mayes C Rubeo; **Marvel Studios**; 119; $250m; $760m

Notes: There are a slew of uncredited cameos in the film, including Idris Elba as Heimdall, Matt Damon, Luke Hemsworth and Sam Neill reprising their roles as Asgardian actors from **THOR: RAGNAROK**, now joined by Melissa McCarthy, and Stellan Skarsgard and Kat Dennings returning as Erik Selvig and Darcy. Daley Pearson appears as Darryl, Thor's housemate from the comedy shorts *Team: Thor, Team: Darryl* and *Team: Thor 2* made in 2016, 2017 and 2018 respectively. India Rose Hemsworth, playing Love, is the daughter of Chris Hemsworth, and Cameron Chapek, Tristan Hemsworth and Samson Alston play the baby, kid and teenage Thors (you can probably guess who Tristan Hemsworth's father is...). Elsa Pataky, Chris Hemsworth's wife, makes a cameo appearance as "wolf woman", one of Thor's former lovers. One of the Zeusettes is played by Indiana Evans who, like Chris Hemsworth, got her start in *HOME & AWAY*. Similar to **DOCTOR STRANGE IN THE MULTIVERSE OF MADNESS**, this film was banned in certain Asian countries due to Marvel refusing to remove LGBTQ content. Bao, the God of Dumplings is a reference to **BAO**, the Pixar short film. A number of changes were made to the design of Gorr in order to stop him looking like Voldemort.

Should I Stay To The End? Yes, definitely. The post-credits sequence gives us the fate of Jane Foster, but the mid-credits sequence reveals that Zeus is not dead, and that he is sending Hercules to slay Thor (with Brett Goldstein taking on the role of Hercules).

It's All Connected: Set in 2025, **THOR: LOVE AND THUNDER** confirms a few things from the past, including the reason for Jane and Thor breaking up (essentially living very different lives made it impossible for the relationship to work), but more importantly it confirms that Jane was a victim of the snap. Valkyrie remains King of New Asgard, a position she struggles with at the beginning of the film – still keen to meet her end in a spectacular way and go to Valhalla – though by the end of the film she seems to have found something to live for, so would prefer not to die. Thor begins the film travelling with the Guardians doing good where they can. One such mission on Indigarr sees him given the gift of Toothgrinder and Toothgnasher, two very large goats. When he gets an SOS regarding Sif, he sets out to find her – she has been fighting Gorr the God Butcher, someone who has slain many Gods with his Necrosword. Gorr's next target is New Asgard and there he takes a lot of Asgardian children, including Heimdell's son.

Jane has stage four cancer, and is getting help with her treatment from both Darcy and Erik Selvig. She travels to New Asgard and finds the remains of Mjolnir. Years earlier Thor asked the hammer to protect Jane, and so when she gets there it reassembles and grants her the powers that Thor wields, allowing her to become the Mighty Thor. Thor, the Mighty Thor, Valkyrie and Korg go to Omnipotence City on a boat drawn by the two goats and the power of Stormbreaker, where they meet a number of gods, including Bast, the panther God, and Zeus the Olympian. There are also two Celestials at the city, which suggests they might be gods for certain species. The quartet fight – with Korg getting broken up in the process – before they set off to again in their quest to find Gorr, the children of New Asgard and Eternity, whom Gorr seeks.

Gorr once had a family, including a daughter named Love, and when his gods let her die, he found the Necrosword and vowed vengeance. The final confrontation sees Jane transform into the Mighty Thor, something which is slowly killing her – as Thor she is invulnerable, but the cancer continues to grow, becoming more devastating to her when she is just Jane. As Jane and Gorr both lay dying in front of Eternity – a cosmic entity capable of altering reality – Gorr decides not to ask Eternity for Thor's death, but instead for Love's resurrection. When Gorr dies, Thor agrees to look after Love. The two get their own ship and continue to fight evil across the universe. Meanwhile Jane's afterlife is Valhalla, where she is met by Heimdell.

Comic Notes: *The Mighty Thor:* A lot has happened to Jane Foster since her entry in way back in *It's All Connected Volume 1*, so let's recap a little. In *Thor #1 (Oct, '14)* the new Thor appeared, though the idea of Jane being Thor was actually first played with in *What If…? #10 (Aug, '78)* where she appeared as Thordis. A storyline entitled "Original Sin" saw Thor lose the right to wield Mjolnir (it's a long story, but blame Nick Fury…) and an unknown woman picked the hammer up, later revealed to be Jane Foster. She had lost her son and ex-husband in a car accident and had breast cancer, and though Thor was able to reclaim Mjolnir, he opted to leave it with Jane as she wielded the power so well. He also helped protect her from Odin, who was unhappy she had the hammer. The storyline was similar to the movie, in that the hammer powers Jane, but the constant transformation meant the cancer grew stronger in the weakened Jane. It's also worth noting that the movie does a very good job of recreating the comic book costume. She continued as Thor, fighting in the second Secret Wars, acting as Earth's representative in Asgard and joining the Avengers. Similar to the movie, however, there comes a point where a final transformation will be too much, but in order to protect others she sacrifices herself and Mjolnir. Jane is resurrected, but hands over the last bit of Mjolnir to

Thor so he can reclaim his power. When Malekith wipes out the Valkyrior, Jane uses an alternate Mjolnir to become Thor one more time. This hammer is also shattered, but she keeps a piece that allows her to become the first in a new wave of Valkyrior – the new Valkyrie.

Gorr the God Butcher: making his first appearance in *Thor: God of Thunder* #2 *(Jan, '13)*, and created by Jason Aaron and Esad Ribic, the comic Gorr isn't too far removed from the final version seen in the movie. He possesses All-Black the Necrosword, forged from the head of a dead Celestial, and can create sharp tendrils capable of killing any gods (the sword was created by Knull, who was the dark god of the Symbiotes). His backstory is quite similar to the movie version, though in the comics his family is expanded upon, and while he was stopped from killing Thor, he went on to kill more gods until several temporal versions of Thor were able to kill him. He would be resurrected by Loki to kill Thor, but beaten again and driven insane. It's worth noting that Nick Fury whispered to Thor that "Gorr was right" which was the reason Thor lost the right to wield Mjolnir.

Zeus: is obviously the Greek God, though the Marvel version was created by Lee and Kirby in *Venus* #5 *(Jun, '49)*. He is, to all intents and purposes the, historical god with the same backstory, but there is a slight difference in that the nexus between the dimension of Olympus and the prime dimension is at Mt Olympus. Here the Eternals had their city, and so the two groups worked together, though a war did break out between the Olympians and Asgardians until Zeus and Odin ended it. He would later meet Thor when the Asgardian was battling Hercules', Zeus' own son. Zeus was seemingly killed by the Japanese god Amatsu-Mikaboshi, but was in fact imprisoned by Pluto. When Hera attempted to destroy and recreate the universe, Zeus returned to stop her, though both he and Hera were killed by Typhon. Pluto used Zeus to fight Amatsu-Mikaboshi, in the process restoring the god, though Hera depowered him when he cheated on her. Hercules helped him regain those powers, but Nyx later killed him. Again. So far for good. So far. In short, he's not really anything like the movie version.

Hercules: is, of course, another character who is essentially the historical figure, though again, it was Lee and Kirby who brought him to life in the comics *(Journey into Mystery Annual #1 (Oct, '65)* to be precise) and the movie version looks quite similar. He has a strong rivalry with Thor, though he shares a surprising bond with Hulk, feeling the two are out from the same ilk. Outside his rivalry with Thor, he has been in The Avengers, the Champions and the Defenders. During the "Chaos War", Hercules lost his powers, and though

Zeus offered to restore them when Zeus' own powers were returned, Hercules said no. Hercules then started working at a bar, which strangely, is a job he never seemed to leave. Ironically this is despite finding a way to get his powers back. Most recently he has started a relationship with Noh-Varr.

Eternity: looks almost exactly like the comic version, which first appeared in *Strange Tales #138 (Nov, '65)* created by Lee and Steve Ditko. Along with his sister Infinity, they were born in the Big Bang. Eternity is a cosmic entity that embodies the multiverse, but is currently in its 8th incarnation. It has encountered a number of humans, though it has no agenda as such, but has been captured and imprisoned a surprising number of times. It has several children, each as abstract as it is, including Empathy, Eon, Eulogy, Epiphany, Enmity, Expediency and Entropy. It's worth noting that Entropy has once killed Eternity, before becoming the new Eternity, which is all part of Eternity's life cycle. Most recently Eternity's jailer has been the First Firmament, who is effectively Eternity from the previous universe. Eternity was ultimately freed by Galactus.

Bast: is the Panther Goddess, though in the comics she is often portrayed as a man. She has an odd run, appearing as an idol as far back as *Fantastic Four #52 (Jul, '66)*, and then mentioned as the Panther God or the Panther Spirit, until *Black Panther Vol 3 #21 (Aug, '00)* establishes clearly that it is Bast (Christopher Priest and Sal Velutto were responsible for this final interpretation, though Stan Lee and Jack Kirby came up with the character in the beginning). Bast, as you can imagine, looks different to the comics, where she also has a sister, Sekhmet, who is the Lion God of Wakanda. She is one of the orisha, the Wakandan Pantheon, and she has a connection to whoever is the Black Panther.

And: it's not entirely clear, but Love, Gorr's daughter and Thor's adopted daughter, might be a version of the comic character Mistress Love, another cosmic entity more powerful than Odin and Galactus but less powerful than Eternity and the Living Tribunal. Toothgrinder and Toothgnasher (or Tanngnjóstr and Tanngrisnir) also come from the comics. Both first appeared in *Thor Annual #5 (Aug, '76)* and although created by Steve Englehart and John Buscema are based on the actual goats that pull Thor's chariot in Norse mythology. Sadly, Toothgnasher was killed, but happily Loki resurrected him. Omnipotence City first appears in *Thor: God of Thunder #3 (Feb, '13)* created by Jason Aaron and Esad Ribić. Like the movie it's a nexus for all gods and was built by the first Elder Gods (or possibly even those who came before them). In the same issue, Thor finds the body of Falligar the Behemoth, a scene which is almost exactly recreated in the movie.

Ratings: *IMDB:* 6.4; *Rotten Tomatoes:* 64%; *Metacritic:* 57

Review: It's strange to buck the trend, but while it has received a lot of dislike, **THOR: LOVE AND THUNDER** is probably a better film than **RAGNAROK**. The latter film occasionally tended to sideline the powerful moments with a throwaway line, but arguably Waititi gets the balance better in this film, as the shocking or emotional moments aren't robbed by humour, though there is certainly much of this in the film. As such, this film tugs at the heart more than its predecessor, and giving Jane Foster a strong role seems especially rewarding. Though it seems to be an acquired taste, this is definitely one of, if not the best of the **THOR** films.

THOR WILL RETURN

I AM GROOT
[Season 1]*(10 August 2022 - Disney+)*

Regular Cast: *Vin Diesel (Baby Groot), Bradley Cooper (Rocket)*[1.5]
Writer/Dir.: Kirsten Lepore; **Prod:** Carrie Wassenaar; **Music:** Danielle Luppi; **Exec.Prod:** Brad Winderbaum, Kevin Feige, Louis D'Esposito, Victoria Alonso, James Gunn, Kirsten Lepore; **Ed:** Dan Urrutia**; Marvel Studios**; 5

Episodes:

1.1 GROOT'S FIRST STEPS
Growing up in his pot plant, Groot is angered when his robotic carers become more interested in a bonsai tree.

Cast: Fred Tatasciore (Additional Voices)

1.2 THE LITTLE GUY
On an alien world, Groot's treehouse is destroyed by larger animals, and then he discovers a race of creatures even tinier than he is.

Cast: Bob Bergen, Terri Douglas, Scott Menville, Kaitlyn Robrock, Fred Tatasciore, Kari Wahlgren, Matthew Wood (Additional Voices)

1.3 GROOT'S PURSUIT

Disturbed by noises on the ship, Groot encounters a creature that becomes a copy of him. Naturally this leads to a dance off.

Cast*:* James Gunn (Wrist Watch Voice), Trevor Devall (Iwua), Terri Douglas (Additional Voices)

1.4 GROOT TAKES A BATH
Another alien world gives Groot the perfect mud bath that allows him to grow a lot of foliage.

Cast: Kaitlyn Robrock, Fred Tatasciore (Additional Voices)

1.5 MAGNUM OPUS
With a collection of odds and ends, Groot builds an explosive which he blows a hole in the ship, much to Rocket's annoyance.

Cast: Fred Tatasciore (Additional Voices)

Notes: The Marvel logo is sped up by Groot using his remote at the beginning of each episode.

Should I Stay To The End? It's not necessary, but there's a cute payoff in the final episode, showing us what Groot was trying to do when he built the explosive.

It's All Connected: The five episodes take place, presumably in the six months between volumes one and two of **GUARDIANS OF THE GALAXY** (Groot's picture has himself, Rocket, Gamora, Quill and Drax, but no Mantis so it's definitely before the second film, and definitely after the first as it is Baby Groot, after all). There's no connection to anything else, aside from the appearance of Rocket in the final episode.

Ratings: *IMDB:* 6.7; *Rotten Tomatoes:* 87%; *Metacritic:* 68

Review: Five fun slices of Groot adventures, by himself, and it's very enjoyable. It's not particularly deep, but it's a great way to kill a few minutes. Even if it wasn't worth the watch, it's so short you're never going to waste time watching it.

SHE-HULK: ATTORNEY AT LAW
[Season 1]*(Disney+)*

Regular Cast: *Tatiana Maslany (Jennifer Walters/She-Hulk), Josh Segarra (Augustus "Pug" Pugliese)*[1.2-1.3,1.5,1.8], *Jameela Jamil (Titania)*[1.1,1.4-1.6,1.9], Ginger Gonzaga (Nikki Ramos), Megan Thee Stallion (Herself)[1.3], Jon Bass (Todd/Hulk Todd)[1.4-1.5,1.8-1.9], *Mark Linn-Baker (Morris Walters)*[1.2,1.4,1.8-1.9], *Tess Malis Kincaid (Elaine Walters)*[1.2,1.8-1.9], Rhys Coiro (Donny Blaze)[1.4], Griffin Matthews (Luke Jacobson)[1.5,1.8], Patti Harrison (Lulu)[1.6], *Steve Coulter (Holden Holliway)*[1.8], *special guest star Mark Ruffalo (Bruce Banner/Hulk)*[1.1-1.2,1.9], *special guest star Charlie Cox (Matt Murdock/Daredevil) [1.8-1.9], special guest star Benedict Wong (Wong)*[1.3-1.4,1.9] *with Renée Elise Goldsberry (Mallory Book)*[1.3,1.5-1.6,1.8-1.9] *and Tim Roth (Emil Blonsky/The Abomination)*[1.2-1.3,1.7-1.9]

Prod: Melissa Hunter; **Music:** Amie Doherty; **Exec.Prod:** Kevin Feige, Louis D'Esposito, Victoria Alonso, Brad Winderbaum, Wendy Jacobson [1.6-1.9], Kat Coiro, Jessica Gao; **Created by** Jessica Gao; **DOP:** Florian Bailhaus [1.1-1.4,1.8-1.9], Doug Chamberlain [1.5-1.7]; **Prod.Des.:** Elena Albanese; **Costumes:** Ann Foley; **Marvel Studios**; 30

Episodes:

1.1 A NORMAL AMOUNT OF RAGE *(18/8/2022)*

On a drive with her cousin, Bruce Banner, Jennifer Walters is forced off the road by a spaceship and gets Bruce's blood in her own bloodstream, causing her to become a Hulk. Bruce is convinced she wants to be a super-hero, but in truth she just wants to return to her normal life. After some training, Bruce agrees to Jennifer returning to her job in New York, but her first case back is shattered by the arrival of Titania.

Cast: *Steve Coulter (Holden Holliway), Drew Matthews (Dennis Bukowski),* Brandon Hirsch (Defense Lawyer), George Bryant (Judge Price), Monica Garcia Bradley (Bathroom Girl #1), Tiffany Denise Hobbs (Bathroom Girl #2), Quincy Giles (Skeevy Guy), Cabot Basden (Skeevy Guy #2), Toni Bryce (Bathroom Girl #3), Arrianna Marie Hagan (Bathroom Girl #4), Vincent Van Hinte (Skeevy Guy #3), Maliah Arrayah (On-Set She-Hulk Reference)
Dir: Kat Coiro; **Writer:** Jessica Gao; **Ed:** Jamie Goss, Stacey Schroeder, Zene Baker

1.2 SUPERHUMAN LAW *(25/8/2022)*

Fired from her job at the DA's office, Jennifer tries to get a new job, but is surprised to be employed by Goodman, Lieber, Kurtzberg & Holliway. They are starting a super-human division, and want She-Hulk to be the face of it. Despite accepting the job, Jennifer is disappointed to discover they don't want her as such, and even more problematic, they want her to represent Emil Blonsky. After meeting with Blonsky, Jennifer contacts Bruce to let him know she is going to take the case.

Cast: *Steve Coulter (Holden Holliway), Candice Rose (Aunt Melanie), Michael H Cole (Uncle Tucker),* Nicholas Crillo (Cousin Ched), *Drew Matthews (Dennis Bukowski),* Keith Flippen (DA Boss), David Kronawitter (Local News Reporter), Derrick Haywood (Eyewitness), Matt Skollar (Entry Security), Krystin Goodwin (LA Reporter), Bruce Blackshear (Supermax Guard), David Marshall Silverman (Potential Employer #1), *Elizabeth Becka (Aunt Rebecca),* Vas Sanchez (Pedro the Barender), Holly Belcastro (Eyewitness #2), Jovana Lara, John Gregory, Rachel Brown (News Anchors), Maliah Arrayah (On-Set She-Hulk Reference)
Dir: Kat Coiro; **Writer:** Jessica Gao; **Ed:** Jamie Goss, Stacey Schroeder, Tim Roche, Zene Baker

1.3 THE PEOPLE VS EMIL BLONSKY *(1/9/2022)*

As Jen and Nikki attempt to track down Wong to confirm Blonsky's claims that he was taken from his cell with no choice, Pug finds himself having to defend Bukowski in a case where the ADA was fooled by an elf into thinking he was dating Meghan Thee Stallion. Despite being assured that Wong will testify, Jen finds herself facing a difficult parole board without her star witness.

Cast: *Steve Coulter (Holden Holliway), Nick Gomez (Wrecker), Justin Eaton (Thunderball), Drew Matthews (Dennis Bukowski),* Peg O'Keef (Runa), David Kronawitter (Local News Reporter), Matt Skollar (Entry Security), George Bryant (Judge Price), Sharon Reed (Cable News Reporter), Jason Turner (Gideon Wilson), Mahdi Cocci (Jefferson Coop), Freddy Boyd (Gossip Reporter), Rory Asplund (Social Media Man #1), Travis Bobbitt (Social Media Man #2), Caleb Thomas (Social Media Man #3), Amanda Salas (Entertainment News Anchor), Paul Ryden (Parole Officer #1), Nicci T Carr (Parole Officer #2), Robert Stevens Wayne (Emotional Guard), Burke Brown (Literacy Program Guy), Jennifer Van Horn (Prison Counsellor), Ruth Kaufman (Lauren

Jesper), John Gregory (News Anchor), Bob DeCastro (News Interview Anchor), Jessica Rodriguez, Karla Martinez, Raul Gonzelez (Anchors from Despierta America), Maliah Arrayah (On-Set She-Hulk Reference)
Dir: Kat Coiro; **Writers:** Francesca Gailes & Jacqueline J Gailes; **Ed:** Stacey Schroeder

1.4 IS THIS NOT REAL MAGIC? *(8/9/2022)*
Jen struggles with the dating scene, and reluctantly accepts the fact that she might have to use her She-Hulk identity to find a date. Meanwhile, Wong is furious when Donnie Blaze, a former student at Kamar-Taj, uses his magic to make money and demands that Jen help him stop Blaze. They take Blaze to court, but are unable to convince the judge to give an injunction, despite Wong's star witness – a party girl named Madisynn who got caught up in Blaze's antics.

Cast: Patty Guggenheim (Madisynn), Britt George (Married Guy), Leon Lamar (Cornelius P Willows), Ryan Powers (Alan), Mike Benitez (Hank Sanderson), David Otunga (Derek), Eddy Rioseco (Noah), Michel Curiel (Arthur), Caroline Henry (Amberleigh), Amanda Salas (Entertainment News Anchor), Suzanne Salhaney (Judge Hanna), Bob DeCastro (News Interview Anchor), Adam Murray (Delivery Person), Maliah Arrayah (On-Set She-Hulk Reference)
Dir: Kat Coiro; **Writer:** Melissa Hunter; **Ed:** Jamie Gross

1.5 MEAN, GREEN AND STRAIGHT POURED INTO THESE JEANS *(15/9/2022)*
Back before the courts again, Jen is represented by Mallory Brook as they try to stop Titania from using the name She-Hulk, but unfortunately Jen's public derision of the name works against her as Titania's lawyer suggests she genuinely doesn't want the name. Meanwhile Nikki and Pug contact a specialised costumier to help make outfits for Jen that can adapt to both her physical forms.

Cast: *Steve Coulter (Holden Holliway),* Nicholas Cirillo (Cousin Ched), Brandon Stanley (Eugene Patilio), David Otunga (David), Eddy Rioseco (Noah), Michel Curiel (Arthur), Eli N Everett (Security Guard), Darin Toonder (Robert Wallis), Vas Sanchez (Pedro the Bartender), Charis Jeffers (Autograph Fan), Thao Thanh Nguyen (Young Clerk), Mary Kraft (Judge Earley), Bob DeCastro (News Interview Anchor), Maliah Arrayah (On-Set She-Hulk Reference)
Dir: Anu Valia; **Writer:** Dana Schwartz; **Ed:** Stacey Schroeder

1.6 JUST JEN *(22/9/2022)*

Jen is a little surprised to be invited to be a bridesmaid at the wedding of a friend she hasn't seen in ages, but when she arrives as She-Hulk, she is asked to be just Jen for the wedding. However, when Titania turns up as a guest for the groom, Jen is convinced that it's to start something. Sure enough it is, but by the time it happens, Jen is very drunk. Meanwhile Mallory and Niki represent Mr Immortal in his case against his former spouses who are suing him after discovering he is definitely not dead.

Cast: Nicholas Cirillo (Cousin Ched), Trevor Salter (Josh Miller), *David Pasquesi (Mr Immortal),* McKenzie Kurtz (Heather), Abigail Esmena (Bridesmaid #2), Heidi Rew (Ex-Wife #1), Lucia Scarano (Ex-Wife #2), Bree Shannon (Ex-Wife #3), Schwanda Winston (Ex-Wife #4), Gregory Nassif St John (Ex-Husband #1), Daniel Annone (Bartender), Sean Goulding (Lab Worker #1), Justin Randell Brooke (Lab Worker #2), Maliah Arrayah (On-Set She-Hulk Reference)
Dir: Anu Valia; **Writer:** Kara Brown; **Ed:** Jamie Gross

1.7 THE RETREAT *(29/9/2022)*

As Jen waits to hear back from her new boyfriend, she gets a call informing her that Emil Blonsky has a fault on his ankle monitor, and so heads up to see what is happening, which results in Man-Bull destroying her car. With little option she has to wait in Blonski's retreat for a tow, but finds herself drawn into the strange little group of villains trying to become better people, which has the surprise bonus of addressing her own lovelife.

Cast: *Nick Gomez (Wrecker), Justin Eaton (Thunderball),* Trevor Salter (Josh Miller), *Nathan Hurd (Man-Bull), Joseph Castillo-Midyett (El Aguila), Terrence Clowe (Saracen),* John Piruccello (Chuck Donelan), *Jordan Aaron Ford (Porcupine),* Tow Truck Guy (David R Sardi), Maliah Arrayah (On-Set She-Hulk Reference)
Dir: Anu Valia; **Writer:** Zeb Wells; **Ed:** Stacey Schroeder

1.8 RIBBIT AND RIP IT *(6/10/2022)*

Jen is assigned to represent the hero "Leapfrog" in court, but awkwardly in a suit against Luke, her tailor. The law suit fails thanks to Ryan's lawyer Matt Murdock, who reveals that Leapfrog didn't follow the user instructions. When Leapfrog calls her, in trouble, she learns Daredevil is in California, trying to deal with her client. Despite fighting

– and discovering Daredevil is Murdock – Jen accepts that Leapfrog has kidnapped Ryan and joins forces with Murdock to stop him.

Also Starring *Brandon Stanley (Leapfrog)*
Cast: Trevor Salter (Josh Miller), Anthony S Goolsby (Robber #1), Charles Barden (Robber #2), Ryan Monolopolus (Goon #2), Si Chen (Barbara Wells), Peter Leake (Presenter), Vas Sanchez (Pedro the Bartender), Justin Eaton (DODC Officer), Maliah Arrayah (On-Set She-Hulk Reference)
Dir: Kat Coiro; **Writer:** Cody Ziglar; **Ed:** Jamie Gross

1.9 WHOSE SHOW IS THIS? *(13/10/2022)*
At life's lowest ebb, Jen opts to take up Emil on his offer and heads to his retreat, even as Nikki digs deeper into the Intelligensia. Thanks to a helpful video, Nikki and Pug are able to access the Intelligensia, but Jen is shocked to discover that their motivational speaker is none other than Emil – and the Intelligensia meeting is actually at his retreat. And then Hulk and Titania and Daredevil arrive…and then Jen decides things have gone too far and sets off to meet with the writers.

Also Starring *Drew Matthews (Dennis Bukowski)*
Cast: *Nick Gomez (Wrecker),* Candice Rose (Aunt Melanie), Michael H Cole (Uncle Tucker), Nicholas Cirillo (Cousin Ched), David Kronawitter (Local News Reporter), Kristyn Goodwin (LA Reporter), Maxton Jones (Bro #1), Joshua Fu (Bro #2), Mitchell Ryan Miller (Bro #3), Mike Kaye (Bro #4), *Elizabeth Becka (Aunt Rebecca), Wil Deusner (Skaar),* Eden Lee (Writer Jessica), Justin Miles (Writer Zeb), Matt Wilkie (Receptionist), Christine Renaud (Brittany), Rusell Bobbitt (Interviewee), Michael Zeb Wells (Ham Guy), Sean Earley (EPK Interviewer), John Gregory, Rachel Brown, Jovana Lara (News Anchors), Maliah Arrayah (On-Set She-Hulk Reference)
Dir: Kat Coiro; **Writer:** Jessica Gao; **Ed:** Jamie Gross, Stacey Schroeder, Zene Baker

Notes: The opening title cards are occasionally changed to reflect the storyline – the second episode swaps the title to *SHE-HULK: ATTORNEY FOR HIRE*. The fifth episode is *SHE-HULK: BY TITANIA* and the sixth is *JUST JEN: ATTORNEY AT LAW*. For the final episode, the title becomes *THE SAVAGE SHE-HULK* and the opening sequence is almost a shot-for-shot remake of the 1978 *THE INCREDIBLE HULK* series, complete with voice over and the original theme music. A website mentions that a man with blades in his hands was in a bar room brawl, which seems unlikely to be anything other than a reference to Wolverine. Goodman, Lieber, Kurtzberg & Holliway is a reference to the comics (indeed all four partners appear there), with Goodman a nod to Martin Goodman, Marvel's first publisher, Stanley Lieber (better known as Stan Lee), and Jacob Kurtzberg, the artist more famously known as Jack Kirby. The music again plays an important part in the series, and obviously Megan Thee Stallion's "Body" plays out the credits in the third episode. The first episode titles are played over "Who's That Girl" by Eve; the third's "Seize the Power" by Yonaka; the fifth's is "Say my Name" by Tove Stryke; the seventh's is "IDGAF" by Dua Lipa; the ninth's is "We Run This" by Missy Elliott. All other episodes use the "She-Hulk" theme. The last episode also briefly features the Black Panther theme. In the scene where She-Hulk meets the writers, several real-life production figures are present, including Jessica Gao, Wendy Jacobson and Cody Ziglar. Interestingly, Michael Zeb Wells is credited as the Ham Guy, but he is also a writer on the series, as well as a writer on the comic book series. Weirdly, the writers who speak are actors playing Jessica and Zeb (presumably Gao and Wells). The Knowledge Enhanced Visual Interconnectivity Nexus, or KEVIN, is obviously a reference to Kevin Feige. Kevin Feige was given the opportunity to voice KEVIN, but elected not to.When She-Hulk leaves her television series and goes to **MARVEL ASSEMBLED** she moves through the Disney+ menu screen in a fashion very similar to when she moves through panels in her comic series.

Stan Spotting: No appearance, but as mentioned in the notes, the L in GLK & H is a reference to Lee.

Should I Stay To The End? Several episodes have mid-credit sequences, though most of the time they are played for fun rather than having any significance to the overall story. The first simply sees Jennifer trick Bruce into revealing the truth about Steve Rogers' virginity, while the second has her helping her family around the house. In the third – and arguably the most controversial – Jennifer has a meeting with Megan Thee Stallion, and they twerk (shock, horror!). In the fourth, Wong and Madisynn watch tv together discussing Wong's favourite alcoholic drink. There are no more until the final episode which is probably worth watching, as Wong clearly frees Blonsky from prison and takes him to Kamar-Taj.

It's All Connected: this one is a doozy.

There are a lot of connections to the MCU as a whole. Jennifer Walters is Bruce Banner's cousin, and Bruce reveals that he has a device that can turn him back to Bruce (he is wearing it in the end credits of **SHANG-CHI**

AND THE LEGEND OF THE TEN RINGS and this explains why he appears as Banner, but also still has his wounded arm). His arm is no longer wounded and he exits the series on a Sakaar ship. He doesn't turn up again until the final episode where he introduces to his family, his son Skaar. Jennifer's family includes her mother Elaine and father Morris, another cousin named Ched, her uncle Tucker and her aunts Melanie and Rebecca. In the comics Bruce's mother's name Is Rebecca, so this might be that very person. When the Sakaar ship arrives on Earth it causes Jennifer to crash the car and she and Bruce get wounded, with his blood getting into her blood stream. Curiously, her physiognomy allows her to have her own personality with a Hulk's body – essentially the "Smart" Hulk that Bruce had to create. She trains with Bruce but returns to her normal life, where she is an Assistant District Attorney. During a case where she turns into She-Hulk and defends the jury there, she is fired from being an ADA because she brings a bias to a courtroom. She is employed by Holden Holliway of GLK&H to act as the front of their superhuman division – or more accurately She-Hulk is.

In this new position she represents Emil Blonsky, who is released from prison after having been there ever since **THE INCREDIBLE HULK**, though Wong is required to attest to the fact that he released Blonsky for them to fight in **SHANG-CHI AND THE LEGEND OF THE TEN RINGS**. She represents Wong in a law suit against Donnie Blaze, a former acolyte at Kamar-Taj, and is required to represent Leapfrog in a lawsuit against Luke Jacobson (Jacobson being the tailor to the superheroes). She brings to the firm her paralegal Nikki Ramos, and both Anthony Pugliese and Mallory Brook work on her team (though the latter has little time for Jennifer, despite representing her against Titania in a lawsuit over who owns the rights to the name She-Hulk). Blonsky later sets up his own retreat which Jennifer goes to, meeting Saracen, El Aguila and Man-Bull. She also meets Wrecker, a member of a gang who attack her earlier in the series, alongside Thunderball and two others. As it turns out, however, all of these villains are actually attempting to redeem themselves, including Blonsky. When she is forced to deal with Leapfrog, Jennifer finds an ally in the form of Matt Murdock (who represents Jacobson in court), as She-Hulk and Daredevil save the day. Throughout the series Jennifer tries to find a relationship, but is disappointed on several levels as most men want She-Hulk and aren't interested in Jennifer. Murdock, however, becomes the fling that actually has long term potential, and he is invited to the family dinner that Hulk shows up at.

Throughout the series she is plagued by an online hate group called the Intelligensia, led by Todd, who She-Hulk briefly dates and then is forced to represent in court. The final episode sees Todd uses Jennifer's blood to become Hulk Todd, and then he and Titania fight She-Hulk, Hulk and

Daredevil, while the Abomination is also there. And this is where it gets weird. There's no real way to explain how characters can break the fourth wall and have that work within the continuity of the series. Ultimately you either accept it or you don't. As such, the finale is actually skipped over and Todd is arrested (and found guilty if the title sequence artwork is anything to go by). This all comes around by Jennifer interacting with the series writers, and then the robot that controls all of Marvel's output – KEVIN. Clearly this is very meta, and again you either accept it or you don't. KEVIN does note that this is Jennifer's only opportunity to interact with it in this manner.

This book accepts that the sequences are meta and not intended to be part of the fiction, in the same way that the comics have similar sequences where She-Hulk speaks to the artist or writer. So don't expect an in-universe explanation for what happened.

Comic Notes: *Jennifer Walters/She-Hulk:* made her first appearance in *The Savage She-Hulk #1 (Feb, '80)* – giving rise to the alternate series title in the last episode – and was a district attorney who was shot by Nicholas Trask's hitmen, but her life was saved when Bruce Banner, who was visiting, gave her a blood transfusion (this explains the in-joke when a reporter asks the MCU She-Hulk if she got her powers during a mob hit). She-Hulk looks very much like the comic version, but the original version of Jennifer was actually a red headed, white woman. There turn out to be a lot of these in She-Hulk stories… Like the series, her powers are similar to the Hulk's though not as dramatic, but unlike Banner, in the comics Walters decides to embrace her alternate identity and remains in the form of She-Hulk (though, in fairness, unlike her cousin she doesn't lose her personality). Her solo career as a superhero leads her to join the Avengers, and then to replace the Thing in the Fantastic Four. She also has a "grey" version of her Hulk which is similar to Banner's green version, as it has a severely reduced intelligence. She supported Tony Stark during "Civil War", though advised both sides as a lawyer, and represented Speedball in court after his actions triggered the desire for the Superhuman Registration Act. Stark later has her depowered to stop her interfering in plans to send the Hulk away from Earth, though she sued Stark for his actions. She would later retire from being a superhero when Bruce Banner was killed by Hawkeye, and as her transformations into She-Hulk were only into the grey version, she was worried she would become dangerous like her late cousin. Thanks to the Leader, however, she gained control again, but was later killed by the Cotati. She was resurrected, ironically thanks again to the Leader. In *The Sensational She-Hulk* series, written by John Byrne, She-Hulk would address the comic reader, or Byrne or editor Renée Witterstaetter (indeed in one issue she abducts Byrne and with Witterstaetter heads out to find a better writer). This is actually listed as one of She-Hulk's powers in the *Official Handbook of the Marvel Universe*, but is not often seen after Byrne's run, though she was once asked about it and replied she couldn't do it, but appeared to be addressing the audience when she did.

Titania: wears purple in the comics, but is also a redheaded white woman, appearing first in *Secret Wars #3 (Jul, '84)* and created by Jim Shooter and Mike Zeck. Her real name is Mary MacPherran and is actually the second Titania (the first was member of the Grapplers). Originally a scrawny, short girl, she later pretends to be Spider-Woman (based on the colour of her hair), but when their part of the world is grafted into Battleworld, she is taken by Doctor Doom and mutated. Her best friend is Marsha Rosenberg, who is transformed into the plasmic Volcana, while Mary became the bulked-up Titania. During the Secret Wars her arrogance at her new found powers is shattered when she is easily defeated by Spider-Man, and she fears him for quite some time. She becomes romantically involved with the Absorbing Man, and later when she gets cancer, he kidnaps Jane Foster to help her, but a fight with Thor results in Titania using the last of her strength to save Foster. Captain America is moved by this and gives the Absorbing Man a gift which cures Titania's cancer. During Secret Wars, one of her fights was with She-Hulk, and this led to a long-standing rivalry between the two and at one point she took the Infinity power gem to fight Walters. Curiously, when Walters convinces her that she beat She-Hulk, Titania is disturbed that her life consequently lacks any meaning and when Walters takes the power gem, she lays out Titania with a single punch. Needless to say, there is very little in the comics that feeds into the influencer storylines of the television series, though the She-Hulk rivalry is very clear.

Elaine & Morris Walters: Morris first appears in *Savage She-Hulk #2 (Dec, '79)* created by David Kraft and Mike Vosburg, where he looks very different to his television counterpart, and is actually a county sherriff. Nick Trask's hitmen kill his wife Elaine off page. Interestingly he once got Jennifer turned back from She-Hulk as a gift from St Nick. Elaine physically makes an appearance in *Sensational She-Hulk #53 (May, '93)* where she briefly interacts with her daughter, thanks to the Green Goblin's gas. Again, she looks nothing like the tv version.

Augustus Pugliese: or Pug as he is known to his friends is an NYU graduate in the comics, but worked as a bouncer, so looks quite different to the television Pug. He dedicates his life to helping superhumans after Spider-Man saved him, and does indeed work at Goodman, Lieber, Kurtzberg & Holliway. He had feelings for She-Hulk, but took a potion to suppress those feelings, which obviously did not turn out well. He first appears in *She-Hulk #1 (Mar, '04)* created by Dan Slott and Juan Bobillo.

Mallory Book: is known as Mal to her friends, and is a beautiful defence attorney with GLK&H. She's also been nicknamed as "the Face that's Never Lost a Case", but she has a big problem with Jennifer. Also, as a red-headed white woman, she physically looks nothing like her tv counterpart. She was wheelchair bound thanks to an incident with Titania, but perhaps most interestingly, she was the chairwoman of Fourth Wall Enterprises, a corporation seeking to end all metafictional characters. Like Pug, she first appears in *She-Hulk #1*, created by Slott.

Holden Holliway: Looks not dissimilar to the comics version, if you added a beard, and did indeed recruit She-Hulk to the Superhuman Law division of GLK&H, primarily because his superhuman granddaughter became a criminal. He ultimately left GLK&H to look after his granddaughter after she was wounded by Titania. He first appeared in *She-Hulk #1*, also created by Slott and Bobillo.

Dennis Bukowski: or Joachim as his first name was once claimed to be, was an ADA who faced Jennifer in court where he prosecuted Lou Monkton. He doesn't have a beard, but is not dissimilar to the tv version. As his case involved the Walters, it's not surprising his first appearance was in *Savage She-Hulk #2,* created by Kraft and Vosburg.

Rebecca Banner: is the Auntie Rebbeca at the table who first appeared in *Incredible Hulk #267 (Oct, '81)* created by Bill Mantlo and Sal Buscema, and who married Brian Banner. Given that the tv version barely makes comment, the comic version is vastly different. She is the mother of Bruce, though Brian never wanted children and was physically abusive to both her and Bruce. After years of abuse, Rebecca attempted to leave, but the struggle with Brian resulted in Rebecca's death. She was briefly resurrected during the Chaos War.

Eugene Patilio: is known as Frog-Man in the comics, rather than Leapfrog, though Leapfrog is the identity of his father, Vincent. In the series, of course, Vincent is mentioned as a wealthy client, though in the comics he was destitute and developed the Leapfrog suit to commit crime and become rich. In the comics, Eugene wants to actually be a hero and became Frog-Man to do good. Eugene tried to join a number of superhero groups, unsuccessfully, though he did join Iron Man in a space race to stop the villainous Korvac. He first appeared in *Marvel Team-Up #121 (Jun,'82)* and was created by J M DeMatteis and Kerry Gammill. The suit in the television series is pretty close to what it was in the comics.

The Wrecking Crew: When She-Hulk is attacked at the end of episode three, the group attacking her seem to be the Wrecking Crew, a group of four individuals who first appeared in *The Defenders #17 (Nov, '74)*, created by Len Wein and Sal Buscema. In the comics the four are all costumed, but like the tv versions, they carry signature weapons, making it easy to identify them. *Wrecker* who carries a crowbar, predates the crew, appearing first in *The Mighty Thor #148 (Jan, '68)* created by Stan Lee and Jack Kirby. In the comics, Dirk Garthwaite is enchanted by an Asgardian, rather than his weapon, and as such has superhuman strength. When the crowbar was later struck by lightning, it took on the enchantment allowing various other powers. He was beaten by Thor before joining the Wrecking Crew and has worked both with them and alone since then. *Thunderball* carries the ball and chain, and is really Dr Eliot Franklin. He was noted to be the "black Bruce Banner" thanks to his impressive intellect but was imprisoned after building a miniaturised gamma bomb. When Wrecker's crowbar was struck by lightning, the enchantment passed onto the Crew's weapons, and Franklin became Thunderball. Eliot has a soft spot for Damage Control accountant John Porter, because he recovered the ball and chain, and even betrayed the rest of the Crew to save Porter. The other two members of the Crew are *Bulldozer* (who has the helmet) and *Piledriver*, who in the comics doesn't have a weapon. Piledriver is Brian Philip Calusky, who gets oversized hands from the Asgardian enchantment. Bulldozer is Henry Camp and was in the Army before starting a life of crime. Bulldozer was given strength from the enchantment, and built a helmet so he could protect his head. In the comics he had a daughter, Marci, who became the second Bulldozer after her father died from unknown causes. The Wrecking Crew as a whole have joined other teams, such as the Masters of Evil and the Lethal Legion and even the Thunderbolts, and were last seen working with a group of supervillains infiltrating Doctor Doom's castle.

Mr Immortal: is a character the tv series has taken quite a liberty with. In the comics he is a much younger man, and is usually costumed in red, white and blue as part of the Great Lakes Avengers (indeed he has served as their leader). His real name is Craig Hollis, and his mother made the cosmic entity Deathurge promise to look after Craig. Deathurge effectively made Craig immortal, though Craig was then haunted by the deaths of his parents and his lover. He became a superhero, but when he failed in his first mission, he formed the Great Lakes Avengers to help him. Further deaths, such as his teammate and lover Dinah Saur, deepened Mr Immortal's depression and he fought Deathurge in anger, severing any ties with the entity who had genuinely come to see Mr Immortal as a son. Deathurge later revealed that Mr Immortal's destiny was to evolve into Homo Supreme, and this inspires Craig to return to being a superhero. He first appeared in *The West Coast Avengers #46 (Jul, '89)* created by John Byrne.

Man-Bull: is better known as William Taurens, and his backstory is relatively similar to what the tv version describes – he took an experimental serum made from bull enzymes which turned him into what he is, though the comic version is a fairly traditional minotaur, rather than the television interpretation (indeed he was known as Minotaur briefly). He has battled a number of heros, but over time became progressively more bull like. He has been a background villain a lot, often being seen in villain tournaments, or escaping the Raft with other villains, but according to Toad, Man-Bull was killed during the Hunted series. Most recently he has returned to life to join Wilson Fisk's Thunderbolts. He first appeared in *Daredevil #78 (Jul, '71)*, created by Gerry Conway and Gene Colan.

El Aguila: first appeared in *Power Man and Iron Fist #58 (Aug, '79)* created by Mary Jo Duffy, Trevor Von Eeden and Dave Cockrum as a sort of superpowered version of Zorro. The tv version does a pretty good job of recreating the original costume, though in the comics he is a mutant – Alejandro Montoya – who decides to fight crime, and teams up with Luke Cage, Iron Fist, Misty Knight and Colleen Wing. He was depowered during the "M Day" incident.

Saracen: is radically different to the television version. In the comics he is one of the first vampires, and is actually green. He lives beneath the Vatican, with his servant known only as Boy. Created by Bart Sears, he first appeared in *Blade: Vampire Hunter #1 (Oct, '99)*.

Porcupine: is better known as Alexander Gentry, and the comic costume is almost identical to the television one. He first appeared in *Tales to Astonish #48 (Oct, '63)*, created by Stan Lee and Don Heck, and was a weapons designer for the US government. Because the government refused to pay him what he was worth, Gentry embarked on a life of crime, initially going up against Ant-Man and the Wasp, but later joining the Maggia in a fight against the X-Men, and then working with Batroc against Captain America. A string of defeats follow, and he ultimately decides to sell the suit and retire, but no one will buy it. When he offers it to the Avengers, Captain America makes a suggestion that they use him to trap the Serpent Society, but in the process

Porcupine is killed. He was buried with the Avengers to honor him. Later he turned up in court where She-Hulk had to remind him he was dead.

The Intelligencia: first appeared in *Fall of the Hulks: Alpha #1 (Dec, '09)* created by Jeff Parker and Paul Pelletier. Unlike the vicious online forum from the television series, this is a group of villains including MODOK and the Leader. They created a number of Hulks, including the Red Hulk (from General Ross), A-Bomb (Richard Jones), Amadeus Cho and Red She-Hulk (Betty Ross). They were disbanded by Doctor Doom when he took on the mantle of Iron Man.

Skaar: first appeared in *What if? Planet Hulk #1 (Dec,'07)* created by Greg Pak and John Romita Jr, though the following month he appeared in the canonical *World War Hulk #5.* We barely see him in the television series, but the comic version does look different, with much longer hair and often with white facial markings. He is the son of Hulk and Caiera the Oldstrong, a native of the planet Sakaar. He was actually born in a cocoon which Skaar escaped from after his father left the planet. He uses the "Old Power" which is from the planet itself, focussed through a stone, but his mother tries to use this to stop Galactus. Subsequently, the Silver Surfer restores Skaar's power. When he gets to Earth, his intention is to kill his father, but he realises that the Hulk he is fighting is not the War Hulk that he hates. Strangely, he becomes close to Banner, despite hating the Hulk. Because of his relationship with Banner, he is able to deal with his hatred of the Hulk, and the two form a proper familial bond. Hulk – in his Doc Green persona – depowered Skaar, but the Abomination reversed this. As to how much of this will appear in the MCU remains to be seen.

And: the idea of the Intelligencia creating Hulks comes from the "Fall of the Hulks" storyline published from Dec, '09.

Ratings: *IMDB:* 5.2; *Rotten Tomatoes:* 85%; *Metacritic:* 67

Review: Despite being very divisive, this series is actually brilliant. The casting is superb and the continuity nods from the MCU are very satisfying, resolving issues from the past and setting up the future. But that aside, it's brilliant to see a different approach to becoming a Hulk to what we got from Banner. Whereas Banner fights to keep the Hulk down, Jennifer spends most of the series being forced to not only become She-Hulk but to accept the part of a hero, something she's not comfortable with being, and certainly not at the expense of her own identity. The final shot of the series, however, shows that she has come to terms with her alter-ego and chooses to accept it, though won't let it define her. Very much in the vein of things like **ALLY MCBEAL**, this is definitely a show you'll either love or hate.

WEREWOLF BY NIGHT
(7/10/2022)

With the death of Ulysses Bloodstone, a number of people are summoned to fight for his legacy – the Bloodstone itself. This includes Jack Russell, of all the hunters assembled the one with the greatest number of kills, and Elsa Bloodstone, the only child of Ulysses. The group are sent to hunt down a monster and retrieve the Bloodstone, though Russell is actually there to save the monster – the Man-Thing. As Elsa kills the other hunters, she and Russell make an agreement to save Man-Thing and give Elsa the stone, but Ulysses' widow Verussa has other plans.

Cast: *Gael García Bernal (Jack Russell), Laura Donnelly (Elsa Bloodstone),* Harriet Samsom Harris (Verussa), Kirk R Thatcher (Jovan), Eugenie Bondurant (Azarel), Leonardo Nam (Liorn), Daniel J Watts (Barasso), Al Hamacher (Billy Swan), *Carey Jones (Ted (Man-Thing)),* David Silverman (The Flaming Tuba), Rick Wasserman (Narrator), *Richard Dixon (Ulysses Bloodstone (VO)),* Jeffrey Ford (Additional Man-Thing Vocalizations), Erik Beck (Puppeteer)
Dir/Music: Michael Giacchino; **Writers:** Heather Quinn and Peter Cameron; **Prod:** Leanne Stonebreaker; **Exec.Prod:** Kevin Feige, Stephen Broussard, Louis D'Esposito, Victoria Alonso, Brad Winderbaum; **DOP:** Zoë White; **Prod.Des.:** Maya Shimoguchi; **Ed:** Jeffrey Ford; **Costumes:** Mayes C Rubeo; **Marvel Studios**; 53

Notes: This is the first of the Marvel "Special Presentations". For the most part, the movie is in black and white, though throughout, the bloodstone itself is red, and in the last few minutes, the colour is restored to the rest of the film. To add to the "classic" look of the film, the MCU logo has a different arrangement for the fanfare, and is "ripped" by claws at points, and "cigarette burns" appear at two points in the film, where traditionally the reel changes would have occurred in old films. The film is much gorier than much of Marve's output, though the black and white disguises this. Verussa's comment "Where monsters dwell" is a reference to a Marvel title in the seventies that featured many of the monsters whose heads appear on the walls of Bloodstone Manor. As the film becomes color, the song *Somewhere Over The Rainbow* is played, in a similar manner to what happened in **THE WIZARD OF OZ**.

Should I Stay To The End? Errr…no. There's no mid or post credits sequence.

It's All Connected: This is one of those entries that is actually not all that connected to the MCU. Aside from a brief picture of the Avengers when describing the present day as "the time of heroes" there are no real references to the MCU at all.

We're introduced to the Bloodstone family, headed by Ulysses Bloodstone, who has a gem that is deadly to "monsters". Ulysses is dead as the story starts, his widow Verussa organising the hunt that will determine who gets the Bloodstone next. One of the hunters is Elsa Bloodstone, estranged from her father and step-mother, and who has been trained by others. Her goal is the Bloodstone, which by the end of the movie, she acquires. There are other hunters introduced – Jovan, Azarel and Liorn, though all are killed throughout the movie, and Verussa herself is killed by the Man-Thing – a giant, lumbering beast that the hunters are sent to kill. The Man-Thing ultimately saves Elsa's life when he kills Verussa.

The other hunter we meet is Jack Russell, a man with more kills to his name than any other, though as the story plays out, it is revealed Russell is a werewolf, and also a friend of the Man-Thing (who he knows as Ted). In fact, Russell simply wants to rescue the Man-Thing and then leave. As his goals align with Elsa's, the pair team up.

By the end of the story, Elsa has the Bloodstone and Bloodstone Manor, while Jack and Ted continue their travels together in the wilderness.

Comic Notes: *Jack Russell:* is the first of two Marvel "werewolf by night"s, the second being Jake Gomez. Russell first appeared in *Marvel Spotlight #2 (Feb, '72)*, created by Roy Thomas, Jean Thomas, Gerry Conway and Mike Ploog (thought the *Werewolf by Night* moniker was thought up by Stan Lee). In the comics Jack comes from a line of werewolves, dating back as far as 1795, when his ancestor Grigori was transformed in a fight with Dracula. Jack was told of his heritage on his 18th birthday, just before his mother died as the result of a car crash. He spends most of his time travelling to avoid hurting others, though he did try to seek out the Darkhold in an attempt to end his curse. He has also encountered and allied himself with the more supernatural of Marvel's heroes, such as Moon Knight, Ghost Rider and, of course, Man-Thing. Although he temporarily lost control of his transformations, Morbius helped him, and as such Russell joined Morbius' Midnight Sons. Most recently Deadpool shot him in the head for sleeping with his wife, Shiklah the Queen of the Undead, though Shiklah confirmed this wasn't fatal.

Elsa Bloodstone: is a relatively new character to Marvel, first appearing in *Bloodstone #1 (Dec, '01)*, created by Dan Abnett, Andy Lanning and Michael Lopez. Unlike the movie version, Elsa is not really estranged from her family – she lives in Bloodstone Manor with her mother Elise, and friend Adam (Frankenstein's monster), and like her father Ulysses is a monster hunter. She has a blog, detailing the monsters of the Marvel comics universe. Over time she has joined forces with Dracula to defeat Nosferatu, joined HATE (though worked with the rest of the team to bring down their benefactors, the Beyond Corporation), become part of the Fifty State Initiative, and has become a teacher at the Braddock Academy in the UK. Truthfully, she looks nothing like the television version, and has often been compared to Buffy, the Vampire Slayer – though allegedly any similarities are purely coincidental.

Man-Thing: though the television version looks almost identical to the comic version, given there is virtually no backstory for Man-Thing it's hard to compare him to what was on the printed page. First appearing in *Savage Tales #1 (May, 71)* and created by Stan Lee, Roy Thomas, Gerry Conway and Gray Morrow, he is indeed really known as Ted – or more accurately Dr Theodore Sallis. He was working alongside Bobbi Morse and Paul Allen (and also Curt Connors at one point) on attempting to recreate the Super Soldier Serum (it is genuinely an obsession of government organisations in the Marvel universe). Sallis brings his wife, Ellen Brandt into the laboratory, but she was actually working for the Advanced Idea Mechanics (AIM) group and betrayed him. Crashing his car into the swamp, a combination of science and magic turned Sallis into the Man-Thing. Despite being extraordinarily powerful, it's not clear how much of Sallis' mind remains, though Hank Pym believed Man-Thing was still sentient. Man-Thing has the ability to secrete an acid, but also those that fear him will burn at his touch. He can also actually "ooze" through gaps, meaning he is more a semi-solid sludge, than an actual solid object. He has worked for a number of different organisations, including the Howling Commandos and the Legion of Monsters, but most of the time he prefers to be left alone. Sallis and Brandt also have a son, though the boy was put up for adoption.

Ulysses Bloodstone: has an odd history which is reflected a little in the opening montage. He was actually hunter in the Hyborian Age (the fictional time in Earth's history when Conan existed) and part of a meteor embedded itself into his chest (the Bloodgem), granting him immortality (and the more traditional super strength, heightened senses and regeneration powers). He would go onto fight monsters, acquire a mass fortune and travel the world, all the while searching for his nemesis Ulluxy'l Kwan Tae Syn, an agent of the Hellfire Helix who was sent to acquire the Bloodgem. In the more modern age of superheroes, he joined the Monster Hunters, created his own country on Bloodstone Island, fought alongside the likes of Iron Man, and against the likes of Fin Fang Foom, before finally defeating Kwan Tae Syn, though in the process ending his own life. He first appeared in *Marvel Presents #1 (Oct, '75)* created by Len Wein, Marv Wolfman and John Warner.

Ratings: *IMDB:* 7.2; *Rotten Tomatoes:* 91%; *Metacritic*: 69

Review: There's something quite fun about **WEREWOLF BY NIGHT**, playing mostly on the 1930's horror conventions for a Halloween special. It's also the perfect way to introduce characters like Jack and Elsa who are interesting enough for a one-off, but don't have a huge amount more to offer to the MCU. As such this format works perfectly and hopefully Marvel continue to do more. The special itself, though, is one that will appeal to a certain sensibility – if you like the campy horror and a little gore this is perfect. If not, you can happily skip it and you won't miss out.

BLACK PANTHER: WAKANDA FOREVER
(10/11/2022)

With the passing of T'Challa, Ramonda assumes the throne, but when the CIA use new technology to seek out vibranium, they run afoul of the leader of Talocan, Namor, who possesses another source of vibranium. Namor wants to form an alliance with Wakanda to stop the surface world gaining possession of the metal, and demands they bring the scientist who developed the new technology. When Shuri and Okoye discover that scientist is a 19-year-old girl named Riri, the Wakandans question whether this is the direction they should be heading in.

Cast: *Letitia Wright (Shuri), Lupita Nyong'o (Nakia), Danai Gurira (Okoye), Winston Duke (M'Baku), Florence Kasumba (Ayo), Dominique Thorne (Riri), Michaela Coel (Aneka), Alex Livinalli (Attuma), Mabel Cadena (Namora),* Lake Bell (Dr Graham), Robert John Burke (Smitty) *introducing Tenoch Huerta Mejía (Namor) with Martin Freeman (Everett Ross) with Julia Louis-Dreyfus (Valentina Allegra de Fontaine) and Angela Bassett (Ramonda)*
Dir/Writer: Ryan Coogler; **Writer:** Joe Robert Cole; **Prod:** Kevin Feige, Nate Moore; **Music:** Ludwig Göransson; **Exec.Prod:** Victoria Alonso, Louis D'Esposito, Barry H Waldman; **DOP:** Autumn Durald Arkapaw; **Prod.Des.:** Hannah Beachler; **Ed.** Kelley Dixon, Jennifer Lame, Michael P Shawver;

Costumes: Ruth E Carter; **Marvel Studios**; 161; $250m; $805m

Notes: The Marvel logo changes so that the scenes are all of T'Challa/Black Panther, and the movie is dedicated to Chadwick Boseman. Trevor Noah and Michael B Jordan both cameo as Griot and Kilmonger from earlier films, while Isaach de Bankolé, Danny Sapani, Connie Chiume and Dorothy Steel play the Elders from the previous film. Sadly, this was Steel's last movie role. The Talocans speak a version of Mayan in the film. Daniel Kaluuya was supposed to appear, but scheduling conflicts prevented this. Namor's appearance in the film circumvents a similar problem with the Hulk's movie appearances, in that Disney don't have the rights to distribute a solo Namor film. But, like the Hulk, Namor can appear in other films getting around this clause. Ironically, Tenoch Huerta is unable to swim.

Should I Stay To The End? Yes, as the scene with Shuri on the beach continues to reveal T'Challa's true legacy.

It's All Connected: The majority of the film takes place a year after T'Challa's death, and Ramonda notes that it's been six years since Nakia left them. Nakia wasn't in **INFINITY WAR**, which is 2018, and as **END GAME** is set in 2023 for the most part – and T'Challa is present – the film is probably set in 2024 or 2025. Given Toussaint's age, Nakia must have left Wakanda not long after the first **BLACK PANTHER**, which is 2016, which suggests that Ramonda might have been inaccurate with her six-year assessment (though she may have been thinking of the last time she saw Nakia – more on that in a moment).

      T'Challa's death sees Ramonda take the throne, but curiously without any battle, so the Elders may have all agreed on her ascension rather than demand a traditional replacement. The loss of the heart shaped herb and with it any new Black Panther might also have prompted this. Several countries are taking advantage of the loss of the Black Panther, including France, who tries to attack an Outreach Centre in the hope of getting vibranium. M'Baku sits on the council, and reveals that he promised T'Challa to protect and guide Shuri. Zawavari, who formerly represented the Mining Tribe as their Elder, has succeeded Zuri, effectively as the High Elder. The Border, Merchant and River Tribes Elders remain the same as previously. After losing Shuri to Namor, Okoye is stripped of her rank by Ramonda, and Ayo replaces her as the head of the Dora Milaje. Shuri appears to reinstate her though.

      Thaddeus Ross is no longer the US Secretary of State, though his replacement goes unnamed. Valentina Allegra de Fontaine is the Director of the CIA, and was formerly married to Everett Ross. She doesn't trust Ross' loyalty, and is right, as Ross is deeply indebted to Shuri for saving his life; so much so he gives up government secrets to Ramonda, consequently getting arrested for it. Riri Williams, a child prodigy, develops a machine that can detect Vibranium, and the CIA send a team, protected by Navy Seals, to retrieve vibranium found on the ocean floor. This vibranium belongs to the city of Talocan, ruled over by Namor, or K'uk'ulkan – the winged serpent god. Namor reveals that his mother was part of a tribe that survived smallpox by ingesting what was a variant of the heart shaped herb. This variant changed the physiognomy of the tribe so they had gills and could live underwater (curiously turning their skin blue when they were out of water). Namor was born mutated by the changes: his skin doesn't change colour, he lacks gills but can breathe both above and below water, he has pointed ears and has wings on his feet which allow him to fly. Namor notes that he is a mutant. His two closest confidantes are Attuma and Namora – essentially his generals. Namor's motives are curious – he seeks an alliance with Wakanda to protect their vibranium, but also hopes to destroy the surface world. After the Wakandans and Talocans battle, Shuri shows him mercy, but Namor spins this to Namora, claiming they have formed an alliance for the future.

Namor's mother had a bracelet which was made from the heart shaped herb variant, and after Namor gives the bracelet to Shuri, she uses it to synthesize a new heart shaped herb, which she then takes. In the initial battle with the Talocans, the Wakandans suffer a devastating defeat, which includes the loss of Ramonda. For the final battle, Shuri has gained the power of the Black Panther with the herb. On the Astral Plane she meets Kilmonger, who tells her she needs to choose between being like him or being like T'Challa – initially she chooses Kilmonger, but a vision of her mother makes her choose T'Challa's guidance. She chooses a new version of the Black Panther costume. After being saved from the CIA by Shuri and Okoye, Riri Williams remains in Wakanda to help them against the Talocans, and builds herself an armoured suit, with a heart shaped emblem. When she returns to America, however, Shuri forbids her from taking the suit. Ultimately the tribes assemble to select a new leader, but Shuri opts not to participate in this, and the hint is that M'Baku will take the throne of Wakanda. Shuri herself travels to Haiti to join Nakia, and here she learns that T'Challa and Nakia had a child together, named Toussaint, though his Wakandan name is T'Challa. Toussaint is six years old, and Ramonda had met him around the time he was born.

Comic Notes: *Namor*, is one of Marvel's oldest creations, having first appeared in *Motion Picture Funnies Weekly #1 (Apr, '39)* created by Bill Everett. That comic was actually a give away in theatres at the time, but it didn't catch on, and so in October, 1939 Namor made his first appearance in *Marvel Comics #1*. Truthfully, there's not a whole lot of similarity between the comic and movie versions. While both have the white wings on their ankles and the green swimming trunks, the comic book version essentially looks like Spock from *STAR TREK*. Everett apparently created the character as a response to Carl Burgos' Human Torch. The back story of the character has similarities to what appears in the movie – Namor is the son of a human, Captain Leonard Mackenzie, and an Atlantean woman, Fen, daughter of Emporer Thakorr. Having been created so long ago, Namor's comic book history is *very* extensive. He serves as an interesting character, though, and in the Golden Age of comics is an enemy of the US, though retcons suggest he also fought alongside the Allies with Captain America and the original Human Torch. In the Silver Age of comics, he encounters the Fantastic Four and attempts to rebuild his home, Atlantis which has been devastated. He allies himself with Doctor Doom and Magneto, but his alliances rarely last. By the Bronze Age he has become something of an anti-hero, working with his cousin Namor and her daughter Namorita, but also with the Fantastic Four on occasion, but getting villains of his own in the form of Tiger Shark and Stingray. The Modern Age of comics establish him as a mutant and he variously becomes a member of The Fantastic Four, the X-Men, the Avengers, the Defenders, the Invaders and is a member of the Illuminati (though he forms his own version of this – the Cabal – who are less hamstrung by morals and when they cross to another universe, he is killed, but time travel reverses this). Most recently he was selected as a potential candidate for the Phoenix Force. In essence, however, the movie and comic book versions of Namor are poles apart.

Namora: There's a fairly significant physical difference between the movie and comic versions as well, as the comic version is white with long blonde hair, and tends to wear a green leotard. In the comics she is also half-Atlantean and as such has the foot wings and pointed ears. Namora is Atlantean for Avenging Daughter, which is the name she took on when her father was killed by humans. Her real name is Aquaria Nautica Neptunia. She has a strong desire to sleep with Namor, although this become a little awkward when her backstory was retconned to make her Namor's actual cousin. She was killed by the Lemurian Llyra, and survived by her clone, Namorita (in Atlantis, cloning is frowned upon and so Namora had always passed off Namorita as her daughter). Obviously, she was resurrected (because it turned out she hadn't really died, just been preserved in a coffin) and she joined the Agents of Atlas, before falling in love with Hercules, and then starting a relationship proper with Namor. However, when it turned out the two had been manipulated by the Atlantean elders into hopefully mating to produce a super breed of Atlanteans, the pair split up. She first appeared in *Marvel Mystery Comics #82 (May, '47)*, created by Ken Bald and Bob Powell, and an unknown writer.

Attuma: is another departure from the comics, although physically he looks quite similar to the comic version, especially in regards to the shark helmet. He first appeared in *Fantastic Four #33 (Dec, '64)* created by Stan Lee and Jack Kirby, and is generally Namor's nemesis, believing himself to be the phophesized conqueror of Atlantis. He has on occasion been successful with this, sometimes assuming the Atlantean throne, before invariably losing it to Namor again. After teaming up with the Deviants and Lemurians to conquer the surface world, he tried again by himself, but was killed by Sentry. Of course, he was resurrected…by Dr Doom, and continued to conquer, but was killed a second time by Power Princess.

Riri Williams: is only fifteen in the comics, and lives with her mother after her father's death, though like the movie version she does attend the Massachussets Institute of Technology, and is also a veritable genius. She builds an Iron Man style suit called Ironheart, and is sought out by Tony Stark, who supports her plan to become a super hero. Stark transfers his consciousness into an AI which becomes Riri's guide, as she continues her studies, but also joins the Champions. She is forced to stop her actions thanks to the Underage Superhuman Warfare Act, but when the real Tony returns, she develops a new AI called NATALIE, which then seems to take control of the Ironheart armour, though this turns out to be the work of a Stark intern named André. She makes a cameo appearance in *Invincible Iron Man Vol 3 #7 (May,'16)* before appearing proper two issues later, and Ironheart debuts in *#47 (Apr,'17)*. She was created by Brian Michael Bendis and Mike Deodato.

Aneka: is a member of the Dora Milaje, and Ayo's lover in the comics. She actually led the Dora Milaje until she was stripped of her title for killing a local chieftain who was victimising the women in her village. She was sentenced to death, but escaped and stole the Midnight Angel armor – which does look very similar to what we see in the movie. Thanks to Shuri, Aneka made peace with T'Challa and agreed to serve him. She first appears in *Black Panther Vol 5 #8 (Sep, '09)*, created by Jonathan Maberry and Will Contrad.

And: in the comics it is Ayo, rather than Okoye, that becomes the second Midnight Angel. Shuri becomes Black Panther in *Black Panther Vol 5 #5 (Jun,'09)* but when she went to war with Atlantis, it was Wakanda that devastated Atlantis, not the other way round.

Ratings: *IMDB:* 7.4; *Rotten Tomatoes:* 84%; *Metacritic*: 67

Review: It was never going to be an easy thing to make a Black Panther movie without Chadwick Boseman, but this movie manages to tell a story about T'Challa without actually having the character in it. There are nods to Boseman's passing in the death of T'Challa, but the story itself centers around the grief of losing people. Basset easily steals the entire movie, but Wright does a sterling job of taking on the mantle of Black Panther, while Mejía's performance is a superb way of bringing the character of Namor to life. Not as good as the original, but it comes very close.

BLACK PANTHER WILL RETURN

THE GUARDIANS OF THE GALAXY HOLIDAY SPECIAL
(26/11/2022)

When Kraglin tells the story of how Yondu ruined Christmas for Peter and the Ravagers, Mantis and Drax decide to make things better for Peter by getting him the best Christmas present they can think of – Kevin Bacon. Overcoming a few obstacles, they bring Bacon back to Peter, but Peter demands Mantis take her influence off the actor, freaking Kevin Bacon out. As Kraglin sets out to return Bacon home, their chat results in Kevin deciding to stay to bring Peter joy.

Cast: *Chris Pratt (Peter Quill/Star-Lord), Dave Bautista (Drax), Karen Gillan (Nebula), Pom Klementieff (Mantis) featuring Vin Diesel as Groot, Bradley Cooper as Rocket, Sean Gunn (Kraglin),* the Old 97's (Alien Band) *with Michael Rooker (Yondu)* and introducing Kevin Bacon (Himself), *Luke Klein (Young Peter Quill), Maria Bakalova (Cosmo),* Rhett Miller (Bzermikitokolok), Murry Hammond (Kortolbookalia), Ken Bethea (Sliyavastojoo), Philip Peeples (Phloko), Kyra Sedgwick (Herself), Si Chen (Sobbing Woman), Don McLeod (Statue Guy), Thomas McNamara ("Captain America"), Daniel Bernhardt (Gobot), Michelle Gunn (Tourist Mom), Flula Borg (Bartender), Matthew Withers (Handsome Man), Rusty Schwimmer (Sara), Helene D'Auria (Dispatcher), Tinashe Kajese (Officer Fitzgibbon), Barry Curtis (Officer R Bobbitt), Rachel Luttrell (Upside-Down Cop), Giovannie Cruz (Orloni Peddler), Stephen Blackehart (Steemie), Sarah Alami (Gloob), Terence Rosemore (Gurb)
Dir/Writer: James Gunn; Line **Prod:** Nikolas Korda; **Music**: John Murphy; **Exec.Prod:** Sara Smith, Simon Hatt, James Gunn, Brad Winderbaum, Victoria Alonso, Louis D'Esposito, Kevin Feige, Stephen Broussard; **DOP:** Henry Braham; **Prod.Des.:** Beth Mickle; **Ed:** Greg D'Auria, Gregg Featherman; **Costumes**: Judianna Makovsky; **Marvel Studios**; 42

Notes: The story was pitched to Kevin Feige during the making of **GUARDIANS OF THE GALAXY VOL 2** and James Gunn wrote it in three days. After the usual "A Kevin Feige production" credit, we get "A James Gunn special" credit. The opening and closing scenes are flashbacks and are animated, and also at a slower frame rate to give the feel of the *STAR WARS HOLIDAY SPECIAL* animated sequences. The Old 97's appear in the film as a group of aliens who have learnt musical instruments from Earth, and they perform two songs, "I Don't Know What Christmas Is (But Christmastime is Here)" and "Here it is, Christmastime", the latter performed with Kevin Bacon. Barry Curtis, who plays one of the police officers in the car that Drax flips, is the head of security for Marvel Studios, and also appeared in **CAPTAIN MARVEL** as a security guard. The man drinking deeply on Knowhere as the Santa deflates is Mark Hamill.

Should I Stay To The End? It's not necessary, but there's a fun little moment between Groot, Rocket and Cosmo.

It's All Connected: It's not clear exactly when this takes place, but it's after **THOR: LOVE AND THUNDER** as the Norse god is not with them, and Gamora has definitely died. Additionally, the crew are using the Bowie as their ship, rather than the Benatar. When Drax and Mantis are in Los Angeles, there's a play that Kingo is appearing in and Mantis is close enough friends with Steve Rogers to hug him (even though it's not Steve Rogers). Curiously Nebula's gift to Rocket is actually Bucky's arm, though how she has it remains a mystery.

The Guardians have bought Knowhere from the Collector and Nebula notes there is a lot of work to be done. This would possibly suggest they are still cleaning up after Thanos' attack, though given that would be, chronologically speaking, well over five years earlier, that would seem a little surprising. The Guardians also now seem to count Cosmo amongst their numbers. The dog is making full use of her telepathic and telekinetic abilities. Perhaps most importantly, though, Mantis reveals to Peter that Ego was her father and consequently she and Peter are siblings.

Comic Notes: Not in this one.

Ratings: *IMDB:* 7.3; *Rotten Tomatoes:* 89%; *Metacritic:* 78

Review: This is mindless for the most part, with nothing of any particular note happening, but it's not the worst way to spend 45 minutes. Most of the Guardians barely make an appearance, though Gillan still manages to shine with some excellent line delivery. There is a moment at the end that is actually emotional and delivers, but for the most part this is less a Christmas feast, and more the nuts in the Christmas stocking.

IV COMIC BOOK TIE-INS

As per the previous volume, this book is only really concerned with the movies and films rather than any additional tie-ins, but as the comics occasionally flesh some details out, for the sake of completeness here are the continuing MCU Marvel comics.

Black Widow Prelude (2 issues – Jan, '20 – Feb, '20)
Story: Peter David; Art: C F Villa
The story of Natasha's history.
Eternals: The 500 Year War (7 issues – Jan, '22)
Story: Dan Abnett, Aki Yanagi, Jongmin Shin, Ju-Yeon Park, David Macho, Rafael Scavone, Yifan Jiang; Art: Geoffo, Matt Milla, Joe Sabino, Rickie Yagawa, Carlos Macias, Do Gyun Kim, Fernando Sifuentes, Magda Price, Pete Pantazis, Marcio Fiorito, Felipe Sobreiro, Gunji
A series that looks at a number of flashbacks telling the story of the Eternals in 1520.

There have been other comics published around the MCU, though these ones are not necessarily considered canonical as such. However, and again for reasons of OCD and completeness, here they are.

Iron Man: Fast Friends (2 issues – Sep, '08)
Story: Paul Tobin; Art: Ronan Cliquet
A look at the friendship between Tony Stark and James Rhodes.
The Incredible Hulk: The Fury Files (2 issues – Oct, '08)
Story: Frank Tieri; Art: Salvadore Espin
A prequel to **The Incredible Hulk**.
Nick Fury: Spies Like Us (1 issue – Dec, '08)
Story: Joe Caramagna; Art: Hugo Petrus
A look at one of Fury's secret missions.
Iron Man 2: Fist of Iron (1 issue – Nov, '10)
Story: Paul Tobin; Art: Patrick Olliffe, Scott Koblish and Khoi Pham
Tony encounters a group of thieves on his way to a meeting.
Captain America & Thor: Avengers (1 issue – Jul, '11)
Story: Fred Van Lente; Art: Ron Lim
Set during WW2, Steve leads the Howling Commandoes against Hydra, while Thor, Loki and Sif rescue Fandral.
The Avengers Initiative (1 issue – May, '12)
Story: Fred Van Lente; Art: Ron Lim

An introduction to the Avengers.

Iron Man: The Coming of the Melter (1 issue – May, '13)

Story: Christos Gage; Art: Ron Lim

Iron Man and War Machine confront the Melter.

Captain America: Homecoming (1 issue – Mar, '14)

Story: Fred Van Lente; Art: Tom Grummett

Captain America and Black Widow battle terrorists in New York.

Guardians of the Galaxy: Galaxy's Most Wanted (1 issue – Jul, '14)

Story: Will Corona Pilgrim; Art: Andrea Di Vito

Rocket and Groot become the galaxy's most wanted.

Agents of SHIELD: The Chase (1 issue – Jul, '14)

Story: George Kitson; Art: Mirko Cook, Neil Edwards and Mirco Pierfederici

A retelling of the **Agents of SHIELD** episode *Seeds*.

Avengers: Operation Hydra (1 issue – Apr, '15)

Story: Will Corona Pilgrim; Art: Andrea Di Vito

The Avengers take on Hydra.

Ant-Man: Larger Than Life (1 issue – Jun, '15)

Story: Will Corona Pilgrim; Art: Andrea Di Vito

A prequel to **Ant-Man**, featuring Hank Pym.

Captain America: Road to War (1 issue – Apr, '16)

Story: Will Corona Pilgrim; Art: Andrea Di Vito

A prequel to **Captain America: Civil War** as the new Avengers fight Ultimo.

Doctor Strange: Mystic Apprentice (1 issue – Oct, '16)

Story: Will Corona Pilgrim; Art: Andrea Di Vito

Stephen Strange tries to find his astral self while he studies in Kamar-Taj.

V THE FUTURE

Nothing seems to be slowing the Marvel train down, regardless of the television situation (which seems bad for Netflix, but great for Hulu…who knew?). Here's the forthcoming movie/television slate as we know it.

PHASE FIVE

ANT-MAN AND THE WASP: QUANTUMANIA
(17/2/2023)

Sucked into the Quantum Realm, Scott Lang finds himself forced into a deal with the mysterious Kang.

Cast: *Paul Rudd (Scott Lang/Ant-Man), Evangeline Lilly (Hope Van Dyne/ Wasp), Michael Douglas (Hank Pym), Michelle Pfeiffer (Janet Van Dyne), Kathryn Newton (Cassie Lang), Jonathan Majors (Kang), Randall Park (Jimmy Woo)*
Dir: Peyton Reed; **Writer:** Jeff Loveness; **Prod:** Kevin Feige; **Marvel Studios**

Notes: Billy Murray has also been cast in the film, and the villain MODOK will make an appearance.

WHAT IF…?
[Season 2] *(Disney+)*
Marvel Studios

Notes: The second season that follows alternate dimensions for Marvel. The first episode will involve Captain Carter fighting the Hydra Stomper.

SECRET INVASION
[Season 1] *(Early 2023, Disney+)*

Cast: *Samuel L Jackson (Nick Fury), Cobie Smulders (Maria Hill), Ben Mendelsohn (Talos), Martin Freeman (Everett K Ross), Don Cheadle (James Rhodes/War Machine)*
Marvel Studios

Notes: Kingsley Ben-Adir, Olivia Colman, Emilia Clarke, Killian Scott, Christopher McDonald and Carmen Ejogo have all been cast in the series. Dermot Mulroney has been rumoured to be playing the US President. Thomas Bezucha and Ali Selim are the directors of the series. It is six episodes long and will be based loosely on the comic series of the same name.

GUARDIANS OF THE GALAXY: VOL 3
(5/5/2023)

Cast: *Chris Pratt (Peter Quill/Star-Lord), Zoe Saldana (Gamora), Dave Bautista (Drax), Vin Diesel (Groot), Bradley Cooper (Rocket), Karen Gillan (Nebula), Pom Klementieff (Mantis), Elizabeth Debicki (Ayesha), Sean Gunn (Kraglin Obfonteri), Sylvester Stallone (Stakar Ogord), Will Poulter (Adam Warlock), Chukwudi Iwuji (High Evolutionary), Maria Bakalova (Cosmo), Michael Rosenbaum (Martinex)*
Dir/Writer: James Gunn; **Prod:** Kevin Feige; **Marvel Studios**

Notes: Daniela Melchior and Nico Santos have also been cast. The film was delayed for some time after Gunn was removed from Marvel due to old tweets he had posted that were deemed inappropriate. Vocal support helped return him to the position, though his work on **THE SUICIDE SQUAD** delayed the film again.

ECHO
[Season 1] *(Mid 2023, Disney+)*

Regular Cast: *Alaqua Cox (Maya Lopez),* Zahn McClamon (William Lopez), *Vincent D'Onofrio (Wilson Fisk/The Kingpin), Charlie Cox (Matt Murdock/ Daredevil)*
Marvel Studios

Notes: Marion Dayre is the head writer for the series, while Sydney Freeland and Catriona McKenzie will direct.

THE MARVELS
(28/7/2023)

Carol Danvers, Monica Rambeau and Kamala Khan switch places with each other.

Cast: *Brie Larson (Carol Danvers/Captain Marvel), Teyonah Parris (Monica Rambeau), Iman Vellani (Kamala Khan/Ms Marvel), Samuel L Jackson (Nick Fury)*
Dir: Nia DaCosta; **Writer:** Megan McDonnell; **Prod:** Kevin Feige; **Marvel Studios**

Notes: Saagar Shaikh, Zenobia Shroff and Mohan Kapur will return as the Khan family, and Goose will also appear. Zawe Ashton has been cast as the villain, though the part has not been revealed. Park Seo-joon has also been cast in the film.

LOKI
[Season 2] *(2023, Disney+)*

Regular Cast: *Tom Hiddleston (Loki)*
Exec.Prod: Kevin Feige, Louis D'Esposito, Victoria Alonso, Tom Hiddleston, Kate Herron, Michael Waldron; **Created by** Michael Waldron; **Marvel Studios**

Notes: Eric Martin will be the head writer for the new season. Sophie di Martino, Gugu Mbatha-Raw and Owen Wilson are all expected to return.

IRONHEART
[Season 1] *(Late 2023, Disney+)*

Cast: *Dominique Thorne (Riri Williams/Ironheart)*
Marvel Studios

Notes: Anthony Ramos, Harper Anthony, Manny Montana and Lyric Ross have all been cast, with the latter playing Riri's best friend. Sam Bailey and Angela Barnes are directing. It will be six episodes long.

AGATHA: COVEN OF CHAOS
[Season 1] *(Late 2023, Disney+)*

Regular Cast: *Kathryn Hahn (Agatha Harkness)*
Marvel Studios

Notes: Jac Shchaeffer is head writer and will also be executive producer on the series.

DAREDEVIL: BORN AGAIN
[Season 1] *(Early 2024, Disney+)*

Cast: *Charlie Cox (Daredevil), Vincent D'Onofrio (Kingpin)*
Marvel Studios

Notes: A soft reboot of the *DAREDEVIL* Netflix series, which will have Matt Corman and Chris Ord as the head writers. It will be eighteen episodes long.

CAPTAIN AMERICA: NEW WORLD ORDER
(3/5/2024)

Cast: *Anthony Mackie (Sam Wilson/Captain America), Danny Ramirez (Joaquin Torres/Falcon), Carl Lumbly (Isaiah Bradley), Tim Blake Nelson (Samuel Sterns/The Leader), Shira Haas (Sabra), Harrison Ford (Thaddeus "Thunderbolt" Ross)*

Dir: Julius Onah; **Writers:** Tim Spellman, Dalan Musson; **Prod:** Kevin Feige; **Marvel Studios**

THUNDERBOLTS
(26/7/2024)

Cast: *Sebastian Stan (Bucky Barnes/The Winter Soldier), Florence Pugh (Yelena Belova/Black Widow), David Harbour (Alexei Shostakov/Red Guardian), Hannah John-Kamen (Ava Starr/The Ghost), Wyatt Russell (John Walker/US Agent), Olga Kurylenko (Antonia Dreykov/Taskmaster), Julia Louis-*

Dreyfus (Valentina Allegra de Fontaine)
Dir: Jake Schreier; **Writer:** Eric Pearson; **Prod:** Kevin Feige; **Marvel Studios**

BLADE
(6/9/2024)

Cast: *Mahershala Ali (Blade)*
Writer: Stacy Osei-Kuffour, Beau DeMayo; **Prod:** Kevin Feige; **Marvel Studios**

Notes: Bassam Tariq was originally brought on board to direct the film, but dropped out, necessitating the delay of the film.

PHASE SIX

DEADPOOL 3
(8/11/2024)

Cast: *Ryan Reynolds (Wade Wilson/Deadpool), Hugh Jackman (Logan/ Wolverine)*
Dir: Shawn Levy; **Writers:** Rhett Reese, Paul Wernick; **Prod:** Kevin Feige; **Marvel Studios**

Notes: The third film in the series was confirmed not long after Disney bought out Fox, but it wasn't until September 2022 when Reynolds released a video confirming that Jackman was joining the cast. Originally slated for September, 2024, it was pushed back when **BLADE** was moved. It is expected Leslie Uggams will also return as Blind Al.

FANTASTIC FOUR
(14/2/2025)

Dir: Matt Shakman; **Writers:** Jeff Kaplan, Ian Springer; **Prod:** Kevin Feige; **Marvel Studios**

Notes: Jon Watts was originally lined up to direct the film, but decided to take a break from superhero films.

AVENGERS: THE KANG DYNASTY
(2/5/2025)

Cast: presumably *Jonathan Majors (Kang)*
Dir: Destin Daniel Cretton; **Writer:** Jeff Loveness; **Prod:** Kevin Feige; **Marvel Studios**

AVENGERS: SECRET WARS
(1/5/2026)

Cast: presumably *Jonathan Majors (Kang)*
Writer: Michael Waldron; **Prod:** Kevin Feige; **Marvel Studios**

There are three other films in Phase Six that have yet to be accounted for, to be released on 25 July, 2025, 7 November 2025 and 13 February, 2026.

CONFIRMED BUT UNPLACED

ARMOR WARS

Rhodey sets out to stop Tony Stark's technology from falling into the wrong hands.

Cast: *Don Cheadle (James Rhodes/War Machine), Walton Goggins (Sonny Burch)*
Writer: Yassir Lester; **Prod:** Kevin Feige; **Marvel Studios**

Notes: The was long in development as a television series for Disney+, but the decision was made in in September, 2022 to turn it into a movie instead. Filming will take place in 2023, suggesting that it might be one of the missing films in Phase Six.

SHANG-CHI 2

Cast: unknown, presumably *Simu Liu (Shang-Chi), Awkwafina (Katy)* and *Meng'er Zhang (Xu Xialing)*
Dir/Writer: Destin Daniel Cretton; **Prod:** Kevin Feige; **Marvel Studios**

Notes: The first film was quite successful, but Cretton's commitment to **AVENGERS: THE KANG DYNASTY** has pushed this film back.

ETERNALS 2

Cast: unknown, presumably *Gemma Chan (Sersi), Angelina Jolie (Thena), Kumail Nanjiani (Kingo), Lauren Midloff (Makkari), Barry Keoghan (Druig), Bryan Tyree Henry (Phastos)* and possibly *Harry Styles (Starfox) and Patton Oswalt (Pip the Troll)*
Prod: Kevin Feige; **Marvel Studios**

Notes: The original wasn't exactly a huge success for Marvel, but Patton Oswalt has claimed that a sequel is in development and producer Nate Moore has confirmed that the characters will be returning. There has been speculation that any return wouldn't be in a movie titled **Eternals 2**, with a great deal of rumour suggesting the title will be **The Celestials: End of Time**, based on Marvel securing that name for a web address.

Untitled Wakanda Series
[Season 1] *(Disney+)*

Cast: *Danai Gurira (Okoye)*
Marvel Studios

Notes: Developed by Ryan Coogler, this series is set in Wakanda.

MARVEL ZOMBIES
[Season 1] *(Disney+)*

Marvel Studios

Notes: A continuation of the episode of *WHAT IF...?*

WONDER MAN
[Season 1] *(Disney+)*

Cast: Ben Kingsley (Trevor Slattery)
Marvel Studios

Notes: Part of the deal Destin Daniel Cretton has with Marvel to develop new series. Andrew Guest will serve as the head writer.

Untitled Nova Series
[Season 1] *(Disney+)*

Marvel Studios

Notes: Sabir Pirzada is the head writer on a Richard Rider/Nova series.

VI *MCU TIMELINE*

This timeline is not definite, nor perfect. For the MCU, a perfect timeline is utterly impossible. This timeline uses the best information available to create a reasonable sequence of events. Evidence can be found to both support and attack some of the dating. When an event is in grey, it means the event is merely mentioned in on screen. *If an event is italicised, the event is a flashback seen on screen.* Underscored events are speculative.

Pre-Universal Creation

> 13,800,000,000 BC

I The Dark Elves exist prior to the creation of the universe. (**Thor: The Dark World**)

Pre-Twentieth Century

c. 13,800,000,000 BC

I The universe is created; the Infinity Stones – six singularities that are the basic nature of reality, power, the mind, time, space and the soul - along with it. (**Guardians of the Galaxy**) These singularities hold the prime timeline in place. (**Avengers: Endgame**)

c. 2,500,000 BC

I A vibranium asteroid crashes into Earth where Wakanda will ultimately be founded. (**Black Panther**) A second asteroid may have also crashed into the sea. (**Black Panther: Wakanda Forever**)

c. 30,100 BC

I Enoch comes into existence. (***Agents of SHIELD 5.10 Past Life***)

c. 28,000 BC

I Enoch is sent to Earth. (***Agents of SHIELD 5.5 Rewind***)

| Five tribes come together in East Africa and form Wakanda. **(Black Panther)**

28,000BC < Uncertain Dates <2988 BC

| *A Kree faction uses Terrigan mists to create Inhumans, beginning with Alveus (the Hive) who is banished to an alien world. (**Agents of SHIELD 2.8 The Things We Bury**)*
| Odin defeats Surtur. **(Thor: Ragnarok)**

2988 BC

| *The Convergence. Malekith begins his campaign to destroy the Nine Realms.* **(Thor: The Dark World)**

2988 BC < Uncertain Dates < 79 AD

| Odin and Hela subjugate the Nine realms. Hela's ambition grows too great and Odin imprisons her. **(Thor: Ragnarok)**
| The Hand is formed in K'un-Lun to gain immortality. They discover how to use Dragon bones to do so. A rival group called the Chaste is formed to stop them. **(*Daredevil 2.8 Guilty as Sin*; *The Defenders 1.4 Royal Dragon*)**

79 AD

| The Hand cause the eruption of Vesuvius. **(*The Defenders 1.4 Royal Dragon*)**

79 AD < Uncertain Dates < 1197 AD

| *Hela escapes and the Valkyrior stop her, with only Valkyrie surviving.* Valkyrie goes into self-exile on Sakaar. **(Thor: Ragnarok)**
| Thor is born.
| *The Asgardians fight the Frost Giants, and Odin and Frigga adopt Loki.* **(Thor)**
| The Kree begin wars with the Skrull and Nova Empires. **(Captain Marvel; Guardians of the Galaxy)**

1197 AD

| The Berserker splits his staff. **(*Agents of SHIELD 1.8 The Well*)**

1316 AD

I The Ancient One is born. (**Doctor Strange**)

1409 AD

I <u>Odin hides the Tesseract on Earth.</u>
TIMELINE NOTE: According to the official Marvel timeline.

1413 AD

I Lorelei's terrorism of the Nine Realms is stopped by Sif. (**Agents of SHIELD 1.15 The Yes Men**)

1793 AD

I Leland Wilson allows his brother Ewin to kill him in a duel, saving his family and the city as they are the first Divine Pairing. (**Cloak & Dagger 1.3 Stained Glass**)

1839 AD

I *Hydra attempts to cross the universe and meet Alveus via the Monolith.* (**Agents of SHIELD 3.2 Purpose in the Machine**)

Twentieth Century

1904 AD
October

I Werner Reinhardt is born. (**Agents of SHIELD 2.8 The Things We Bury**)

1911 AD
May

I Agnes Cully is born. (**Agent Carter 2.3 Better Angels**)

1917 AD
March

| Sebastian "Bucky" Barnes is born. (**Captain America: The Winter Soldier**)
TIMELINE NOTE: The movie shows the Smithsonian memorial, which actually gives Bucky's birth year as both 1916 and 1917.

1918 AD
July

| Steve Rogers is born. (**Captain America: The First Avenger**)

1920 AD

| *Agnes Cully starts her experiments. (**Agent Carter 2.4 Smoke & Mirrors**)*

1921 AD
April

| Peggy Carter is born. (**Agents of SHIELD 3.20 Emancipation**)

1927 AD

| Dottie Underwood is born. (**Agent Carter 1.5 The Iron Ceiling**)

1931 AD – ALTERNATE TIMELINE

| ***Agents of SHIELD 7.1 The New Deal – 7.2 Know Your Onions***

1932 AD

| In Germany, Abraham Erskine begins work on the Super Soldier serum. (**Captain America: The First Avenger**)

1934 AD

| *Agnes Cully is discovered at a cinema and changes her name to Whitney Frost to begin acting. (**Agent Carter 2.4 Smoke & Mirrors**)*

1936 AD
August

I Alexander Pierce is born. (**Captain America: The Winter Soldier**)

October

I Sarah Rogers, Steve's mother, dies. (**Captain America: The Winter Soldier**)

1937 AD

I *Dottie Underwood trains in the Red Room.* (***Agent Carter 1.5 The Iron Ceiling***)

1940 AD

I *Peggy Carter cancels her wedding when her brother dies at war and joins MI5.* (***Agent Carter 2.4 Smoke & Mirrors***)

I Johann Schmidt is injected with the super solder serum, becoming the Red Skull. (**Captain America: The First Avenger**)

1941 AD

I Howard Stark works on the Manhattan Project. (**Iron Man**)

1942 AD

I Johann Schmidt locates the Tesseract. (**Captain America: The First Avenger**)

I Werner Reinhardt is tasked by Schmidt to find more magical objects. (***Agents of SHIELD 2.1 Shadows***)

1943 AD
June

I Steve Rogers becomes Captain America, and changes his initial mission of publicity machine to become a proper soldier, and leads a group called the Howling Commandoes. (**Captain America: The First Avenger**)

1944 AD
May

I A massacre takes place leaving only Peggy Carter a survivor, though Peggy claims this is untrue. (***Agent Carter 2.10 Hollywood Ending***)

June

I *General McInnis uses Midnight Oil on Finow in Germany. Johann Fennhoff is the only survivor. He is later captured by Leviathan. (**Agent Carter 1.6 A Sin to Err/1.7 SNAFU**)*

1945 AD

I Arnim Zola is captured. (**Captain America: The First Avenger**)
I Captain America defeats Schmidt, but is apparently lost when his plane goes down. (**Captain America: The First Avenger**)
I *Peggy Carter takes control of the Howling Commandoes and shuts down other Hydra bases, arresting Werner Reinhardt in the process. (**Agents of SHIELD 2.1 Shadows/2.8 The Things We Bury**)*
I Thaddeus Ross is born. (**The Incredible Hulk**)
TIMELINE NOTE: In a deleted scene, Ross claims he was 27 when he left Vietnam, but the latest US troops pulled out was 1973. As actor William Hurt was 23 in 1973, Thaddeus Ross can't have left 'Nam earlier and so this is approximately his birth year.

1946 AD
April/May

I ***Agent Carter Season 1***
TIMELINE NOTE: The climax takes place on the first anniversary of VE Day: 8 May, 1946.

1947 AD
July

I ***Agent Carter Season 2***
TIMELINE NOTE: A newspaper gives the date of July, 1947.
I *Agent Carter (Marvel One-Shot)*
TIMELINE NOTE: The caption states this takes place a year after **Captain**

America: The First Avenger, but it also ends with Peggy Carter joining Howard Stark to create SHIELD, which is not how the television series ends. In some ways it seems to contradict the series, though there's no reason to assume that this doesn't fit with Thompson's death and someone new taking control of the SSR New York office. Therefore, the "year later" caption has been ignored.

1948 AD

I Video is shot of an Iron Fist defending the gates of K'un-Lun. (***Iron Fist 1.10 Black Tiger Steals Heart***)

1949 AD

I Arnim Zola is forced to work for SHIELD, and uses this opportunity to rebuild Hydra within it. (**Captain America: The Winter Soldier**)

1950 AD

I Nick Fury is born. (**Captain Marvel**)

c 1952 AD

I *Steve Rogers's time travelling to return the Infinity Stones brings him back to the 1950's where he meets up with Peggy Carter and marries her.* (**Captain America: The Winter Soldier; Avengers: Endgame**)

TIMELINE NOTE: Peggy is interviewed in 1953, which is then seen at the Smithsonian. In the interview she talks of how it was thanks to Steve Rogers she met her husband. The insinuation in **Endgame** is that Steve married Peggy, however, in the flashback she doesn't look as old as she did in 1970, so presumably Steve's decision to stay with Peggy was in a time after Peggy's time with the SSR (ie after 1947) but before the interview (ie before 1953). The special effects team believed that Rogers was physically 106 when he handed over the Captain. If he was 27 when he went into the ice in 1945 and was much the same when he was revived in 2012, then he would have been physically 38 in 2023, and as such lived with Peggy for about 68 years. This suggested he returned to her in about 1955. Given the interview, however, we can allow for a few years discrepancy.

Much speculation has been made as to whether this is an alternate timeline (which directors Joe and Anthony Russo believe) or the prime timeline (which was the intention of writers Markus and McFeely). There is no reason not to believe that Rogers was present during the events of the seventy years from '53 – '23, knowing that he had to keep his true identity secret because of the temporal implications (he seems to understand the argument that Banner and Stark give), and it has been confirmed that there were two versions of Rogers at Peggy's funeral. When the youthful Rogers returns in 2012, Peggy would understand the need to stay quiet. It has also been confirmed that Bucky knew what Rogers was planning all along. Therefore, this book assumes that Rogers returned to the primary timeline and stayed there.

1955 AD – ALTERNATE TIMELINE

I *Agends of SHIELD 7.3 Alien Commies From the Future – 7.4 Out of the Past*

1956 AD

I Alisa Jones is born. (*Jessica Jones 2.3 AKA Sole Survivor*)

1960 AD

I Karl Malus is born.
TIMELINE NOTE: Malus is 57 at the time of his death, and started university in 1978.

1961 AD

I Felix Blake is born. (*Agents of SHIELD 1.16 The End of the Beginning*)
I Meredith Quill is born. (**Guardians of the Galaxy Vol 2**)

1962 AD

I William Rawlins is born. (*The Punisher 1.8 Cold Steel*)
I Harold Meachum is born. (*Iron Fist 1.1 Snow Gives Way*)
I Midtown School of Science and Technology is established. (**Spider-Man: Homecoming**)

1963 AD

I Anton Vanko defects to the US and helps Howard Stark develop Arc

technology. **(Iron Man 2)**
TIMELINE NOTE: Presumably this was a result of having worked with him at the SSR in the forties.

1964 AD
July

I Phil Coulson is born. (***Agents of SHIELD 2.13 One of Us***)

1965 AD
December

I Wendall Rand is born. (***Iron Fist 1.1 Cold Steel***)

1967 AD
June

I Anton Vanko returns to the USSR, but is exiled to Siberia. **(Iron Man 2)**

1968 AD
February

I Ivan Vanko is born. **(Iron Man 2)**

March

I Heather Rand is born. (***Iron Fist 1.1 Cold Steel***)

October

I James Rhodes is born. **(Iron Man Three)**

1969 AD
December

I Bruce Banner is born. **(The Incredible Hulk)**

1970 AD
February

I *Gideon Malick meets the current head of Hydra, Daniel Whitehall and joins the organisation.* (**Agents of SHIELD 3.16 Paradise Lost**)

April

I Tony Stark and Steve Rogers travel from 2023 and steal the space stone, though Rogers returns it to the same point, negating an alternate timeline created from this point. (**Avengers: Endgame**)

I Tony Stark is born. (**Iron Man; Avengers: Endgame**)

1971 AD
March

I <u>Emil Blonsky is born.</u>

1972 AD
Uncertain date

I Arnim Zola's consciousness is uploaded to a computer on his death. (**Captain America: The Winter Soldier**)

June

I Mr Giyera is born. (**Agents of SHIELD 3.8 Many Heads, One Tale**)

October

I Marcus Daniels is born. (**Agents of SHIELD 1.19 The Only Light in Darkness**)

1973 AD
September

I *Howard Stark records a video for Tony alongside his opening video for the Stark World Exposition.* (**Iron Man 2**)

November

I *Wilson Fisk kills his father.* (**Daredevil 1.8 Shadows in the Glass**)

December

I Jasper Sitwell is born. (**Captain America: The Winter Soldier**)

1973 AD – ALTERNATE TIMELINE

I *Agends of SHIELD 7.5 A Trout in the Milk – 7.6 Adapt Or Die*

1974 AD
April

I The Stark World Expo is held, and will be the last for 36 years. (**Iron Man 2**)

1977 AD
May

I Herman "Shades" Alvarez is born. (*Luke Cage 2.12 Can't Confront on Me*)

November

I Kevin Thompson (aka Kilgrave) is born. (*Jessica Jones 1.8 AKA WWJD?/ 1.9 AKA Sin Bin*)

1978 AD

I Helmut Zemo is born. (**Captain America: Civil War**)

November

I Ego meets Meredith Quill and falls in love. (**Guardians of the Galaxy Vol 2**)

1980 AD
Uncertain Dates

I *Ego makes a number of trips to and from Earth, impregnating Meredith Quill.* (**Guardians of the Galaxy Vol 2**)
I Hope Van Dyne is born. (**Ant-Man**)
I Robert Coleman is born (*Jessica Jones 2.1 Start at the Beginning*)
I Peter Quill is born. (**Guardians of the Galaxy**)

July

| Franklin Nelson is born. (***Daredevil 3.3 No Good Deed/Daredevil 3.4 Blindsided***)

1982 AD
April

| Maria Hill is born. (***Agents of SHIELD 1.1 Pilot***)

July

| JT James is born. (***Agents of SHIELD 3.19 Failed Experiments***)

1982 AD – ALTERNATE TIMELINE

| ***Agends of SHIELD 7.7 The Totally Excellent Adventures of Mack and the D***

1983 AD
January

| Grant Ward is born. (***Agents of SHIELD 1.1 Pilot***)

May

| Gordon undergoes terrigenesis. (***Agents of SHIELD 2.11 Aftershocks***)

1983 AD – ALTERNATE TIMELINE

| ***Agends of SHIELD 7.8 After, Before – 7.12 The End is at Hand***

1984 AD
Uncertain Dates

| Natasha Romanoff is born. (**Captain America: The Winter Soldier**)

April

| Aaron Davis is born. (**Spider-Man: Homecoming**)

1985 AD
Uncertain Dates

| Calvin Johnson meets and marries Jiaying. (***Agents of SHIELD 2.18 The Frenemy of My Enemy***)
| Matt Murdock is born. (***Daredevil 1.7 Stick***)
| Trish Walker is born. (***Jessica Jones 1.8 AKA WWJD?***)

April

| Lincoln Campbell is born. (***Agents of SHIELD 3.22 Ascension***)

June

| *Kevin Johnson/Kilgrave gains his powers.* (***Jessica Jones 1.9 AKA Sin Bin***)

October

| Jessica Jones is born. (***Jessica Jones 1.8 AKA WWJD?***)

1986 AD
Uncertain Dates

| Ulysses Klaue steals vibranium from Wakanda. (**Avengers: Age of Ultron**)
TIMELINE NOTE: It is stated repeatedly in **Black Panther** that it has been thirty years since Klaue stole the vibranium. Taking that at face value the theft must have occurred in 1986 (though the official timeline suggests 1987).

September

| Ward Meachum is born. (***Iron Fist 1.9 The Mistress of All Agonies***)

1987 AD
Uncertain Dates

Ι *Hank Pym becomes Ant-Man. Janet Van Dyne will later join him as the Wasp, before she shrinks and is lost in the Quantum Realm on a mission.* (**Ant-Man; Ant-Man and the Wasp**)

August

Ι *Leo Fitz is born.* (***Agents of SHIELD 1.12 Seeds***)

September

Ι *Jemma Simmons is born.* (***Agents of SHIELD 1.7 The Hub***)

1988 AD
July

Ι *Daisy Johnson is born.* (***Agents of SHIELD 1.12 Seeds***)

Uncertain Dates

Ι *Meredith Quill dies, and Peter Quill is abducted.* (**Guardians of the Galaxy**)

1989 AD
March

Ι *Werner Reinhardt is released from jail by Alexander Pierce and subsequently kidnaps Jiaying, using her DNA to extend his life and incurring the wrath of Calvin Johnson/Zabo.* (***Agents of SHIELD 2.8 The Things We Bury***)

June

Ι *Pym resigns from SHIELD.* (**Ant-Man**)
Ι *Wendy Lawson gets Carol Danvers to fly her experimental jet to a secret laboratory. Yon-Rogg shoots it down, killing Lawson. Danvers is unintentionally given superhuman powers when she tries to destroy the jet.* (**Captain Marvel**)

1990 AD
February

Ι *Philip Jones and Malcolm Ducasse are born.* (***Jessica Jones 2.1 AKA Start*** *at the Beginning*)

April

I *Whitehall lectures Hale's class and she is forced to shoot her dog.* (**Agents of SHIELD 5.15 Rise and Shine**)

Uncertain Dates

I Joy Meachum is born. (***Iron Fist 1.3 Rolling Thunder Cannon Punch/1.8 The Blessing of Many Fractures***)

1991 AD
April

I Danny Rand is born. (***Iron Fist 1.1 Snow Gives Way/1.8 The Blessing of Many Fractures***)

May

I Lewis Wilson is born. (***The Punisher 1.9 Front Towards the Enemy***)

December

I *The Winter Soldier murders Howard and Maria Stark.* (**Captain America: Civil War**)
I Obadiah Stane is appointed acting CEO of Stark Industries. (**Iron Man**)

1992 AD

I *T'Chaka confronts N'Jobu.* (**Black Panther**)
I *Victor Stein and Janet meet.* (***Runaways 1.7 Refraction***)

1993 AD
May

I Ivan Vanko goes to jail for selling plutonium to Pakistan. (**Iron Man 2**)

1994 AD

Uncertain Dates

| *Matt Murdock is blinded. (**Daredevil 1.1 Into the Ring**)*
| *Jack Murdock does not lose in a fight with "Crusher" Creel. Roscoe Sweeney subsequently has Jack Murdock murdered. (**Daredevil 1.2 Cut Man**)*
| *Matt is sent to an orphanage where he later encounters Stick. (**Daredevil 1.7 Stick**)*

1995 AD
Uncertain Dates

| *Stick trains Matt. (**Daredevil 1.7 Stick**)*
| *Stakar Ogord banishes Yondu Udonta from the Ravagers. (**Guardians of the Galaxy Vol 2**)*
| *Elihas Starr and his wife are killed, and Ava Starr affected on a quantum level, when Starr's quantum tunnel experiment explodes. (**Ant-Man and the Wasp**)*
TIMELINE NOTE: It's not entirely clear when this happens. This is a rough estimation based on the actor's ages.
| **Captain Marvel**
TIMELINE NOTE: Nick Fury says that it's been six years since Danvers' test flight with Lawson crashed. Stan Lee is reading the script for **Mallrats**, in which he appears, and which was released in 1995.

July

| *Grant Ward's oldest brother tries to kill his other brother. (**Agents of SHIELD 1.8 The Well**)*
| *Misty Knight's best friend Cassandra is murdered. (**Luke Cage 1.9 DWYCK**)*

c September

| *Natasha Romanoff, Yelena Belova, Alexei Shostakov and Melina Vostokoff are forced to abandon their US personas and flee the country. On their return to Russian custody, the girls are entered into Dreykov's Red Room program, Melina begins a research project and Alexei is imprisoned. (**Black Widow**)*

1996 AD

| *Stick trains Elektra. (**Daredevil 2.12 The Dark at the End of the Tunnel**)*

1997 AD

I Kaecilius goes to Kamar-Taj to deal with the death of his wife. (**Doctor Strange**)

I *Black Bolt accidentally kills his parents, manipulated by Maximus.* (***Inhumans 1.8 ...And Finally: Black Bolt***)

I Dorothy Walker forces Trish into acting work. (***Jessica Jones 2.4 God Help the Hobo***)

1998 AD

I Robert Coleman is experimented on giving him super speed. (***Jessica Jones 2.2 Freak Accident***)

I Clint Barton is sent to assassinate Natasha Romanoff. He arrests her instead. (**The Avengers**)

TIMELINE NOTE: This may be the Budapest incident the two frequently discuss.

1999 AD
Uncertain Dates

I *Grant Ward is recruited by John Garrett.* (**Agents of SHIELD 1.21 Ragtag**)

I *Jonah recruits Geoffrey Wilder.* (**Runaways 1.5 Kingdom**)

July

I *After recovering from a coma, Jessica moves in with the Walker family.* (***Jessica Jones 1.11 AKA I've Got the Blues***)

December

I *Tony Stark misses his meeting with Aldrich Killian on New Year's Eve.* (**Iron Man Three**)

Twenty-First Century

2000 AD
April

I *Jessica's family is killed in a car accident. (**Jessica Jones 1.7 AKA Top Shelf Perverts/1.8 AKA WWJD**)*
I Jessica and Alisa are taken to IGH where Karl Malus works on both, giving them superpowers. Work on Alisa takes much longer and she is listed as dead along with the rest of the family, while Jessica is adopted by the Walkers. (***Jessica Jones 2.7 AKA I Want Your Cray Cray***)

2001 AD
Uncertain Dates

I David Lieberman kisses Sarah for the first time. (***The Punisher 1.8 Cold Steel***)
I Will Daniels and his team are transported to Maveth via the Monolith. (***The Punisher 3.5 4,722 Hours***)
I Peter Parker is born. (**Spider-Man: Homecoming**)

June

I Michelle Jones is born. (**Spider-Man: Far From Home**)

June

I Danny Rand breaks his arm in a skating accident. (***Iron Fist 1.3 Rolling Thunder Cannon Punch***)

October

I *Wendell and Heather Rand are killed in a plane crash and Danny is taken to K'un-Lun. (**Iron Fist 1.1 Snow Gives Way**)*
TIMELINE NOTE: A newspaper date is actually given as 2002, but the gravestones of the older Rands are obscured so it's not clear when the crash took place. It is repeatedly said in the first season of ***Iron Fist*** that the crash was fifteen years earlier, placing it in 2001.

I Ned Leeds is born. (**Spider-Man: Far From Home**)

2002 AD

I Coulson works with Camilla Reyes in Peru. (***Agents of SHIELD 1.2 0-8-4***)

2003 AD
August

I *Murdock and Nelson begin law at Colombia University. (**Daredevil 1.10 Nelson V Murdock**)*

November

I *Coulson and May stop Anton Vanko taking an alien artefact at the Burkov Mining Facility. (**Agents of SHIELD 4.14 The Man Behind the Shield**)*

2004 AD
January

I Harold Meachum dies, but is resurrected by the Hand and lives a new, secret life. (***Iron Fist 1.8 The Blessing of Many Fractures***)

June

I *Grant Ward is retrieved from the forest by Garrett and becomes a HYDRA sleeper agent in SHIELD. (**Agents of SHIELD 1.21 Ragtag**)*

September

I Fitz and Simmons attend SHIELD's Science & Technology Academy. (***Agents of SHIELD 2.3 Making Friends and Influence People***)

2005 AD
Uncertain Dates

I *Alisa Jones awakens from her coma with a new face. (**Jessica Jones 2.7 I**

Want Your Cray Cray)

I *Trish Walker releases the single* I Want Your Cray Cray. (***Jessica Jones 2.7 I Want Your Cray Cray***)

I *Banner tests the Bio-Tech Force Enhancement project on himself, unwittingly giving him the ability to become the Hulk. Ross' involvement in the project results in a vicious showdown, and Banner heading to South America to escape persecution.* (**The Incredible Hulk**)

TIMELINE NOTE: Purely speculative, but these events may broadly be the movie **Hulk**. The dating is a little confusing as there is surveillance footage from 2004, as well as a newspaper ending in 06, though the former doesn't necessarily come from the incident, and the latter isn't necessarily the year. The bulk of **the Incredible Hulk** takes place in 2010, five years after the gamma incident, placing it in 2005.

I *Jessica Jones begins a relationship with Stirling Adams which ends when Alisa Jones murders him.* (***Jessica Jones 2.7 I Want Your Cray Cray***)

October – December

I *Matt Murdock and Foggy Nelson gatecrash a party where they meet Elektra Natchios. Matt and Elektra begin a relationship which ends when she takes him to Roscoe Sweeney and tries to get Matt to kill Sweeney.* (***Daredevil 2.5 Kinbaku***)

2006 AD
Uncertain Dates

I Bruce Banner tries to kill himself. (**The Avengers**)

TIMELINE NOTE: This is a deleted scene from **The Incredible Hulk** which is then referred to in **The Avengers**. The 2006 date is speculative, but in 2006, Banner was on the run attempting to contact Betty, so this timeline assumes it was around the same time.

I Frank Castle and Billy Russo are assigned to the same taskforce. (***The Punisher 1.6 The Judas Goat***)

April

I Hope MacKenzie is born and dies four days later. (***Agents of SHIELD 4.11 Wake Up***)

2007 AD
July

| The Ranshakov brothers escape prison and establish themselves as gang lords. (***Daredevil 1.4 in the Blood***)

2008 AD
January

| **Iron Man**
TIMELINE NOTE: On screen evidence places the movie in 2008, even though the official timeline resets it to 2010. The events occur over a significant period of time, so Stark's confession about Iron Man could be set in early 2009.
| *Romanoff and Barton are sent to assassinate Dreykov, and though Romanoff can see Antonia Dreykov in the building, she gives the order to destroy it.* (**Black Widow**)
TIMELINE NOTE: A deleted scene from **Black Widow** states that Budapest was eight years earlier.

Uncertain Dates

| *Coulson and May are sent to add Eva and Katya Belyakov to the Index. Subsequently Maria Hill reassigns May to desk duty.* (***Agents of SHIELD 2.17 May***)

2009 AD
Uncertain Dates

| Coulson is put in charge of Project TAHITI. (***Agents of SHIELD 1.20 Nothing Personal***)
| Natasha Romanoff encounters the Winter Soldier. (**Captain America: The Winter Soldier**)

| *Detective Connors murders Billy Johnson. Nathan Bowen drives off a bridge into the sea. Tyrone Johnson rescues Tandy Bowen. (**Cloak & Dagger 1.1 First Light**)*

TIMELINE NOTE: There is significant evidence for this to occur in 2007 or 2008, but Adina's vision giving Tyrone's year of birth as 2000 seems like the most obvious piece of evidence that can't be ignored. As it's set in February, and Tyrone's birthday is in June, it must be 2009.

2010 AD

| **Iron Man 2**

TIMELINE NOTE: This movie takes place six months after **Iron Man** – though more accurately the "six months later" caption occurs while Ivan Vanko works on the Whiplash armour, which could push the movie forward to 2010. More importantly, Stark says the last expo was 36 earlier – as a poster gives the date for this as 1974, this would place the movie in 2010. During **Iron Man 2** Coulson gets summoned to New Mexico, presumably because of Thor's hammer.

| **The Incredible Hulk**

TIMELINE NOTE: The comic *Fury's Big Week* puts this movie at the same time as **Iron Man 2**, though there is nothing in the actual films to either support or deny this.

| Thor leads his friends in a fight against the Frost Giants consequently having his power stripped from him. (**Thor**)

| *A Funny Thing Happened on the Way to Thor's Hammer (Marvel One-Shot)*

| *Coulson finds Thor's hammer. (**Iron Man 2**)*

| Loki takes the opportunity to create a rift in Asgard and sends the Destroyer to Earth. It is defeated and Thor returns to Asgard, stops the Giants and banishes Loki, destroying the Bifrost in the process. (**Thor**)

TIMELINE NOTE: The comic *Fury's Big Week* places this movie in the same week as **Iron Man 2**, and the movie does seem to follow closely. It is around a year before **The Avengers**.

December

| *The Consultant (Marvel One-Shot)*

| Roxxon's tanker, *Norco*, has a disastrous oil spill. (**Iron Man Three**)

2011 AD
June

| Thaddeus Ross has a heart attack. (**Captain America: Civil War**)

October

| Aaron Davis is arrested for the first time. (**Spider-Man: Homecoming**)

2012 AD
January

| Aldrich Killian begins his appropriation of The Ten Rings using Trevor Slattery as The Mandarin. (**Iron Man Three**)
| Dinah Madani and Ahmad Zubair work together in Kandahar, Afghanistan. (***The Punisher 1.9 Front Towards the Enemy***)
| *Lucy and Joseph Bauer find the Darkhold.* (***Agents of SHIELD 4.5 Lockup***)

February

| *Eli Morrow is introduced to the Darkhold and his obsession with it begins. Robbie Reyes is killed in a car crash, but a Ghost Rider transfers the Spirit of Vengeance to him in order to save Gabriel Reyes' life.* (***Agents of SHIELD 4.6 The Good Samaritan***)

April

| Chad Davis explodes from his Extremis injection. (**Iron Man Three**)

April

| *Steve Rogers' body is recovered and unfrozen.* (**Captain America: The First Avenger**)

May

| **The Avengers**
TIMELINE NOTE: **Thor** was a year before **The Avengers** according to Nick Fury, but he may have been rounding down when making that estimate. This movie explicitly takes place in 2012 according to **Endgame**.

188

I Steve Rogers, Tony Stark, Bruce Banner and Scott Lang arrive to collect the mind stone, the time stone and the space stone. They succeed with the first two, but fail to collect the last, which Loki takes and escapes with, creating an alternate timeline. The mind and time stones are returned to their correct time periods, cutting off the other alternate timelines that were created by their removal. (**Avengers: Endgame**)

I *Adrian Toomes clean-up operation is taken off them by Damage Control.* (**Spider-Man: Homecoming**)

I *Phil Coulson is resurrected using the TAHITI Project. This is kept top secret.* (***Agents of SHIELD 1.11 The Magical Place***)

I Ben Urich writes about the Chitauri Invasion. (***Daredevil 1.3 Rabbit in a Snowstorm***)

June

I *Item 47 (Marvel One-Shot)*

July

I Scott Lang extorts VistaCorp and is arrested, found guilty and sentenced to jail for five years. (**Ant-Man**)

September

I *Shades is sent to Seagate Prison.* (***Luke Cage 1.4 Step in the Arena***)

November

I Matthew Ellis is elected President. (**Iron Man Three**)

TIMELINE NOTE: Ellis is definitely President by the end of 2012, but in the real world he wouldn't be inaugurated until January 2013. As he is definitely President in **Iron Man Three**, in the MCU he was clearly inaugurated not long after the election. Nico Minoru makes mention of the Obama Administration, meaning Barack Obama must have won the 2008 election. It's not clear if Ellis is Democrat or Republican (though presumably something happened to Obama for him not to run in 2012 if Ellis is a Democrat). Though Ellis is criticised for having done nothing during the Roxxon *Norco* affair, this may be because he was Secretary for the Environment, rather than President.

December

I **Iron Man Three**
TIMELINE NOTE: A newspaper carries the date of 2013, but it seems unlikely that Tony would have had PTSD untreated for over a year, so this is regarded as a misprint.

2012 AD – ALTERNATE TIMELINE
May

I Having escaped the Avengers, Loki is then captured by the Time Variance Authority and sentenced to death. (*Loki 1.1 Glorious Purpose*)

2013 AD
January

I Tony Stark meets with Bruce Banner. (**Iron Man Three**)

February

I *Carl Lucas is sent to prison and meets Reva Connors. (**Luke Cage 1.4 Step in the Arena**)*

May

I Joy Meachum earns her Juris Doctor. (*Iron Fist 1.1 Snow Gives Way*)
I Rafael Scarfe's son kills himself with his father's gun by accident. (*Luke Cage 1.6 Suckas Need Bodyguards*)

August

I *Matt Murdock and Foggy Nelson decide to start their own law firm.* (*Daredevil 1.10 Nelson V Murdock*)
I *Matt Murdock begins his vigilante career.* (*Daredevil 1.10 Nelson V Murdock*)
I *Carl Lucas escapes Seagate after gaining superpowers and changes his name to Luke Cage.* (*Luke Cage 1.4 Step in the Arena*)

September

| *Jessica Jones and Trish Walker reconnect, Walker suggesting her friend become a superhero. (**Jessica Jones 1.5 AKA The Sandwich Saved Me**)*
| ***Agents of SHIELD 1.1 Pilot – 1.2 0-8-4***
| *Luke Cage marries Reva Connors. (**Luke Cage 1.2 Code of the Streets**)*
| *Kilgrave kidnaps Jessica Jones and makes her his total slave. (**Jessica Jones 1.5 AKA The Sandwich Saved Me**)*

October

| ***Agents of SHIELD 1.3 The Asset – 1.7 The Hub***

November

| **Thor: The Dark World**
TIMELINE NOTE: **Endgame** gives this a definitive date of 2013.
| *Thor and Rocket arrive in Asgard from the future to steal the Reality Stone from Jane Foster's body. Though this creates an alternate timeline, it is deleted when Steve Rogers returns the stone to the same temporal-spatial location.* (**Avengers Endgame**)
| ***Agents of SHIELD 1.8 The Well – 1.9 Repairs***
TIMELINE NOTE: *The Well* sees Coulson's team mopping up after **Thor: The Dark World**.

2014 AD
January

| *Jessica Jones kills Reva Connors, in the process gaining some control of life back and seemingly killing Kilgrave in a bus crash. (**Jessica Jones 1.2 AKA Crush Syndrome; 1.3 AKA It's Called Whiskey**)*
| ***Agents of SHIELD 1.10 The Bridge- 1.11 The Magical Place***

February
| *All Hail the King (Marvel One-Shot)*
| ***Agents of SHIELD 1.12 Seeds – 1.16 End of the Beginning***
| **Captain America: The Winter Soldier**

April

| *Ahmad Zubair is assassinated in Kandahar. (**The Punisher 1.3 Kandahar**)*

May

| ***Agents of SHIELD 1.17 Turn, Turn, Turn – 1.22 The Beginning of the End***
| *Phil Coulson instigates Theta Protocol. (**Agents of SHIELD 2.20 Scars**)*

August

| **Guardians of the Galaxy**
| Before Quill gets the Orb, Nebula and War Machine ambush him and take it. This creates a new timeline in which alt-2014 Thanos captures the 2023 Nebula and alt-2014 Nebula impersonates her, travelling to 2023 with James Rhodes. Alt-2014 Thanos and the *Sanctuary II* follow her. This alternate timeline is then negated when 2023 Steve Rogers returns the power stone to where it should be for prime-2014 Quill to steal it, though alt-2014 Gamora remains in prime-2023. (**Avengers: Endgame**)

September

| ***Agents of Shield 2.1 Shadows – 2.3 Making Friends and Influencing People***

October

| **Guardians of the Galaxy Vol 2**

November

| *Schoonover's Cerberus Squad is ambushed in Kandahar, resulting in Frank Castle transferring out of Cerberus. (**The Punisher 1.3 Kandahar**)*

December

| Jonathan Pangborn begins recovery from his accident. (**Doctor Strange**)

Uncertain Dates

I William Rawlins is appointed Director of Covert Affairs for the CIA. (mentioned in *The Punisher 1.8 Cold Steel*)

January

I *Daredevil 1.1 Into the Ring – 1.8 Shadows in the Glass*

February

I *Daredevil 1.9 Speak of the Devil – 1.13 Daredevil*
I *Agents of SHIELD 2.4 Face My Enemy – 2.5 A Hen in the Wolf House*

March

I *Jessica Jones 1.1 AKA Ladies Night – 1.5 AKA The Sandwich Saved Me*
I *Agents of SHIELD 2.6 A Fractured House – 2.10 What They Become*

April

I *Jessica Jones 1.6 AKA You're A Winner! – 1.13 AKA Smile*
I *Agents of SHIELD 2.11 Aftershocks – 2.19 The Dirty Half Dozen*
I *Frank Castle returns home from the war.* (*Daredevil 2.4 Penny and Dime*)
I *The Castles spend time together, but are killed by an arranged mob fight.* (*Daredevil 2.5 Kinbaku*)
I *Benjamin Donovan starts his defence of Wilson Fisk.* (*Daredevil 2.9 Seven Minutes in Heaven*)

May

I **Avengers: Age of Ultron**
I *Agents of SHIELD 2.20 Scars – 2.22 SOS*
I Jonathan Pangborn goes to Kamar-Taj to cure his injuries. (**Doctor Strange**)
I Nathaniel Pietro Barton is born. (**Avengers: Age of Ultron**)

June

I *Simmons begins a lengthy period stranded on an alien world trying to survive. She is captured by Will Daniels, and the pair later become friends and lovers.* (**Agents of SHIELD 3.5 4.722 Hours**)
I *Wilson Fisk builds a power base in prison effectively taking control of it.* (**Daredevil 2.9 Seven Minutes in Heaven**)
I Luke Cage starts work at Pop's. (**Luke Cage 1.2 Code of the Streets**)
I *Andrew Garner undergoes terrigenesis.* (**Agents of SHIELD 3.7 Chaos Theory**)

July

I **Ant-Man**

September

I *Simmons determines a way to locate where the portal will open next. She also has an encounter with the Hive.* (**Agents of SHIELD 3.5 4.722 Hours**)

November

I *Daredevil Season 2*
I *Luke Cage 1.1 Moment Of Truth – 1.8 Blown' Up the Spot*
I Sam Wilson attempts to locate Scott Lang. (**Ant-Man**)
I *Agents of SHIELD 3.1 Laws of Nature – 3.2 Purpose in the Machine*

December

I *Luke Cage 1.9 DWYCK – 1.13 You Know My Steez*
I *Agents of SHIELD 3.3 A Wanted (Inhu)Man – 3.8 Many Heads, One Tail*
I Murdock and Stick go to Natchios' funeral, unaware that her body has been taken by the Hand. Murdock later reveals his identity as Daredevil to Page. (**Daredevil 2.13 A Cold Day in Hell's Kitchen**)
I Peter Parker becomes Spider-Man. (**Captain America: Civil War**)

2016 AD

January

| *Agents of SHIELD 3.9 Closure – 3.10 Maveth*

February

| Kaecilius steals the Book of Cagliostro and Stephen Strange has a horrific car crash which severely damages his hands. (**Doctor Strange**)
TIMELINE NOTE: Strange's watch confirms the timing of the accident. The theft is an approximate date, before the crash.
| *Iron Fist Season 1*

March

| *Agents of SHIELD 3.11 Bouncing Back – 3.13 Parting Shot*

April

| *Agents of SHIELD 3.14 Watchdogs – 3.18 The Singularity*
| Stephen Strange undergoes a series of procedures in an attempt to regain the full use of his hands. (**Doctor Strange**)
| Frank Castle assassinates Mickey O'Hare. (*The Punisher 1.1 3 AM*)

May

| *The Defenders Season 1*

May – June

| **Captain America: Civil War**
TIMELINE NOTE: This movie takes place eight years after Tony Stark comes out as Iron Man, according to Vision. We can therefore assume the timing is quite accurate. If Tony admits he was Iron Man in 2009, this places **Civil War** in 2017. However, there is a reference to the Sokovian Accords in *Agents of SHIELD 3.19 Failed Experiments*, making the date 2016. More importantly, Scott Lang finishes his two-year house arrest in 2018; an arrest which was a consequence of breaking the Accords in **Civil War**. Therefore, **Civil War** needs to take place in 2016.
| *When Zemo attacks the UN Jeffrey Mace inadvertently saves someone's life*

*and is crowned a hero. (**Agents of SHIELD 4.5 Lockup**)*

I **Black Widow**
TIMELINE NOTE: This takes place immediately after **Civil War** as Natasha is on the run from Ross.
I ***Agents of SHIELD 3.19 Failed Experiments – 3.22 Ascension***

July

I **Black Panther**
TIMELINE NOTE: This movie is just weeks after **Civil War** as T'Challa is crowned King.

August

I Glenn Talbot begins Project Patriot with Jeffrey Mace to find a new Captain America. Phil Coulson steps down as director of SHIELD, suggesting an Inhuman take his place. (**Agents of SHIELD 4.10 The Patriot**)
I Stephen Strange tracks down Jonathan Pangborn who advises he go to Kamar-Taj in Nepal. There he manages to inveigle himself into the retreat and the Ancient One begins his training. (**Doctor Strange**)
I ***Inhumans Season 1***

September

I Talbot appoints Mace the new director of SHIELD. (**Agents of SHIELD 4.10 The Patriot**)
I *After signing the Sokovia Accords, Elena Rodriguez tracks down Victor Ramon. (**Agents of SHIELD: Slingshot**)*

October

I Coulson and Mackenzie attempt to bring in Quake on Mace's instructions. (**Agents of SHIELD 3.22 Ascension**)

November – December

I ***The Punisher Season 1***

2017

February

I Kaecilius launches his attacks against the Sanctum Sanctorums to bring Dormammu to this dimension. (**Doctor Strange**)

I *Cloak & Dagger Season 1*

TIMELINE NOTE: The placing of this season deals in part with a number of dates regarding Ty's birth, and the deaths of Billy Johnson and Nathan Bowen. A 2016 date clashes with the time that O'Reilly left Harlem (during Misty Knight's leave of absence), and a magazine claims that it is currently 2017. There are facts that don't entirely align (the song *First Light, Lush Life* must have been released earlier in the MCU, as it wasn't released til March, 2017 and is heard in the series; O'Reilly says 2010 was about eight years earlier – both of which could be explained away. However, Fuch's obituary states his year of death as 2018 which is the only obstacle, though this could be a misprint), but the majority of the evidence places this in 2017.

March

I *Agents of SHIELD 4.1 The Ghost – 4.3 Uprising*

April – May

I *Jessica Jones Season 2*

I *Agents of SHIELD 4. 4 Let Me Stand Next To Your Fire – 4.22 World's End*

I *Fitz is arrested by General Hale's troops and imprisoned. (**Agents of SHIELD 5.5 Rewind**)*

August

I *Luke Cage Season 2*

September

I **Spider-Man: Homecoming**

TIMELINE NOTE: The placing of this movie has been particularly problematic and requires evidence to be ignored and re-interpreted. The "Eight Years Later" caption at the beginning of the film cannot be correct as that would place the film in 2020, which absolutely contradicts every other movie released. The official Marvel timeline places **Civil War** in 2017, but this timeline can't reconcile that fact. **Homecoming** would appear to take place not long after **Civil War** (it's described as months), but if it takes place in 2016 that directly contradicts evidence such as Aaron Davis' birth year, which could be a mistake on the police form, but is unlikely. Additionally, having the film set two years before **Infinity War** doesn't really work either. It has to be in September, as that's when Homecoming is, and whilst September, 2016 would make sense of Peter anticipating being summoned again by Tony, September, 2017 works with both pieces of evidence for Aaron Davis, as well as making more sense for the gap between this and **Infinity War**.

October

I *Iron Fist Season 2*
I *Daredevil Season 3*
I *Cloak & Dagger Season 2*

November

I Thor's execution of Surtur leads to a return to Asgard, a trip to Earth to find Odin, the release of Hela and a further trip to Sakaar when he and Loki are flung from the Bifrost. (**Thor: Ragnarok**)
I Danny Rand and Ward Meachum seek Orson Randall. (*Iron Fist 2.10 A Duel of Iron*)
I *Runaways Season 1*
I *Runaways Season 2*

December

I *Agents of SHIELD 5.11 All the Comforts of Home – 5.13 Principia*
I *Runaways Season 3.1 Smoke and Mirrors – 3.5 Enter The Dreamland*

2018
April

I *Jessica Jones Season 3*
I *The Punisher Season 2*

May

I Thor returns to Asgard to confront Hela and release Surtur. (**Thor: Ragnarok**)

TIMELINE NOTE: There is a problem with the idea of **Ragnarok** being set in 2017, but immediately preceding **Infinity War** (as the post-credits scene shows Thanos' *Sanctuary II* encountering the Asgardian ship), as **Infinity War** definitely takes place in 2018. **Ragnarok** takes place over a fairly contained time period, however there is some leeway as it is made clear that time on Sakaar moves differently (the short time between Loki and Thor falling out of the Bifrost is a much larger time difference in their arrival on Sakaar). Therefore, the best solution to the temporal problem would seem to be that the departure from Sakaar propelled Thor and his allies into the future.

June

I *Runaways Season 3.5 Enter The Dreamland – 3.10 Cheat The Gallows*
I **Ant-Man and the Wasp**
I *Agents of SHIELD 5.14 The Devil Complex – 5.22 The End*
I **Avengers: Infinity War**
I Scott Lang enters the Quantum Realm, but once inside, Hope, Hank and Janet are all turned to dust, leaving him stranded. (**Ant-Man and the Wasp**)
I Clint Barton's family are all turned to dust. He becomes a vigilante to balance the books. Erik Selvig is amongst those turned to dust. (**Avengers: Endgame**)
I MJ, Ned and Betty are amongst those turned to dust. (**Spider-Man: Far From Home**)

July

I *Carol Danvers answers the pager and agrees to assist Rogers, Romanoff and Rhodes.* (**Captain Marvel**)
I Danvers rescues Stark and Nebula, and joins Rogers, Banner, Thor, Romanoff, Rocket and Nebula in hunting down Thanos who has used the Infinity Stones to destroy the stones. Thor kills Thanos, but it is too late to undo what he has done. (**Avengers: Endgame**)

August

I Now with the CIA, Madani contacts Castle for help, but he is too busy dispensing his own brand of justice in New York. (***The Punisher 2.13 Whirlwind***)

2018 – ALTERNATE TIMELINE 838
June

I Stephen Strange kills Thanos using the Book of Vishanti. Concerned by his actions, the rest of the Illuminati, with Strange's consent, execute him. Baron Mordo succeeds him. (**Doctor Strange in the Multiverse of Madness**)
TIMELINE NOTE: Though the date isn't stated, it's assumed that the battle with Thanos took place at about the same time.

2019
c April

I <u>Morgan Stark is born.</u>
TIMELINE NOTE: The script for **Avengers: Endgame** gives her age as four.

c June

I *Agents of SHIELD 6.1 Missing Pieces – 6.13 New Life*
TIMELINE NOTE: Although Jeph Loeb claimed that the television series would take place before **Infinity War**, the final few episodes of season five are concurrent with **Infinity War**, and it explicitly stated that a year has passed since they lost Fitz, meaning season six has to take place after **Infinity War**. That said, it's perhaps not totally surprising the snap isn't mentioned as a year has passed and life would have begun to adapt.

2020
May

I Having waited six years for her brother's return, Xu Xianling escapes the Ten Rings. (**Shang-Chi and the Legend of the Ten Rings**).

July

I Coulson's team reunite to celebrate the anniversary of their survival. (*Agents of SHIELD 7.13 What We're Fighting For*)
I Maria Rambeau dies from cancer. (***WandaVision 1.04 We Interrupt This Program***)

October

I *Helstrom Season One*

2021 – ALTERNATE TIMELINE 838
February

I Stephen Strange and America Chavez cross the multiverse and discover Strange is dead in the universe they are in. They find Mordo and the Illuminati, but only Professor Xavier takes Strange's warnings about the Scarlett Witch seriously. Wanda takes control of the body of the 838-Wanda and kills the Illuminati as Strange and America escape with the 838-Christine Palmer. (**Doctor Strange in the Multiverse of Madness**)
TIMELINE NOTE: The date is noted on Strange's X-rays.

2021 – ALTERNATE TIMELINE
June

I *Runaways 3.10 Cheat The Gallows*
TIMELINE NOTE: Although Karolina has a calendar which suggests it is 2022, it is definitely three years since the events of *The Broken Circle,* and given the calendar suggests Karolina is looking at third-year subjects, she couldn't possibly be doing that two years after leaving high school. This suggests it is a draft calendar for the following year.

2023
July

I The Phil Coulson LMD is completed. (*Agents Of SHIELD 7.13 What We're Fighting For*)

October

I **Avengers: Endgame**
TIMELINE NOTE: The majority of **Endgame** takes place five years after **Infinity War**. The Blip (Banner restoring the universe) definitively takes place in mid-October.
I The Avengers Compound is ransacked and a large number of items are taken. (*Hawkeye 1.1 Never Meet Your Heroes*)

November

I *WandaVision Season One*
TIMELINE NOTE: This takes place a few weeks after the Blip and the defeat of Thanos.
I **The Eternals**
TIMELINE NOTE: It is mentioned that the Snap was five years earlier, but the Blip has occurred. There are pumpkins in the American scenes, suggesting it can't be too far past Halloween.

2024

January

I Starfox and Pip arrive on the Domo. (**The Eternals**)
I Gorr begins his quest to kill all gods. (**Thor: Love and Thunder**)
TIMELINE NOTE: These are both approximate dates based on occurring within the vicinity of the main events.

March

I **Shang-Chi and the Legend of the Ten Rings**
TIMELINE NOTE: The majority of this film takes place a few months after December, during the Spring. It is ten years since Shang-Chi was 15.

April

I *The Falcon and the Winter Soldier 1.1 New World Order*
TIMELINE NOTE: The Blip was a few months ago.
I Jane Foster works to find a way to destroy her cancer, becoming the Mighty Thor in the process. (**Thor: Love and Thunder**)
TIMELINE NOTE: Jane's blood tests are done on the 30th of April,

May

I *The Falcon and the Winter Soldier 1.2 The Star-Spangled Man – 1.6 One World, One People*
I **Thor: Love and Thunder**
TIMELINE NOTE: Thor and Jane probably broke up in 2015, and this is definitively 8 years and 7 months after that.

July

| Spider-Man: Far From Home
TIMELINE NOTE: This takes place at the end of the school year, placing it in the July following **Endgame** which takes place in October, moving **Far From Home** to the year after.

November

| Spider-Man: No Way Home
TIMELINE NOTE: The early parts of the film take place not long after **Spider-Man: No Way Home**, but the majority of the film takes place a few months later – specifically after Halloween
| Doctor Strange in the Multiverse of Madness
TIMELINE NOTE: Strange's watch specifically places this in November.
| When a Sakaar courier ship appears, Jennifer Walters is forced off the road, causing an accident in which she gets some of her cousin's blood in her, creating the She-Hulk. Bruce Banner takes a few months to train her. (*She-Hulk 1.1 A Normal Amount of Rage*)
| *T'Challa succumbs to his disease and passes away.* (**Black Panther: Wakanda Forever**)

December

| Clea meets Doctor Strange to get his help. (**Doctor Strange in the Multiverse of Madness**)
| Peter adapts to life as an unknown visiting MJ and his aunt's grave. (**Spider-Man: No Way Home**)
| *Hawkeye Season One*

2025

February

| Marc Spector struggles to come to terms with his mother's death and his Steven Grant persona resurfaces and takes control. Consequently Layla El-Faouly is unable to contact Marc. (*Moon Knight 1.5 Asylum*)

| *She-Hulk 1.1 A Normal Amount of Rage*

| *She-Hulk 1.2 Superhuman Law – 1.4 Is This Not Real Magic?*
| *Moon Knight 1.1 The Goldfish Problem – 1.2 Summon the Suit*

| *She-Hulk 1.5 Mean, Green and Straight Poured Into These Jeans*
| *Moon Knight 1.3 The Friendly Type – 1.6 Gods and Monsters*
| *Ms Marvel 1.1 Generation Why – 1.2 Crushed*

| *Ms Marvel 1.3 Destined – 1.6 No Normal*

| *She-Hulk 1.6 Just Jen*

| *She-Hulk 1.7 The Retreat – 1.9 Whose Show is This?*

| **Werewolf by Night**
TIMELINE NOTE: There aren't many specific indicators as to when this takes place, but the Disney+ timeline puts it before *The Guardians of the Galaxy Holiday Special*.

| **Black Panther: Wakanda Forever**
TIMELINE NOTE: T'Challa and Nakai's child is six years old. Nakia isn't present in **Avengers: Endgame** which suggests that in 2018 she was either pregnant or had given birth. As T'Challa was snapped away, conception must

have occurred in 2018 at the latest. Though this could take place in 2024, there's no reason to believe this doesn't occur in the same timeframe as the surrounding releases.

December

I ***The Guardians of the Galaxy Holiday Special***
TIMELINE NOTE: There aren't many specific indicators as to when this takes place, but it's after the Blip, and the Disney+ timeline puts it right at the end.

2050 – ALTERNATE TIMELINE
March

I Sylvie hides in a timeline where the Roxxcart Mall is devastated by a hurricane. Mobius, Loki and B-15 arrive to capture her, but fail. (***Loki 1.2 The Variant***)

2051

I A Tsunami ends the production of Kablooie chewing gum. (***Loki 1.2 The Variant***)

2077
July

I Lamentis-1 is destroyed by meteorites. (***Loki 1.4 The Nexus Evet***)

2077 – ALTERNATE TIMELINE
July

I Lamentis-1 is destroyed by meteorites as witnessed by Loki & Sylvie. (***Loki 1.4 The Nexus Event***)

2091 – ALTERNATE TIMELINE
c. September

I ***Agents of SHIELD 5.1 Orientation – 5.10 Past Life***

| **Loki Season One**

VIII *MCU RELEASE GUIDE*

PHASE ONE

2008   **Iron Man**

       The Incredible Hulk

2010   **Iron Man 2**

2011   **Thor**

       Captain America

2012   **The Avengers**

PHASE TWO

2013   **Iron Man Three**

       Agents of SHIELD: Season 1 (ABC)

       Thor: The Dark World

2014   **Captain America: The Winter Soldier**

       Guardians of the Galaxy

       Agents of SHIELD: Season 2 (ABC)

2015   *Agent Carter: Season 1 (ABC)*

       Daredevil: Season 1 (Netflix)

       Avengers: Age of Ultron

       Ant-Man

       Agents of SHIELD: Season 3 (ABC)

       Jessica Jones: Season 1 (Netflix)

2016 *Agent Carter: Season 2 (ABC)*

Daredevil: Season 2 (Netflix)

Captain America: Civil War

Luke Cage: Season 1 (Netflix)

Agents of SHIELD: Season 4 (ABC)

Doctor Strange

2017 *Iron Fist: Season 1 (Netflix)*

Guardians of the Galaxy Vol 2

Spider-Man: Homecoming

The Defenders: Season 1 (Netflix)

Inhumans: Season 1 (ABC)

Thor: Ragnarok

The Punisher: Season 1 (Netflix)

Runaways: Season 1 (Hulu)

Agents of SHIELD: Season 5 (ABC)

2018 **Black Panther**

Jessica Jones: Season 2 (Netflix)

Avengers: Infinity War

Luke Cage: Season 2 (Netflix)

Cloak & Dagger: Season 1 (Freeform)

Ant-Man and the Wasp

Iron Fist: Season 2 (Netflix)

Daredevil: Season 3 (Netflix)

Runaways: Season 2 (Hulu)

2019   *The Punisher: Season 2 (Netflix)*

Captain Marvel

Cloak & Dagger: Season 2 (Freeform)

Avengers: Endgame

Agents of SHIELD: Season 6 (ABC)

Jessica Jones: Season 3 (Netflix)

Spider-Man: Far From Home

Runaways: Season 3 (Hulu)

2020   *Agents of SHIELD: Season 7 (ABC)*

Helstrom: Season 1 (Hulu)

PHASE FOUR

2021   *WandaVision: Season 1 (Disney+)*

The Falcon And The Winter Soldier: Season 1 (Disney+)

Loki: Season 1 (Disney+)

Black Widow

What If…?: Season 1 (Disney+)

Shang-Chi and the Legend of the Ten Rings

Eternals

Hawkeye: Season 1 (Disney+)

Spider-Man: No Way Home

2022   *Moon Knight: Season 1 (Disney+)*

Doctor Strange in the Multiverse of Madness

Ms Marvel: Season 1 (Disney+)

Thor: Love and Thunder

I Am Groot: Season 1 (Disney+)

She-Hulk: Attorney at Law: Season 1 (Disney+)

Werewolf by Night (Disney+)

Black Panther: Wakanda Forever *Guardians of the Galaxy Holiday Special (Disney+)*

The Guardians of the Galaxy Holiday Special (Disney+)